THE INFANT MIND

Books by Richard M. Restak

PREMEDITATED MAN:
BIOETHICS & THE CONTROL OF FUTURE HUMAN LIFE

THE SELF SEEKERS

THE BRAIN:
THE LAST FRONTIER

THE BRAIN

THE INFANT MIND

THE
INFANT
MIND

RICHARD M. RESTAK, M.D.

DOUBLEDAY & COMPANY, INC.
GARDEN CITY, NEW YORK
1986

Library of Congress Cataloging-in-Publication Data

Restak, Richard M., 1942–
The infant mind.

Includes index.
1. Infants—Development.   2. Brain.   3. Infant
psychology.   I. Title.   [DNLM: 1. Brain—popular works.
2. Child Development—popular works.   3. Child
Psychology—popular works.   4. Infant—popular works.
WS 105 R4365i]
RJ134.R47   1986   155.4'22   86-2033
ISBN 0-385-19531-1

To My Father

CONTENTS

INTRODUCTION

The intent of this book is to relate behavior to what we know about the human brain—the fetal and infant human brain, specifically.

Psychologists have been experimenting for decades in order to learn what an infant will do under certain circumstances: Will he crawl onto a Plexiglas table? Will he perform as a mimic if an adult sticks out his tongue at him? Will an infant recognize his mother's voice over the babble of competing voices? Although answers to such questions are presently available (*yes* to all three), only recently has anyone asked the equally fascinating and much more fundamental question: Granted that the infant can do all this, what takes place in the infant brain that explains such performance?

About two years ago I took up these questions only to discover that (1) less was known about the infant brain than I had anticipated, and (2) the infant brain is a unique structure, far more than simply an inadequate version of its adult counterpart.

In addition, I discovered that infant brain development involves some counterintuitive notions. Starting with only two cells, merged in the process of fertilization, a geometric progression of cell multiplication ensues from which emerge the first cells destined to become the components of the adult human brain.

Many multiplications later, some of these cells will die off rather than multiply further in order that the optimal number of cells and cell connections can endure and get on with the business of shaping the most complicated organ that we know. Most marvelous of all, behavior unfolds in tandem with the development of the infant brain. As brain structure evolves, function emerges, behavior ensues.

At birth we are hybrids; many of our earliest movements reflect our experiences within the liquid environment that contained and sustained us for the nine months before our Grand Entry. Other movements and activities anticipate accommodations required of us in order to get on in the environment in which we will spend the next seventy-odd years of the "anticipated average life span" that actuarials tell us we have coming to us.

If the brain is altered before birth—indeed, at any time from three or so weeks after conception when "the brain" is nothing more elaborate than a plate of cells and extending to the moment, decades away, of our Grand Exit—behavior is altered accordingly.

Simply put, at every moment of every life the brain reflects the demands that are made on it by the environment in which that brain finds itself. Breathing and movement patterns can be observed in the womb before birth via suitable technological probes. These observations correlate with breathing and movement patterns in newborns. Such comparisons provide a surprise: the fetus isn't merely practicing for what will come later. Rather, the fetus is perfectly adapted to life within the womb. As the environment changes the brain changes: fetal brain merges into infant brain merges into adult brain. Most fascinating of all, this transition isn't incremental; the infant brain is perfectly adapted to the world of the infant.

It is possible to correlate what we know of the infant brain with our observations of what that infant is capable of at different stages of development. Such correlations form the basis for the emerging field of developmental neurobiology. *The Infant Mind* is a first step toward explaining such things as the behavior of a seven-week-old fetus that can be observed kicking its legs against the wall of the uterus, thus producing a somersault as the legs contract the uterine wall, press against it, and generate an active retropulsive motor movement. Neuroscientists now believe such movements spur brain development, especially those structures important for balance, coordination, and dealing with the forces of gravity. Additional correlations between infant behavior and brain organization can be anticipated over the next decade. Thanks to new technology which will be described subsequently in this book, neuroscientists can observe the *living* brain rather than having to wait like vultures to examine under a microscope the brain of a baby that, for some reason, didn't make it. Modern neuroscience enables us to move beyond the traditional sequence within medicine: the study of the dead (pathology) helping to unravel the afflictions that trouble the living.

In their study of the human brain, neuroscientists are now entering a new phase. Attention can now be focused on the well and measures suggested to maintain their wellness. Since science has delved into the mysteries of what goes wrong in the damaged brain, there is now the opportunity to learn about processes far removed from the laboratory or the doctor's consulting room: infant smiles, attention, moods, the early development of "personality."

Not all of this can be correlated with the brain, may never be, perhaps cannot be (depending on the views that one holds regarding the relationship of the mind to the brain). For this reason none of the chapters in *The Infant Mind* portends to Finality: "Everything that anybody would want to know is herein contained," and so on. Instead, I've aimed at conceptions as much as facts, speculations on what it all might mean, my hope being that there will emerge from all of this a mixture of mastery and mystery. We know a lot about the infant brain but what we don't know is so much more than our present paltry knowledge that anyone who waxes "definitive" can depend on earning for himself the snickers of those a decade or two hence.

While there are facts and figures enough here to keep happy those for whom learning facts about something is a form of mastery, there are, at the same time, matters to ponder about which, I trust, will interest those readers who would agree with Thomas Merton that on occasion, "the demand for explanation is due to the desire to be rid of mystery."

The Infant Mind is a mixture of facts known, speculations, mystery, pondering and, finally, experimental research aimed at arriving at additional facts or at least additional leads about what avenues of research promise to tell us the most about the baby's brain.

During the writing of this book I was privileged to meet and correspond with or otherwise communicate with eminent researchers on the infant brain. In the preparation of this book I am particularly grateful for the suggestions or other assistance given by:

D. Frank Benson	Marshall H. Klaus
T. G. R. Bower	Herbert Lansdale
Joseph J. Campos	Bruce Pennington
Harry Chugani	Robert Plomin
Robert N. Emde	Heinz F. R. Prechtl
Nathan Fox	Louis W. Sander
Marshall M. Haith	Daniel Stern
Michael V. Johnston	David W. Shucard

Special thanks to Steven J. Phillips, M.D., Professor of Anatomy, Temple University School of Medicine, for his careful and thoughtful review of the manuscript.

CHAPTER 1

Reflexes

A practiced adult can hold a newborn with one hand and the forearm. The fingertips brace the back of the baby's skull, with the back of the palm supporting the shoulder and the forearms supporting the derrière. But that practiced adult will also tell you without too much prodding and absolutely no exaggeration that no two neonates feel the same when held. Some remain curled and cozy like kittens. Others sprawl or otherwise spill over the boundaries of the human hand. Some are tense as if fearful of being dropped. Others sink deeply as if into a cushion. Some writhe and flail. Some stare and remain motionless.

In appearance each infant is also unique. They are not at all like the infants seen in advertisements: plump, well proportioned, and cheery. Rather, most are tinier than expected, wet, sticky, red. Average weight: seven pounds. Average height: a mere twenty inches. (The legs, constituting a third of the baby's length, are most of the time drawn up, with the feet bent inward at the ankles so that the soles are almost parallel, which makes them appear even smaller.)

Baby proportions are grotesque by adult standards. The head takes up about a quarter of the total body length (Martians in science fiction movies are typically so endowed—one of the reasons for their appeal). The cranial dome is well developed, eyes large, nose flat, head squished slightly out of shape by the recent passage through the birth canal.

Despite the larvallike appearance, Baby Martha born but a moment ago brings with her all of the potentialities associated with a whole human being. Virtually all of the neurons in the human brain are present at birth. Her brain size, however, will undergo early modification. Between birth and the end of year one, the brain will double in size. Between year one and Martha's sixth birthday the brain will double again in size. The brain cells will get bigger, take on insulating sheaths for those cells outside the cortex, and luxuriate in a forest of glial cells that will nourish the brain cells and perhaps establish a communication system among themselves (glial cells are no longer considered simply of nutritive interest—they, too, appear to constitute a communication network).

From the moment of conception, the brain and behavior are inextricably linked; increasingly sophisticated behavior requires an increasingly sophisticated brain. The earliest responses of Baby Martha, therefore, are simple and repeatable. Direct a light into the eye. The pupil constricts, a reflex that will endure over the life span—a permanent failure of pupilary constriction equates with death. With the proper stimulation Baby Martha sneezes, yawns, hiccups, blinks. Anything put in the mouth elicits salivation. Tear ducts bathe the eyes continuously but play no part in crying or temper tantrums. They will come later.

Other brain reflex responses at this stage are important only to the doctor. Tap the baby's knee with a small hammer and the knee will jerk outward. Stroke the bottom of the baby's foot from sole to front and the toes will fan outward in the Babinski reflex. This simple test—the most famous in all of neurology—indicates the immaturity of the baby brain. After a few months the test will produce a different result: the toes will turn downward instead of fanning outward. In the event of brain damage, the Babinski reflex will revert to the way it was in infancy.

Immature, still in the process of establishing millions of neuronal connections (synapses), synthesizing neurotransmitters, growing, increasing in complexity from moment to moment—that's the baby brain. The damaged adult brain is, in a way, a reversion: cells destroyed, neuron connections disrupted, chemical messengers gone awry, the total amount of brain available for use diminished. The Babinski sign is an indicator of this process. Stroke the baby's sole and the toes flare because the baby brain hasn't yet completed its journey. Stroke the sole of the old man after a stroke and toes also flare: journey is over. No new brain cells are forthcoming.

The most startling and disturbing reflex is the Moro response: a baby is held in a horizontal position and suddenly thrust downward. Arms and legs stretch wide, Baby freezes and then hugs the arms inward against the trunk. Sometimes residents and medical students will elicit a Moro response in a newborn just for the hell of it, just to break the boredom of an afternoon in the well-baby clinic. But they don't allow the baby's parents to view their amusement: parents are discomforted by the Moro response, as startled and disturbed as their baby.

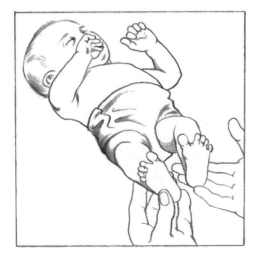

The Babinski response in an infant.

Hold the baby upright so that its feet lightly touch a tabletop and it will make movements up and down as though walking. Hold the baby horizontally on its belly and it'll move for all the world as if swimming. In ages past, seers speculated on the meaning of such performances. It is curious how a baby can almost walk and almost swim despite never having been instructed in these skills. It is even more curious how almost walking and almost swimming disappear only to reappear later in a different form and after much learning and effort. We now explain these arcane mysteries the way Darwin might have explained them. The baby brain goes through a series of stages, expresses a repertoire of motor behaviors based on "circuits" resident in the brain stem. In time, when these lower "centers" are eclipsed by the cerebral cortex, these curious behaviors will cease. From that moment on, the baby is no longer an automaton.

Another reflex displayed routinely by the baby brain: grasping a rod or a finger placed in the palm. A legacy from our apelike ancestors, the grasp reflex is automatic and can't be inhibited. If an infant grasps with one hand but not with the other, the pediatrician or neurologist will look more closely at that baby, will apply his or her experience and logic to divine whether the baby's brain is all that it should be. By three or four months of age, reflex grasping gives way to voluntary grasping: a baby takes only what it wants. This wanting grasping is also primitive; once something is grasped, the baby continues to hold it, can't let go of

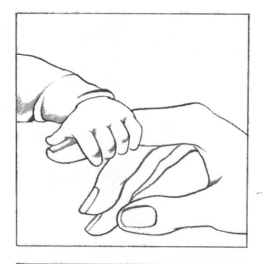

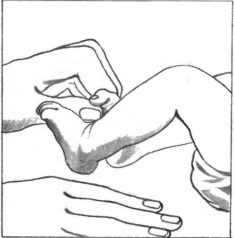

(Above) The grasp reflex of the hands.
(Below) The grasp reflex of the toes.

it. Only the brain of the six month old has advanced far enough along to enable its possessor to grasp what it wants and let go of it when it pleases. The origin of the grasp reflex? Its history is lost in mists of rumor and speculation. But perhaps a contemporary observation can shed some light on the matter.

There is a monkey trap still in use in certain parts of Asia. A coconut is hollowed out and hung by a rope from a tree branch. At the bottom of the coconut a small slit is made just big enough for the entrance of a monkey's *open* hand. A sweet is placed inside the coconut. The monkey approaches and reaches inside the coconut and closes its hand on the sweet—the trap has been sprung. The *closed* fist can't be withdrawn through the slit, and the monkey can't open its hand again to withdraw it. The monkey is irretrievably trapped. Clench the fist, grasp something, and that grasp reflex endures. It happens in monkeys. It happens in newborns.

CHAPTER 2

Fetal Brain

Up to three months of age, the baby does not need the human brain as we think of it (the cerebral hemispheres) for survival. All that's needed is an intact spinal cord below the level of the phrenic nerve. In experiments with animals, if that nerve is cut, or to put it more correctly, both nerves (there's one phrenic nerve on each side of the spinal cord), the animal ceases to breathe. Ceases to live. Ceases to be of any further interest to its investigators.

Babies are sometimes born without cerebral hemispheres, nature having left her task only half done. Prior to the introduction of CT scans these babies often masqueraded as normal. Mother and Father gleefully carried home Timothy or Janice only to discover that their baby at three or four months of age "hadn't a brain," as one of their neighbors, wanting in tact, might put it. How could such a cruel deception be possible?

Brain development, like life itself, proceeds along a continuum from the comparatively simple to the exceedingly complex. If the human infant is to survive, it must be capable from the moment of birth of regulating its blood pressure, breathing, and body temperature—components of the *intérieur milieu* first described by the French experimental physiologist, Claude Bernard. This regulation is prepared for in the womb by brain growth: more brain cells, brain cells multiplying at a dizzying rate. Equally important, neurons in different parts of the brain mature at varying times. The timetable goes like this. Cells lower down the brain stem mature before the neurons higher up. One breathes before one can walk. One walks before one tackles trigonometry.

Second, the neurons specialize along one chemical line or another, secreting messengers, "neurotransmitters," which transform the brain into what Descartes, if he had known any chemistry (he didn't) might have described as an electrochemical "machine." But the fetal brain isn't like any machine Descartes or anyone else after him could ever have dreamed of. Neurons change their chemical affinity according to the influence of additional neurons. It's not at all like the construction of a machine, one part once forged always remaining the same, interfacing with another, the simple gradually benefiting from accretion to produce complexity. Instead, the fetal brain is complex from the very beginning, altering the nature of its complexity the way a Bach fugue gains in complexity: not adding any complexity, but rather delightfully unfolding into alternative forms of complexity.

"The basic circuits are laid down quite early, then expanded and are modified chemically and functionally by ingrowth of new systems," writes Dr. Michael V. Johnston in *The Fetus and Independent Life*. Working with fetal brains, Johnston and others have discovered a panoply of neurotransmitters that stimulate or inhibit the activity of other neurons. First, local circuits are established extending from the lower brain stem to influence the behavior of neurons higher up in the cerebral cortex. Later, as additional neurons are added, already established circuits are altered, the sum of the old and the new, resulting in a profound modification of the fetal brain. This is not just a bigger and more complicated brain as one would expect from thinking of a machine equipped with additional parts, but instead it's a brain organized along fundamentally different patterns.

"The road to independence is marked by major shifts in neuronal influence," states Dr. Johnston. Areas of the brain that are important in early fetal life gradually lose their power to mold the future of the fetal brain. Damage to the brain may allow these once powerful centers to reassert themselves. The brain of an old man who today suffers a stroke may, in a few days, display primitive reflexes that brain has concealed for, lo, eighty years. Damage to the octogenarian's brain can do just that, can once again jumble the "circuits" so that destruction of neurons in the cerebral cortex *dis*inhibits neurons lower down the brain stem.

At all times the brain operates according to algebraic principles: two inhibitory neurons neutralize the effect of two excitatory neurons. But if these inhibitory neurons are destroyed by a stroke or senility, excitability can now run rampant: the old man's hand clutches at whatever it encounters and can't help doing this any more than an infant's hand clutching at a rattle. The "grasp reflex" is what the neurologist calls this strange behavior, this "primitive," "release" mechanism.

The laying down of additional neuronal circuits on top of more primitive ones may help explain the formerly inexplicable. A baby is born under the worst of conditions, is deprived of oxygen for a few precious moments, comes out a "blue baby," sufficiently frightening doctor and nurse into wondering what the final result will be. For one

full year nothing untoward appears. Then one spring afternoon
Mother wheels pram and Baby to the doctor because Baby exhibits
peculiar twitching movements. With grimness and as much gentleness
as he can muster, Doctor explains, "These movements are the result of
the oxygen lack at birth."

"But why now? Why does something like this take a whole year to
develop?" asks Mother, equally grim but not featuring any gentleness.

Doctor, unless he's very clever and well informed, may not know the
answer to this frantic query. He may not be aware that over that year
the areas of the fetal brain damaged at birth have established themselves in neuronal pathways that are now malfunctioning instead of
just simply functioning. "Better that these damaged neurons never be
recruited for inclusion into the circuits of the one year old's brain?"
asks Mother—and perhaps you as well. Of course. But how does one
make such arrangements, persuading the infant brain to include only
healthy cells, disregarding those oxygen-deprived ones at birth?

The infant brain—a product of heredity, chance, and circumstance
—molds and remolds itself as the days merge into weeks then into
months. Cholinergic neurons, neurons in the forebrain, play a role in
the encoding of memory. These neurons aren't functional early on,
and shouldn't be, since nature didn't intend for us to recall our earliest
days lazing about in bassinets and playpens. In the fifteen-week-old
newborn, cholinergic neurons are comparatively inactive at the level of
cerebral cortex. Instead, their activity is clustered within the cerebellum, the coordinative part of the brain. The capacity to reach for the
bottle, to bring hand to mouth—that's what's important in the infant
brain. Not memory. Who would want to recall an endless series of
afternoons spent lying, staring at the ceiling, awaiting the arrival of
Mother or Father or doting Grandmother? Nature is merciful, therefore, in delaying the formation of cholinergic neurons within the memory centers of the cortex and hippocampus. Memory will come later,
when there's something worth remembering. Memory, however, will
always remain a tricky business: senility is apt to come on after the
infant brain has endured and been transformed into the adult brain.
No one is ever granted a guarantee that the infant brain, however
orderly its development and transition into an adult brain, will not at
some future time malfunction. When cholinergic neurons are lost in
Alzheimer's disease, the sufferer regresses to the level of infant, back
to the time when cholinergic fibers weren't yet formed and memory
was, therefore, impossible. "No guarantee," says Nature, even under
the best of circumstances. (Forget about the guarantees entirely if
these cholinergic extensions from the forebrain to every other part of
the brain don't take place at all.) The child, and at a later point the

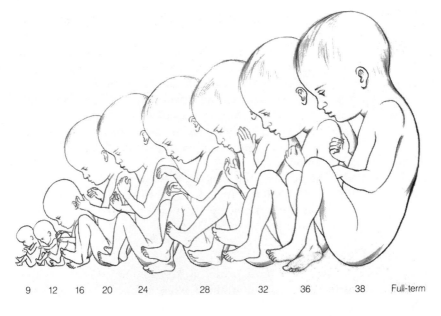

| 9 | 12 | 16 | 20 | 24 | 28 | 32 | 36 | 38 | Full-term |

These nine- to thirty-eight-week fetuses are approximately half actual size. The embryonic period extends to the end of the eighth week. The fetal period runs from the ninth week until birth.

adult resulting from such a failure, won't be educable, won't understand what he's told, and even if he did understand wouldn't be able to remember it anyway.

If normal intelligence and memory are to be expected, then, as in a drama, the development of the infant brain must go just right. Scenes must shift on schedule, actors must recall their lines and deliver them with precision and a feeling for tone and timbre. The infant brain must develop according to time sequence: different neurons coming on stage at the correct moment, delivering their assigned lines and then remaining in place. Eventually all the neurotransmitter systems cooperate in a contrapuntal melody, a most grandiloquent work: the Human Brain. Any slipup and the production will be a failure: a cacophony of voices delivering lines that don't make sense, music played over the wrong time signature.

"At one time the development of neurotransmitter systems was compared to the growth of trees, differentiating over time into large complex units. However, now it seems more accurate to say that during early development many of these systems have fundamentally different organizational patterns than are found in later life," remarks Dr. Michael Johnston.

The infant brain is more than simply a tiny version of the adult brain. Neurochemically it is different. Its circuitry is different. Functions are emphasized in the infant brain that later nature deems less important when infant has been transformed into child and still later into adult. Neurons change brain which changes person which changes behavior. What was once fetal brain becomes infant brain, grows a while, becomes child's brain, grows a while longer until after a while it is finally fitfully fruitfully an adult brain.

In the following section, the basics of brain development are set forth: neuron, synapse, neurotransmitter, the early migration of nerve cells, the formation of the neural plate. Our understanding of these fundamental units and processes make possible an understanding of the infant brain.

Starting with Chapter 19, we will pick up the trail once again, correlating as best we can, what is presently known about the fascinating interweaving of those contrapuntal themes, infant brain and infant behavior.

CHAPTER 3

"What Mysterious Forces . . . Establish These Protoplasmic Kisses?"

"Nature geometrizeth and observeth order in all Things," wrote Sir Thomas Browne in 1643 in *Religio Medici.* His remarks could aptly be applied to the developing brain since, in truth, the geometry of brain cells provides the underpinning for nature's most ordered structure: the human mind.

However simple or complex an organism, its individual brain cells, the neurons, look and behave very much alike. Each neuron is composed of a cell body, or soma, along with several receiving "antennae" called dendrites (from the Greek for "branches," as of a tree), along with a single hair-thin axon which transmits electrical signals for varying distances from the soma. Thus the nerve cell, or neuron, possesses processes concerned with reception (dendrites) as well as transmission (the axon).

The nerve signal, initiated in the soma, traverses the length of the axon at a speed about ten times faster than a well-trained athlete can run a hundred-meter dash.

The "message" from the nerve cell is conveyed via a code based on the variable spacings that separate the successive signals. The signals aren't bigger or louder in any way—what's important are the number of nerve cells and the intervals between them. Samuel Morse had a feeling for the power that can come from alternating short and long sounds. To do this it is also necessary to appreciate the importance of silence—that brief period when no sound provides the context within which subsequent dots and dashes can be manipulated into "We've sprung a leak in the engine room. Need help!"

As the axons approach the end of the line, they splay out, arborize, into increasingly slender and delicate treelike branches. These terminal arborizations are called telodendria (the Greeks provide the quint-

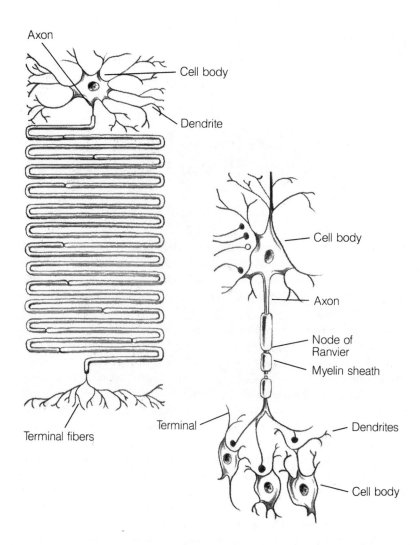

A neuron is composed of a cell body, an axon which carries the nerve impulse, and terminal fibers which form synapses with as many as a thousand other neurons. Most synapses join the terminals of one axon with the dendrites of another neuron. This arrangement enables one neuron to receive incoming signals from hundreds and, in some cases, thousands of neurons. Nerve conduction is enhanced and speeded up by the presence of an insulating myelin sheath which is interrupted periodically at the node of Ranvier.

essential term *telos*, "end"). Looked at through a powerful microscope these ultimate twigs (axonal arborizations) look strikingly like trees in a late fall landscape. And, like trees, they suggest patterns created without a readily identifiable pattern maker.

"If anyone wishes to be dissuaded from wrong thinking about creatures, he should go to look at the trees and notice every intricate detail. These, too, have many aesthetic features but no skill in the arts," wrote Philo of Alexandria sometime around 30 B.C. Were he equipped with a microscope, Philo might have justifiably said something similar about axonal arborization: a fine network of processes oftentimes interlacing into patterns of incredible beauty.

Almost two millennia after Philo a Spanish artist turned neuroanatomist, Santiago Ramón y Cajal, recognized in axonal arborization the same mute beauty. As a result of his study of the human brain Cajal discovered that he had compromised his artistic talents not a bit in switching his allegiance from art to the study of the neuron. After a hard day's work in his lab at the University of Madrid, Cajal lay awake, drawing pad on his lap, pen in hand, bottle of ink at his side. He often stayed awake like that, too excited to sleep, the artist in him revived and intent on capturing these treelike patterns—neurons, too, having "many aesthetic features but no skill in the arts."

The fine points of arborization, the ultimate twigs of this brain-tree, almost but don't quite make contact with dendrites from other neurons. Nor is this matter of *almost* making contact unimportant. In the event of direct contact or fusion between axonal twigs and dendrites, the brain could be considered one huge net with "everything connected to everything else." For the longest time this theory of the brain as a net, or reticulum, held sway. In fact, its most ardent spokesman was awarded a Nobel prize. He had to share it though with Ramón y Cajal who recognized how things really were: individual neurons approaching ever closer but never quite touching. Only an artist could be sensitive to that degree of detail.

At the point of near contact between the axon twig of one neuron and the dendrite of another (many, many dendrites from many, many other neurons actually) is formed what Sir Charles Sherrington, an eminent nineteenth-century physiologist, called the synapse (once again provided from Greek meaning "contact, point of juncture"). When the nerve signal reaches the end of the line, the final branch with its final twig, the message is switched from an electrical to a chemical one. This shift occasions a brief delay at the crossing point, a border check that takes no longer than half a thousandth of a second. At the nerve ending, near the synapse, chemicals are packaged in minute bubblelike structures, the vesicles. The electrical signal activates these vesicles to release their chemicals into the synaptic junction.

At one time it was thought that axons conveyed only excitation (stimulating the next neuron by means of exciting its dendrites) or inhibition (decreasing the chances that a second neuron might "fire"). More recent research indicates, however, that things are not that simple. More than one nerve signal chemical may pass across a single synapse. Further, the chemical may evoke stimulation or inhibition, exciting the adjacent nerve cell or bidding it remain quiescent.

Axons unconnected with other nerve cells do not exist within the brain. The "solitary neuron"—its solitariness based on the fact that it is not fused with other neurons—is, in fact, functionally related to untold numbers of other neurons. Widely separated neurons may join together via their axonal and dendritic arborizations to produce a thought, an impulse, the beginnings of a sonnet. Within milliseconds this active group of neurons may break up to form other groups. Flexibility in functional connections is based on chains of synaptic links: break the link at a critical juncture and the entire chain will dissolve.

One would think that the discovery of the interlocking nature of neurons would be enough to earn its discoverer a Nobel prize or, at the very least, a firm place in history. But how exquisitely ironic are the twists and turns of fate, almost as unexpected and intriguing, in fact, as the axon wending its way through the brain in search of the dendrites upon which it will synapse. For example, B. A. Gudden is remembered today not for his research on neuronal connections, but because of the fact that he died at age seventy-six while attempting, one fine summer afternoon, to rescue from drowning Ludwig, the Mad King of Bavaria.

The formation of a synaptic connection between two neurons is not a guarantee that either neuron will see the journey from toddler to totterer. Nature is too profligate for that. Indeed, many more neuronal connections are formed than can possibly endure. Cajal, in a relaxed moment, once observed excessive outgrowths of the dendritic branches, apparently directed at random. Examination of similar brain tissue from later stages of development revealed a reduction in the number and complexity of these dendritic branches. He immediately recognized that, unknowingly, he had been observing "an epic love story."

"I noticed that every ramification, dendritic or axonic, in the course of formation, passes through a chaotic period, so to speak, a period of trials, during which there are sent out at random experimental conductors most of which are destined to disappear . . . What mysterious forces precede the appearance of the processes, promote their growth and ramification . . . and finally establish these protoplasmic kisses, the intercellular articulations, which seem to constitute the final ecstasy of an epic love story?"

Neuroscientists don't write like Cajal anymore. "Romanticism," "sentimentality," "vitalism"—such are the denigrating terms that are applied to writings such as Cajal's. But how much closer to the mystery and grandeur of brain development does one come by resorting to the exact specification of neurotransmitters or the distance of daily axonal growth in millimeters? Don't think for a moment, however, that Cajal was an incurable romantic. While at one moment he was capable of describing neurons establishing "protoplasmic kisses" he could, when in a different mood, translate his poetic insight into coldly precise and acceptable scientific lingo.

"Communications, more or less intimate, are always established not only between the nervous arborizations but between the ramifications of one part and the body and protoplasmic extensions of another part." (Somehow I think "epic love story" is closer to the truth.)

Precision embedded within flexibility, poetry intermixed with cold-blooded calculation, predictability and chaos—from these dichotomies have evolved the human brain. And nowhere can the scheme of these separate influences be so easily perceived than in the earliest period of brain development.

While the development of synapses is partly a love story, it also proceeds according to a definite and oftentimes invariant plot. "Synapses appear very suddenly and increase rapidly in numbers thereafter," according to Dr. Marcus Jacobson, a neuroanatomist who knows as much as anybody alive about the developing human brain. "The stupendous increase in connectivity, which mainly consists of axodendritic synapses, does not occur at random. All the evidence shows that it is highly selective. Most of the evidence indicates that neuronal connections are determined by genetic and developmental processes that operate without any control from the outside world."

Our knowledge of how neurons connect with one another depended on a mixture of cunning and happenstance. Since the early nineteenth century neuroscientists have known that nerve cells tend to absorb different chemicals. They owed this observation to botanists who had observed years earlier that plants could be "quick-stained" with special solutions. Neurons from the fetal brain can also be stained in this matter, but the process isn't helpful: large sheets of nerve tissue take up the dye, precluding any possibility of differentiating one neuron from another or distinguishing one part of the brain from another.

By chance—perhaps dumb luck describes the event even better—a neuroscientist left some stained brain sections sitting overnight in a diluted solution. In the morning that neuroscientist found displayed at his table a masterpiece: the nerve tissue was neatly separated into gray and white matter.

The gray matter of the human brain consists of soma (cell body), dendrites, and the origins and terminations of the axons. The white matter consists of many bundles of axons ensheathed in an outer covering called myelin. This myelin acts as an insulator which thereby increases the speed of nerve conduction along the axon. It's also responsible for the designation "white matter" since neurons ensheathed in myelin are paler when stained than those bereft of myelin sheaths. The myelin clothes the axons as they weave and wend their way from their site of origin at the soma to their destination, Cajal's "protoplasmic kisses."

Early neuroscientists were able to study neurons by tracing their axonal pathways by means of special stains. If the axon of the nerve cell is deliberately severed a short distance from the cell body, the axon degenerates from the site of the cut outward. A stain was devised in the late nineteenth century which selectively adhered to the degenerated myelin sheaths that cover the axons. The paths of the axon could then be traced in this way for short distances within the brain.

In the case of the fetal brain, the brain age could be correlated with the different timetables of myelination which vary according to the age of the fetus. With the youngest fetus hardly any myelination was detected at all. With increasing age more and more myelination appears, though not anywhere near the total myelination that occurs over a lifetime. In order to comprehend that, it would be necessary for a scientist to set out a series of brains according to a strict chronology, whereby a fetal brain of eight weeks is plopped down beside a brain of ten weeks, twelve weeks, fourteen weeks—as many weeks as interest the investigator. Only in this way can the timetable of myelination be derived.

CHAPTER 4

Altering the Pattern

Every cell in the human body is potentially immortal. Indeed, if scientists could envision how to stop the effects of time and age on protein and genetic structure, one might well live forever (of course, some of us might pass up the chance with a polite "Thanks but no thanks." But science can't be built upon the wishes of such naysayers).

Our immortality has been adumbrated by experiments with cell lines: a cell is removed from its niche within the body and housed in a laboratory dish filled with the equivalent of chicken soup. Such orphan cells have grown, multiplied, and then multiplied again and again until finally the researchers grew bored with the endless multiplications and brought the experiment to a halt.

Odd but true, that body cells can live longer in glass containers than they can in the original containers they were designed as a part of. "Was born. Grew. Lived for a while. Died." Such is the universal epitaph which fits the eighty-year-old man laid to rest this winter morning, fits every cell of which that octogenarian was composed.

Not every body cell has the same degree of mortality, however. Some are more mortal than others. Skin cells slough off and are replaced each time we comb our hair, bathe, spend too much time in the sun. Liver cells regenerate with facility also. (The only exception: the alcoholic who destroys his liver cells faster than that destruction can be accommodated, since a proper interval is required, it seems, before new cells can be generated.) But in this matter of immortality and regeneration the brain is unique along lines that at first seem counterintuitive: all cells in the human brain are generated before birth. Nothing is added, but during life much is taken away: the Alzheimer afflicted, minus millions of neurons, sits in his den for long periods as if pondering. Even a trained brain doctor might be fooled into mistaking that silence for "pondering" until he discovers that the simple question, "What day is it?" elicits only additional silence.

Since the brain generates each of its denizen neurons only once and that generation occurs prior to the extrusion of the brain through the narrow birth canal in the female pelvis, this, in its turn, establishes the final practical limit on just how big that brain can be. A bigger brain without a modification of that maternal pelvis would result in the entrapment of that brain within the womb until such time as a surgeon could pull out through the belly what the midwife or obstetrician dared not try to extract from below.

Between sixteen and twenty weeks after the fertilization of the egg, nerve cell division is completed—all neurons celebrate their birthdays and christenings long before we celebrate ours. Put at its baldest, we are born with a brain in which neurons can only diminish in number and never increase—a sobering thought to occupy our attention on an overcast November afternoon.

In its absolute size the brain grows at a pace unknown throughout the rest of creation. The human infant pops out or is pulled out with a brain weighing in the range of three hundred grams—20 percent of the weight of the same brain on that day twenty years later when its possessor may stand nervously in the delivery room awaiting the arrival of *his* contribution to the next generation.

Fifteen to twenty years after birth is the accepted period during which the human brain continues to develop. No new neurons grow after birth but plenty of new connections, synapses, happen between and among the neurons. The increase in brain weight reflects this increase in the complexity of neuronal connections. In a cat eight days old the typical neuron may make a few hundred synapses. A month later that figure has jumped to thirteen thousand. And here, you must remember, we're speaking of a mere cat.

Neuroscientists still occasionally argue incidentally about whether or not human brain cells just might proliferate somewhere, sometime, somehow in the period after birth. In March 1983, developmental neuroscientists from all over the world gathered to settle the question once and for all during a closed meeting in Geneva, Switzerland. At the conference table, over wine, on the ski slopes, in the boudoirs, these scientists tossed about the question: How can we be certain that all brain cells are generated before birth? The holdouts emphasized that wonderful word "certain" and drew it out ever so delicately while shifting the emphasis, all the while fully aware that no one can ever be *absolutely certain* about anything, least of all something as complicated as the human brain. But on this occasion and in this Swiss retreat there was a surprise. One of the participants, Pasko Rakic, a neuroanatomist at the Yale University School of Medicine, told of a new surgical procedure whereby substantial portions of fetal monkey brain could be

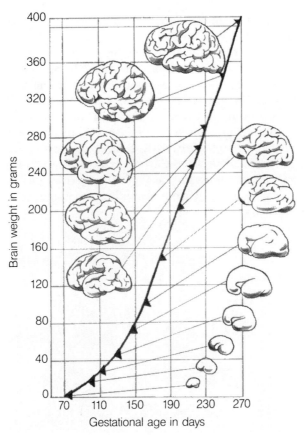

Growth curve of the human brain plotted on a scale starting at the tenth week of gestation (seventy days) and extending until birth.

removed, the monkey returned to the womb, and the pregnancy allowed to proceed to completion. By administering a radio isotope at the time of the surgery, Rakic provided a marker whereby the experimenter could detect the generation of additional brain cells. Briefly, if more cells were generated in order to make up for the missing tissue, they would contain traces of the isotope within their boundaries. Cells containing that isotope were never detected. How then did the neuroscientist account for the brain's adaptation to the removal of fetal brain tissue? Rakic suggested that the remaining cortex had become rearranged and its synaptic connections drastically altered. Along with this, the removal of brain cells in one area was thought to change the rate of neuronal death in other areas, thus "altering the pattern of their connections."

In other words, no new or additional brain cells but, instead, fewer cells dying in neighboring areas accompanied by additional connections between brain cells in areas not affected by the original fetal neurosurgery. Put in even simpler terms: at birth you have all the brain cells you're ever going to have, and they will continue to die off at an unspecified rate throughout your lifetime. Do such pronouncements strike you as depressing? If they do, think of the matter another way. The neuron perfectly mirrors our own situation. No second chance for it, no second chance for us. It is born with us, lives with us a while, and dies with us. We and our neurons are united across the boundary of a common mortality.

CHAPTER 5

Paradox

Human brain development presents an inherent paradox. How can two cells, one from the father, one from the mother, joined at fertilization give rise to such a tremendous variety of body cells? This is particularly intriguing when it's recalled that the genetic endowment of each body cell is exactly the same as every other.

Each time a living cell divides to form two daughter cells the entire library of genetic information is copied and transferred. Each "book" in the library consists of a gene: a string of DNA, the long, unbranched molecule containing the code for replication of the entire organism. The code is based on a four-letter alphabet, *A, G, T,* and *C,* with the letters corresponding to the first letter of the so-called nucleotide bases: adenine, guanine, thymine, and cytosine. Any three of the four letters are sufficient when combined to encode the message for a single amino acid, the building block of proteins. Three hundred bases thus contain enough information for a string of a hundred amino acids in a protein. Combine a sufficient number of proteins in a unique sequence and you have Danny Kaye. With a different protein combination based on another unique combination of amino acids you end up with Bruce Springsteen. Individuality is very much a matter of chromosomes, permutations of the four-letter code strung out along the length of DNA (actually two strands wound together in the famous double helix structure discovered by James Watson and Francis Crick in 1953). Individual variation, almost infinite, is ultimately traceable, therefore, to variations in the "message" conveyed by a four-letter code. Within a single organism there is also a tremendous degree of variation; body cells differ according to their placement and function. This is the paradox of human development.

Two theories uneasily coexist to express this paradox. To the molecular biologist—student of life at the level of the tiniest particle of matter whose existence everyone can agree upon—development depends on preferential gene expression: different genes being switched on at different times.

Embryologists—those less concerned with physics and more comfortable in the biology laboratory—speak of "deeper mysteries" that must be penetrated via higher levels of understanding. "The developmental biologist is looking for a strategy of genetic control that makes an arm different from a leg—that enables genes to be used in different ways in different tissues," says Peter Lawrence of the British Medical Research Council.

Both theories agree, however, that how an embryo constructs its "body plan" remains one of the great mysteries of human biology. Each part of the young embryo contains cells that must somehow "decide" to become a particular structure with a particular relationship to all other body parts. This pattern is revealed slowly, almost imperceptibly, on the basis of a series of "decisions" that funnel an individual cell down one developmental pattern rather than another. At this point we do not know on what basis this "decision" is made.

Consider for the moment the lonely zygote at thirty hours: two cells exactly alike in genetic composition. The genetic information encoded within the DNA, transmitted via the parental chromosomes to the new organism at the moment of conception, controls the structure of all the proteins in the cell along with the synthesis of all of its enzymes and chemical "messages" that will come into play within the cell. Individual variations—my green eyes and your blond hair—are the consequences of differences in enzymes and protein synthesis. Within only a few divisions, the growing embryo is converted into a bundle of cells containing highly organized, cyclical chemical reaction systems. Since the product of one reaction system may form the raw material for another completely different biochemical sequence, the stage is set at a very early moment for individuality and uniqueness.

It's been estimated that we have sufficient DNA in our cells to encode for several thousand times as many proteins as have so far been identified. In essence, embryonic cells possess far more potential for genetic variation than they actually express. But specialization of individual cells is a price that must be paid in order for the organism as a whole to endure; some cells must exist to convey information (neurons) while others must be content with more humble roles—conducting oxygen or perhaps only filtering urine.

My comparison of the brain cell and the kidney cell, the neuron and the nephron, wasn't arbitrarily chosen. The kidney cells, nephrons, are functioning by twelve to thirteen weeks of gestation. In order to do that the fetal kidney's biochemical milieu (a variant of the interior milieu of the French scientist, Claude Bernard) must be fully operational. Even in the youngest kidney ever studied, that of about ten weeks of gestational age, the enzyme patterns are strikingly similar to those found in the adult kidney. When it comes to things renal, whatever slight differences exist between the ten-week fetus and the eighty year old disappear by twenty-one weeks; the neonate is equal to the octogenarian getting up during the night for his third trip to the bathroom.

In the brain, things proceed more slowly, more in line with an organ that one day will be able to carry out experiments aimed at discovering what's happening in nephron and neuron, how they differ and, since they're alive, how much they have in common.

The early fetal brain pattern of one enzyme that neuroscientists have particularly fancied (the nonspecific esterase system it's called) is usually present from about eight to twenty weeks. Thereafter, slowly . . . slowly . . . slowly the adult pattern emerges. As the neuron matures and nerve cell processes become ensheathed in myelin coverings, the fetal brain pattern gradually shifts to its adult counterpart. By three months after birth the adult brain pattern is firmly in command and the fetal pattern barely detectable, its mission accomplished: the immature neurons have completed their process of division. It's likely that many stillbirths—responsible for the anguished, angry, bewildered faces of mothers who have done everything right but still have "lost the baby" —are the results of defects within these functional enzymes. A slight modification of the fetal enzyme pattern and neurons cease to divide or divide too often or too imperfectly. The mother of one such fetus came from a family of fifteen children. Six of these were—as the doctors euphemistically termed it—"mentally subnormal."

Genes and enzymes, two ballroom dancers moving in perfect synchrony to music that differs from moment to moment and from one body cell to another. It's speculated that developmental rhythms follow a timetable, conform to the dictates of a "body clock." But if this is true, then the clocks are set differently in kidney cells and brain cells, in skin cells and liver cells. Some enzyme systems may appear only when the tissue is fully mature. In other cells these same enzyme systems provide the necessary goad for further growth toward maturity. Thus structure and function are more intimately connected than was ever suspected in those "good old days" (not too far in the past) when Anatomy was nailed onto one laboratory door of the medical school and Physiology placed upon another door halfway down the hall. Neuroscientists now are more aware that they need to be less rigid in their definitions. Manipulate the interior of a neuron—rearrange its furniture a bit—and enzymes go on strike, neurons cease to divide—and hence the anguish and anger of "I lost the baby." Interfere with one enzyme system (perhaps with a drug such as thalidomide) and other body cells instead of just neurons cease to divide. Translation: a child is born who must look forward to a lifetime of "tailored clothes" to camouflage the absence of arms or legs.

CHAPTER 6

Neural Plate

At between three and four weeks after conception a line of cells along the back of the zygote begins to stand out from its neighbors. From this sheet, the neural plate, will arise the most special parts of a human being: dreams, illusions, griefs, tenderness, lust.

This neural plate at first folds into a long and hollow tube. Within seconds of this transformation neuronal cells begin a process of multiplication that starts out on the order of the number of spectators in a good-sized football stadium and eventually exceeds the number of stars in the Milky Way.

By four weeks of age the main divisions of the brain are already established: forebrain (destined to produce cerebral hemispheres), midbrain, hindbrain, and spinal cord. Although these descriptive names are helpful they are nothing more than arbitrary sobriquets. One could easily describe them in different ways as did Anton van Leeuwenhoek in 1683. "The Humane Foetus tho no bigger than a Green Pea, yet is furnished with all its parts." A contemporary of Leeuwenhoek's, Sir Christopher Wren, the very same Wren of St. Paul's Cathedral and the Ashmolean Museum, had, at a slightly earlier time, visualized the adult brain by injecting wine and colored dyes into its feeding arteries. (Was the dome of St. Paul's an outgrowth of Wren's interest in the overarching vaults of the cerebral hemispheres?)

By eight weeks the swellings destined to form the major portions of the brain are sufficiently visible that after some instruction even a neophyte can point and exclaim, "There! Those are the future cerebral hemispheres, and that outpocketing along the back of the brain is the cerebellum."

By eighteen weeks the main grooves on the outside of the hemisphere have appeared, but the surface is still smooth, as smooth as a baby's cheek.

Later, by twenty-eight weeks, the hemispheres are demarcated: fron-

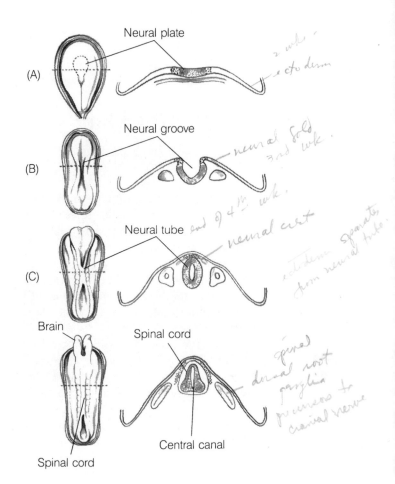

The brain and spinal cord (central nervous system) develop from the neural plate, a flat sheet of cells on the back surface of the embryo. (A) The plate folds in on itself to form the neural groove (B). The neural groove closes into a hollow structure, the neural tube (C). The central canal, enclosed by the neural tube, enlarges at the head end to form the ventricles or cavities of the brain. These drawings illustrate this unfolding process from two points of view: externally and in a cross section at about the level of the middle of the future spinal cord. The processes illustrated here take place between the third and fourth weeks after conception.

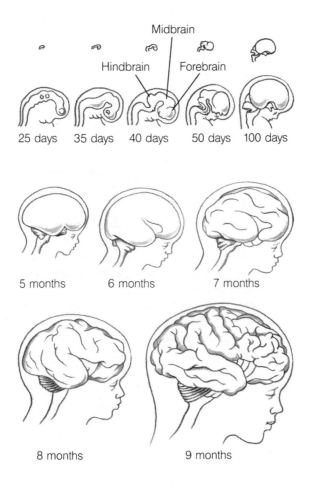

Development of the infant brain. These diagrams are about half of actual size except for the lower two diagrams which are slightly enlarged for clarity. The forebrain which gives rise to the cerebral hemispheres grows out of proportion to the rest of the brain.

tal lobe in front, temporal lobe backward and downward, parietal lobe backward and astride the temporal lobe, separated from it by the lateral fissure also known as the fissure of Sylvius in deference to the seventeenth-century mystic and anatomist, Franciscus Sylvius (Franz de le Boë).

From here on, many of the brain areas bear the names of scientists lucky enough or presumptuous enough to spot something no one else had ever seen before and to promptly post their names, stake their claims on a tiny part of the territory. In the beginning, however, only Latin or Greek names would do to convey the necessary grandeur and wonderment and awe—as if "prosencephalon develops into telencephalon" is saying more than "the forebrain separates into two cerebral hemispheres." But for some reason the early researchers on the terra incognita of the brain favored exotic, convoluted, or simply unfamiliar and often unpronounceable terms. Today we eschew such terminology. You would have stopped reading long ago if I insisted on telling you about how "the rhombencephalon forms two regions, the metencephalon and myelencephalon." No. In the interest of precision we prefer to hear that the forebrain has two lateral extensions (the cerebral hemispheres) connected by an intermediate region.

As the hemispheres grow a hollow space is maintained, the lateral ventricles, which communicates with that intermediate zone, the third ventricle. This, in turn, continues down into a wide tapering of the midbrain called the cerebral aqueduct which, in its turn, is continuous to the opening farther down of the fourth ventricle and then to the central canal of the spinal cord. By clearing out the Greek and Latin in this way, we achieve what we value most: accuracy and precision. But what about the mystery? Did "rhombencephalon" exist as a kind of mantra that conveyed something as important as the anatomical details which made it possible for a Renaissance anatomist to produce an accurate drawing of the brain anatomy? Were these terms as we would interpret them simply a cloak behind which was concealed an abysmal ignorance? Or did the words express an appropriate sense of wonder, mystery, and awe? In this brain, at first barely visible through the most powerful microscope, then green pea sized, then the size of a thumb, then a nut and, even at full maturity, never bigger than a closed fist— how and when during these transformations does the mind emerge, the mind that outvaunts chimps, gorillas, dolphins and, rest assured, the most powerful computer networks that man's brain will ever devise? In short, what happens to the infant that enables it eventually to conquer gorilla and chimp?

For one thing, the infant brain—the fetal brain actually, since infancy

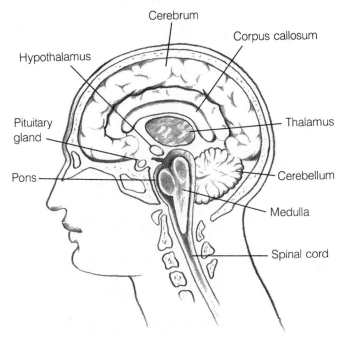

Cerebrum

Corpus callosum

Hypothalamus

Pituitary gland

Thalamus

Pons

Cerebellum

Medulla

Spinal cord

The main divisions of the human brain as seen in a cutaway view from the left side.

begins postnatally when the final "product" of this marvelous process lies cradled in its father's arms—grows out of proportion to the rest of the body.

By week nine the head of the fetus is almost but not quite half the length of the body. At this point within the next ten weeks the fetus will grow at a greater rate than at any time during its life. Between nine and twelve weeks the body length doubles, outpacing the increase in head size which is proceeding now at a slower rate. Coupled with this change, the neck lengthens and extends so that the chin is no longer contacting the body, the fetus no longer bent forward with future face and future forehead touching tiny hands clasped together in front of the chest: a dreaming Buddha floating mysteriously and gently in the amniotic sea.

At thirteen weeks the fetus sucks its thumb, an activity that may continue for two or three or perhaps several years until its mother or care giver or somebody finally says, "Stop! Look out there . . . a whole world to please you if only you can give up that thumb!'' Even the fetus, it seems, requires comfort, solace, some sense of meaning, even though that meaning at such an early stage may involve nothing more complicated than the feel of its own thumb.

CHAPTER 7

Differentiation

Studies on neuron growth and development are influenced by such practical considerations as the number of neurons in the fetal brain that defy the most ingenious attempts at computation and classification, and other constraints having to do with the time required for nerve cell multiplication.

In addition, neuroscientists can't allow themselves, or be allowed, the freedom in experimenting on humans that they employ in their investigations of *Drosophila* (the fruit fly), *Caenorhabditis elegans* (the namatode worm), or *Daphnia* (the small shellfish)—three organisms favored by embryologists in their studies of early brain development. From the investigations of these simple creatures (fewer neurons, less complexity in neuronal organization, no complaints from the subjects, no need to report to ethical review boards, and so on), neuroscientists have discovered quite a bit about how human brain cells develop.

As a first step some cells in the ectoderm, the outer layer of the embryo, are transformed into brain cells. This process of *neural induction* proceeds according to a specific scenario. At an early stage of embryonic development, all cells have the potential to develop into any cell of the body. For example, if one removes cells that ordinarily would develop into neurons and places them in different body regions, these cells become part of where they are put—skin or muscle or intestinal cells. At a certain stage of development, however, neuronal cells assume a specific identity as neurons and as nothing else. This occurs at about fifteen to sixteen days after fertilization when the embryo is in the form of a ball, a gastrula. The mesoderm lies on the outside of the ball and begins to creep inward along the inner lining. Picture your fingers slipping inward as they peel and separate the skin from the body of an orange. As the fingers—the mesoderm—advance, the ectoderm, overlying and forming the outer layer, is transformed into tissue which is irreversibly, intensely neuronal.

Anyone who has ever thought about the nature of identity can benefit from pondering on the process of neuronal induction. Ectoderm destined to become nervous tissue can only do so under the influence of a layer—the mesoderm—which alone has nothing "nervous" about it. It's speculated that the mesoderm exerts its formative influence by means of a chemical factor which it releases, thereby consigning the overlying ectodermal cells to the role of neurons.

A German investigator Hans Spemann transplanted mesoderm from one embryo into the center of the embryonic cavity of a second embryo. The result? The formation, off to the side, of a secondary nervous system. His conclusion? The transplanted mesoderm induced within the host embryo a given number of cells that went on to become neurons instead of skin cells. Another researcher, Johannes Holtfreter, also a German and also a fancier of exotic and meticulously conducted experiments, decided to examine the question quite the other way around—what happens when mesoderm is prevented from creeping inward (no initial break is made in the surface of the orange so that the fingers can't edge inward along the lining). By flooding the embryo with a salt solution, this German caused the mesoderm to drift off to other parts of the petri dish. This unfortunate embryo failed to develop any nervous system at all.

After only three weeks of life the brain is a mix of the arbitrary and the rigidly defined. Primordial tissue must have the potential to spawn every conceivable cell in the body. At the same time, ectoderm must be attentive so that it may be shaped by the chemistry of mesoderm, cell influencing cell through the intermediary of chemicals no chemist has yet discovered much less been capable of synthesizing. A gene produces a chemical that, in turn, activates yet another gene so that the process of differentiation can go on—the delicate pirouette of chance and necessity. If the process is allowed to do what it does, everything proceeds according to schedule: forebrain, hindbrain, and spinal cord inching their way toward deliverance and light.

Chance and necessity, determinism and freedom—these pesky dualisms have their counterpart in the events that unfold in the first months of life. The developing embryo at three weeks has its basic brain, some day to be associated with the mind—or is it already associated? Sperm and egg together forming zygote, forming embryo, forming fetus, forming an infant. At three weeks the process is irreversibly started, this tiny creature, itself, the product of chance and necessity, on its way to encounter and, with luck, understand and learn to cope with the world of chance and necessity in which eight short months later it will find itself.

CHAPTER 8

Good Migrations

Between twenty-one and twenty-four days the neural tube is completed, the result of the fusion of the edges of the folded neural plate, the forerunner of cells that eventually will think and will oftentimes forget. At this early stage of three weeks the embryo is empowered with a rudimentary brain charged with the mandate to fashion between then and thirteen weeks a structure that is identifiably and indubitably brainy in appearance. From three weeks onward the process of multiplication begins. By the time you've read this paragraph a quarter of a million brain cells have multiplied in each and every growing fetus in the world.

As we have seen, neurons migrate from the simple sheet of cells which then divide and divide again. More important than this feat of multiplication, however, is how the neurons wind up in their final position within the brain. Such knowledge could not be derived simply from observing neurons through a microscope. Too remote. Too static a procedure. Microscopic slides reveal only dead cells. Indeed, a neuron's ability to take up and retain a conventional histologic stain is positive proof of its morbidity. A butterfly entrapped for subsequent display within a collector's folio teaches little about the beauty of flight. A box filled with slides of fetal brain cells is equally unrevealing of how the brain reaches its hundred billion population. An understanding of neuron multiplication awaited the development of a nonbiologic technique, a vibrant dynamic tool that captures movement and life.

Recently it has become possible to visualize within the living brain patterns of fetal brain cell growth and development. In this technique the fetal brain cells of a monkey are exposed to a brief pulse of radioactively labeled thymidine (thymidine is a component of DNA). The thymidine is subsequently taken up into the chromosomes of the multiplying brain cells. Those brain cells that incorporate the labeled thymidine within their DNA remain permanently labeled. Whenever these cells reach their ultimate destination, therefore, they can be located. For instance, labeled neurons are found in the visual cortex only in monkeys that have been exposed to the isotope between forty and a hundred days of fetal life. Based on this observation a neuropathologist from Harvard concluded that all the neurons destined for the primary visual cortex (at least in the monkey, and we have no reason to doubt something similar can be said of humans as well) are generated during a two-month period in the middle of gestation. Neurons labeled at different times in the gestational cycle wind up in different areas of the fully developed brain. In order to do this, neurons must migrate from their positions along the ventricular wall to their final destination, oftentimes over unbelievably vast distances.

In order to get some feeling for the complexity of neuronal migration, picture a tissue approximately the width of a human hair. Within this tissue are aligned a small number of neurons with their cell bodies close to the inner layer of the tissue and their cell processes extending toward the outer wall. Those neurons farthest from the inner ventricular wall start making additional DNA. As this genetically controlled process unfolds, the neurons move back toward the inner ventricular surface. At this point mitotic cell division occurs. Where there was one neuron there are now two, the first halting step toward the eventual hundred billion figure. These two cells now migrate outward, away from the inner wall where new DNA is synthesized in each cell. Like dancers successfully and rhythmically repeating a series of highly organized and strictly defined movements, the neurons repeat again and again their cycle: the migration inward toward the ventricular wall, cell division, the migration outward, the building up once again of DNA, the passage inward to the ventricular wall, cell division, movement outward. Soon two becomes four, becomes eight . . . sixteen . . . thirty-two . . . sixty-four. The process of multiplication seems like it could go on forever, just as dancers feeling the rhythm can effortlessly and joyfully repeat the steps they know by heart that have become as natural and effortless as breathing.

But at a certain point which differs from one brain to another—indeed, displays quantum differences within different portions of the same brain—the process of repetition stops. Brain cells lose the capacity to synthesize more DNA. And, at this point, like impatient, rebellious teenagers, these cells that have ceased to divide no longer pause in their outward migration but form a new layer of cells outside the confining boundaries of the ventricular wall. These cells—now forming the intermediate zone—will never again divide. For them the dance of seemingly unending multiplication is over; they are at the "end of the line"—but what a marvelous ending it is. From these cells will be selected those neurons that will survive eighty or ninety years that will be responsible for dreams and illusions, triumphs and disappointments, that will outlast every other cell in the body, that will simply and marvelously endure until the end, that moment on a cold December afternoon when the old man or woman is finally laid to rest within the frozen ground.

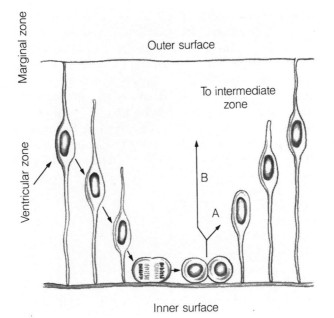

Migration of nerve cells in the developing embryo. Cells in the ventricular zone move toward the inner surface, become rounded in shape, and then divide. After cell division the daughter cells either move back out again to repeat the cycle (A) or (if the cells have stopped dividing) they may become a permanent part of the intermediate zone in the wall of the brain (B).

The physicist who unravels the mystery of matter, the orator who moves his audience to passionate rebellion, the mystic, the seer, the saint, the sinner—is any one of them more than the sum total of these rebellious neurons?

Neuroembryologists tell us that no one knows what turns off the mechanism of cell multiplication. No scientist can tell us who told a certain neuron to multiply no more, to move outward and become a part of what another neuroscientist once called the "enchanted loom":

the adult human brain. One thing is certain, however. The time is not capriciously established. Sometime, somewhere, somebody has set a limit that varies for each of the dancers. Some make their exit early, moving outward to populate the intermediate layer wherein they await further instructions about how they should proceed to their rightful places. Some of these neurons can be dubbed adult neurons (the human brain cell does not undergo a period of adolescence; one moment it's "immature" and the next moment "mature" or "adult").

Most scientists also speak of the neuron as female. "After mitosis (cell division) the daughter cells reform their peripheral processes, and their nuclei return to the deeper layers of the epithelium before reentering the mitotic cycle," one has written. I've never encountered any reference to "son cells," only "daughter cells," which perhaps was appropriate terminology to use in an earlier age when "sensitive," "responsive," and "delicate"—and the neuron is all of these—were attributes considered primarily feminine. No one believes that now. A brain is a brain is a brain. Undoubtedly the neurons making up that brain exist on a more ethereal realm than can possibly be predicated by our paltry pronominals.

CHAPTER 9

The Evolving Brain

The migration of neurons . . . the passage of being . . . the conveyance of meaning, purpose, and delight can be altered irretrievably by a medication taken early in pregnancy or a dose of radiation ("If you are pregnant, mention this to the radiologist" it says on the wall of a cubicle where you undress in preparation for X rays) or a virus manifesting itself as perhaps something as trivial as a "cold" which can be barely recalled nine months later. But the most mysterious interference with "good migration" is inherent in the genes themselves. Thanks to the influence of forces no one completely understands but many are eager to speculate about (cosmic rays, the effects of ongoing nuclear radiation from atomic blasts twenty-five years past) genes can malfunction: they don't turn on at the correct moment, but too early or too late. Programs that shouldn't become operative do so while necessary programs languish like eager young girls waiting to be courted. Under ordinary conditions an untold number of influences are at work directing this cell here and that cell over there. The orchestration must be perfect; there is no room for dissonant notes or missed notes; all improvisations must be kept to a minimum.

A brain scientist had this to say about the consequences of neurons migrating too early, too late, or too capriciously. "If this complex process of migration is disturbed by genetic factors or toxins, the cells may not reach the proper position. If it is extreme, the fetus will be aborted. If it is milder, the pathologist would detect this malformation. However, if it is even milder, it will not come to the pathologist but to the psychiatrist." Think of this: an adult couched in the office of a Freudian disciple, the talk drifting on to neuronal migration patterns. Did the tiny neuron "decide" to move at an inauspicious time or perhaps not move at all? Where's the blame? Who or what was responsible for such malfeasance? Listen again to our neuroscientist as he muses about what to all appearances is a "normal adult brain."

"It would be what we call a 'normal brain' and yet some cells or the processes of some cells will not be in the appropriate position at the appropriate time and, as a result, there would be a relatively slight malfunction of the brain."

What might be the result of such a "slight malfunction"? Is angst the result of a faulty neuronal migration pattern? Are neurons that have gone awry responsible for an eight-year-old child's problem with reading or sitting still or inverting his letters? (Such performances are inevitably those of a "he": the male brain is defiant of antitrust laws and establishes an early monopoly on mirror writing, hyperactivity, and dyslexia.)

"The question is simple but the answer is complicated," says our neuroscientist. He bids us consider the cerebral cortex, the overarching mound of brain tissue, avacadolike in consistency and in appearance reminiscent of a gnarled walnut. (Whenever we speak of the brain and compare it to something else we inevitably draw on mixed metaphors, juggle the senses so that, taken together, touching and seeing can give us some adumbration of what the brain is really like—not the feel of the walnut and the sight of the avacado but the other way around.)

The cortex is generated in about sixty days, the task well on its way to completion at the time the expectant mother makes her way to the obstetrician to confirm her suspicions about why her menstrual periods have ceased and how that change explains why she is feeling sick to her stomach every morning.

If one takes the number of cells in the human cerebral cortex and applies simple mathematical formulas, one can predict that it takes forty to forty-two multiplications to form the cortex. This doesn't take into account the fact that some brain areas are generated in very short periods while others take much longer. For this reason, some parts of the brain need perhaps eighty to a hundred generations, while others need only five to ten.

Several years ago one brain scientist attempted to inject some uniformity into the process of explaining brain growth. In a laboratory in Lausanne, Switzerland, he began counting all the neurons in one fetal brain. Some say he committed suicide six months into the project (the batteries were low in his calculator and the whole thing just went "piff"), while another source assures me that he's still counting, sitting alone in his laboratory not far from the banks and investment houses where Swiss gnomes also count for a living, favoring, however, the computation of francs rather than neurons.

In any case our neuroscientist assures us that "it is so difficult to count that I would not suggest that. Even if it is a good way, I do not think it is a practical way."

But despite his cautions let us proceed a bit with a numeration which must be tempered lest it drift into numerology. After all, numbers provide a sense of security, a talisman that can be clutched to our breasts so that we might enlighten our understanding. But numbers can also be deceptive, often telling us nothing at all. By ten years of age a child has lived 3,650 plus days. But how many of these days does he remember? On what particular day did he learn to sit, to walk, to control his bowels and bladder? Such insights do not come from the simple review and recitation of numbers. One must look beyond numbers in order to achieve meaning.

Starting at two and a half weeks after the fusion of egg and sperm, neurons start multiplying at a rate that boggles our understanding. Not even the national debt gives us a hint of what such a multiplication process implies. Assuming that the adult human brain contains on the order of a hundred billion neurons and that no neurons are added after birth, we can calculate that neurons must be generated in the developing brain on an average rate of more than two hundred and fifty thousand per minute.

Additional numbers: the total genetic information in mammalian cells is about 10^5 genes. The number of neural interconnections, however, is 10^{15}. The conclusion? The development of the brain cannot proceed simply according to a genetic "plan" or "map." It is not "all in the genes," as the reductionists would have us believe.

To appreciate the difficulties involved in relating genes to structure, consider the lowly fruit fly. Pioneering biologists once made heroic efforts to infer how genes regulate the various bodily appearances that fruit flies exhibit. With only five thousand genes the fruit fly seemed a perfect laboratory model. Simply correlate fruit fly variations with observations on genetic variability, and, presto, the mysteries of that humble creature would be revealed. About halfway through the project, however, the futility of such an enterprise became obvious. Exhaustive descriptions of all the thousands of mutations to which fruit fly embryos are heir filled a weighty tome familiarly known as "the Red Book." Several hundred pages and nervous breakdowns later the project was abandoned. Even in an organism with comparatively few genes, the number of variations in external appearance is mind-boggling.

Put another way, brain development doesn't proceed like a play: setting, action, dialogue, conflict, dénouement, resolution. Rather, the brain is a mix of rationality and planning coupled with whim, circumstance, feelings, perhaps even karma.

Assume for a moment that the amount of information required to produce the fully developed brain and all of its complexity and detail cannot be contained within the genes alone. As a corollary also assume that no one is capable at the moment of specifying how many of the total number of genes are involved in specifying the structure of the brain. Genes specify programs of brain cell growth, migration, and interaction which result, according to Marcus Jacobson, in a "self-assembly of neural circuits without requiring genetic control of the cell movements and interactions or genetic specifications of all the details of the fully-developed structure."

Put more simply, the genes influence the human brain in the manner of a president who sets policy but leaves the general day-to-day implementation of his policy to subordinates. In the absence of this flexibility, the resulting brain is rigidly confined and can produce only a limited behavioral repertoire (that's why we're setting traps for the lobster rather than the other way around).

Pondering the influence of genes on the brain—a preliminary pondering before anyone can usefully ponder the relationship of the brain to thoughts—induces in the true ponderer a question. What is the relationship between genes, proteins, and brains? Genes modify proteins which, in turn, modify neuronal networks which modify brains which, if one proceeds far enough along the line of one thing modifying another, would, some believe, lead up to a neuronal version of *The Critique of Pure Reason.* But as Kant realized, the structure of the Mind (writ large) determines the thinking processes that Mind is capable of. Getting at that structure and how it comes about in all of its majesty is the task currently preoccupying neuroembryologists.

One-to-one correspondences are the stuff of gene-protein interactions: if the gene fumbles the ball, the resulting protein product disruption results in a young mother, barely recovered from the delivery, trying to fathom through an anesthesia haze what the pediatrician is telling her about her baby, the baby that she hoped would be "perfect," but instead, it seems, suffers from a genetic disease, phenylketonuria (PKU). The pediatrician must now explain to her how a gene-protein misunderstanding has resulted in a child whose body cells can't handle the amino acid phenylalanine and how an accumulation of that substance threatens to result in severe mental retardation in an otherwise "perfect baby." No pediatrician in the world can work the equation backward: explain to the distraught mother how one can track mental retardation to protein disturbances to the specific fumbling by the genes and finally relate that to what went wrong at the level of DNA. The fundamental building block of the brain, the neuron, still keeps its secrets, sphinxlike, despite the neuroscientists' best efforts. "The path of migration of the neuron, the direction of growth of its axon and dendrites, the orientation of the dendritic branches, and the precise location of synapses have not been traced back to the genes," Dr. Jacobson has written in a book the pediatrician is likely to read before explaining to the mother. "Mutations have been found that affect a large variety of structures and functions in the developing nervous system, but in no case has the causal nexus from mutant gene to mutant phenotype been unraveled." In plain words, the words one would use to the distraught mother if totally candid, "We don't know at this point all the reasons why your baby has been born with PKU."

CHAPTER 10

Preformation

Aristotle began one of the most lengthy debates in the history of science: Is the development of an animal based on preformation (from the beginning all the parts are present in miniature and will automatically appear in due time) or is development dependent on the effects of the environment? As often happened, Aristotle was better at asking questions than he was at supplying answers.

On the whole, Aristotle and other philosophers at the time tended to favor preformation. One sunny afternoon in Rome two thousand years ago, Seneca summed up the philosopher's viewpoint: "In the seed are enclosed all the parts of the body of the man that shall be formed. The infant that is borne in his mother's wombe hath the rootes of the beard and hair that he shall weare one day. In this little masse likewise are all the lineaments of the bodie and all that which Posterity shall discover in him."

With the invention of the microscope, the advocates of preformation declared a victory of sorts: "Look there at the human sperm. Don't you see a tiny man at the head end? And if you still have doubts look at the tiny horse enclosed within this horse sperm."

Close observations of embryos, however, revealed a striking contradiction to the claim of the preformationist: embryos, regardless of the species, resemble embryos of other animals more than they resemble the adults of their own kind. This is in striking contradiction to a view favored throughout the eighteenth century: the embryos of higher species recapitulate the adult features of lower forms (a human embryo was at an earlier stage a turtle).

Another philosopher, Ernst Haeckel, confidently enshrined that "man is at one point a turtle" to the status of a dogma: "Ontogeny recapitulates phylogeny." One of Haeckel's students, W. Roux, the son of a fencing master at the University of Jena, challenged his mentor to a duel (a purely intellectual one, with words and concepts substitut-

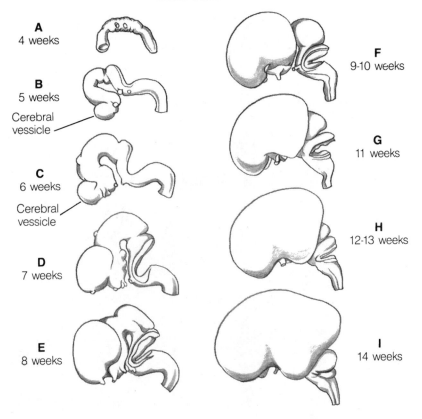

A
4 weeks

B
5 weeks
Cerebral
vessicle

C
6 weeks
Cerebral
vessicle

D
7 weeks

E
8 weeks

F
9-10 weeks

G
11 weeks

H
12-13 weeks

I
14 weeks

The human brain at different developmental stages as seen from the side. Magnification varies from a factor of 20 in A to only about 1.5 in I. The cerebral vessicle gradually enlarges from a small "bump" at five weeks to its final eminent position and size at fourteen weeks.

ing for swords). Roux repeated an experiment originally attempted by Haeckel.

A fertilized frog's egg was isolated at the point of its initial cleavage into two cells. Roux killed one of these cells and awaited developments. Suppose, for the sake of making a point, that the creature that grew from the remaining cell constituted half an embryo. What conclusions would you draw? Roux believed that he observed just that sequence and, therefore, concluded that each cell developed independently and possessed only the information necessary to create a part of the future frog.

Three years later Roux himself was challenged by another neuro

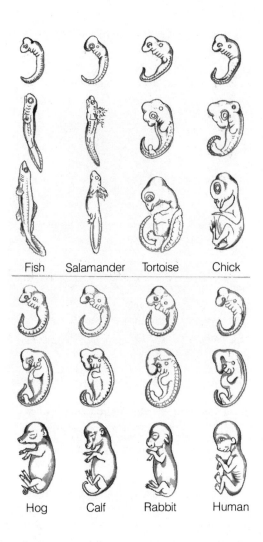

Fish Salamander Tortoise Chick

Hog Calf Rabbit Human

The appearance of vertebrate embryos at various stages of development have many similarities. This suggests that these different animals share the same basic mechanisms of development and, perhaps, a common ancestor.

type who, according to the most updated information now available, knew nothing about fencing but quite a bit about early embryonic development. A clever German working at the Zoological Station in Naples, H. Driesch brought an antivivisectionist spirit to Roux's earlier experiment: instead of killing one of the two original cells (sea urchin this time instead of frog), Driesch merely separated them by a constricting band, a separation carried out with the vigor and sense of purpose of a surgeon setting out to individuate Siamese twins. Under these circumstances, each of the isolated cells developed into a complete, albeit slightly smaller, example of the breed. This "induced twinning of amphibian eggs," as it was dubbed in textbooks of embryology, is considered today a milestone on our journey toward understanding human biology. Incidentally, you may ask, why had Driesch succeeded in the very experiment that Roux had carried out only three years earlier? Most probably, although one can't be sure at this point, the cell which Roux had attempted to kill remained in contact with its mate, provoking an abnormal developmental pattern.

Despite Driesch's success as an experimentalist, he "converted" in his later years to a lofty mysticism. "The harmonious equipotential system" (Driesch's words) represented by the embryo defied analysis, Driesch lectured his students, philosophy students. (Driesch later in life shifted from the laboratory to the amphitheater where he encountered budding philosophers who knew nothing about budding sea urchins.) In short, Driesch was a vitalist, convinced that no system based on pushings and pullings and classical mechanics could ever explain why the separation of two sea urchin eggs at the two-cell stage produces two of the creatures instead of only one. But we should not be too critical of Driesch. Mechanical reductionism (life is no different from any other physical system) continues to vie with a presently unpopular vitalism (there's something unique about living creatures that will never be fully explained simply on the basis of chemistry and physics). Nor is it likely that the last word has been said on the subject of whether or not there is something unique about living creatures.

Around the turn of the century, not long after Driesch's experiment on the sea urchin, Henry V. Wilson, a marine biologist, took a sponge, perhaps the simplest multicellular organism on earth, and separated its cells by pressing the sponge through a mesh. When the separated cells were mixed in solution, they reassembled, once again to form a functioning sponge. In order to make his point with even more flair, Wilson mixed cells of two different species, one red, one blue. He observed the cells of this purple mass separate once again into groups of red and blue. Finally each group assumed the structure of a sponge. The lesson? An organism's cells can somehow "recognize" one another and, if given the chance, will seek one another out, like cozying up to like.

Brain cells too, like immigrants, prefer their own, aggregating together and exhibiting a camaraderie that they don't and can't have with outsiders. Nor are these ghettos unique to nerve cells. Cells from different tissues throughout the body prefer to commingle with one another when given a choice (liver cells prefer other liver cells to kidney cells and so on). If you'd like to learn more about this process you may ask an eighty-five-year-old man who carried out the definitive experiments in the 1950s. His name is Johannes Friedrich Karl Holtfreter—he is still alive and was until recently in his laboratory at the University of Rochester.

Our neuroscientist discovered some years ago that in the embryo different types of cells when separated from one another by the experimenter's machinations reassemble if given half a chance. Subsequent efforts to explain this sociability of one neuron toward another neuron of the same brain area have led to a search for "cell adhesives."

Do the cells exhibit a stickiness like fingers to fresh taffy? Or do nerve cell membranes contain embedded within their structure receptor sites designed to bind with complementary sites within the membranes of a "sister cell"? A decade ago a scholarly tome on the subject of neuronal recognition implied that nerve cells might fraternize with one another on the basis of "intercellular adhesive selectivity." One neuroscientist, S. Roth, even attempted to isolate the rascal molecule. His failure prompted a critic to query, "What hath Roth got?"

While Driesch and Wilson provided proof that cells possess the ability to recognize their cohorts, neither investigator was able to provide an explanation for their observations. This awaited the efforts in the 1940s of Roger W. Sperry of the California Institute of Technology who later would win a Nobel prize for his work on the separate functions of the cerebral hemispheres (the "split brain" research). Sperry shifted attention away from sea urchins and sponges. To him the brain and the brain alone was a suitable experimental subject since its construction is the most complicated feat of biological development.

Whereas one liver cell is pretty much like another, does the same thing, looks and acts like other liver cells, the landscape of the brain is infinitely more complex. The cerebral cortex, for instance, consists of precisely interconnected nerve cells and nerve cell processes. Often nerve cells and neuronal patterning can alter dramatically within a span of only a few millimeters. Brain cells, therefore, must be more discriminating than any other cell in the body in terms of locating and adhering to a select group of similar cells.

Sperry examined the way connections are formed among nerve cells in the retina and other cells within the brain of a goldfish. Under ordinary conditions the retinal cells project their axonal extensions backward from the retina to the midbrain. There the retinal cells link up with their target cells. As a result of this linkage it's possible to plot a map wherein retinal cells can be superimposed upon a grid of the midbrain to yield the entire visual field. If a certain number of retinal cells are missing, the absence of connections within the midbrain results in a distortion of the visual field.

Sperry cut the axon emanating from the goldfish's retina. As expected, the axonal connections to the midbrain atrophied as well and eventually disappeared. Each retinal cell then regenerated its axon, growing millimeter by millimeter back to its original target site in the midbrain. The linkup was precise and identical to what had existed prior to Sperry's experimental alteration. No matter how many times Sperry severed the retinal to midbrain connections, they grew back in exactly the same distribution. In one variation of the experiment, Sperry even bent the budding axonal fibers in the wrong direction. Undeterred, the fibers simply unbent themselves and headed back to their appointed places in the midbrain.

Sperry reasoned that each retinal cell was chemically programmed to seek out, embrace, and otherwise adhere to its corresponding bonding site in the midbrain. "Early in development the nerve cells, numbering in the billions, acquire and retain thereafter individual identification tags, chemical in nature, by which they can be recognized and distinguished from one another," Sperry wrote. "Growing fibers become extremely selective about the chemical identity of other cells and fibers with which they will associate. Lasting functional hookups are established only with cells to which the growing fibers find themselves selectively matched by inherent chemical affinities."

"Inherent chemical affinities" is the operative phrase in Sperry's description that describes the process whereby the retinal cells somehow divine where it is intended that they establish their connections. Sperry concluded that "the final course laid down by any given fiber reflects the history of a continuous series of decisions based on differential affinities between the various advanced elements that probe the surroundings and the diverse elements that each encounters."

In simpler terms nerve cells possess chemical codes of their own, can interpret the codes of others and, based on their chemical affinities, can seek out appropriate cells with which to establish connections. During development it is believed a receptor molecule on the outer membrane of the nerve cell "recognizes" other cells that fit it exactly, like a lock in a key.

Overall, the developing neuron is controlled by two factors. Its moment-to-moment function depends on the gene, DNA, deep within the body of the neuron. But since the neuron must at the same time exhibit an exquisite sensitivity to the environment (seeking out and recognizing its complementary cells), the neuron must also be capable of monitoring and responding to changes in the environment.

It seems likely that the cell surface receptors monitor the environment and report back to the genes which are then modified accordingly. Since each cell contains the same strand of DNA in its nucleus, differences in cell activity, most likely, result from inhibition of specific genes. It is speculated that the cell surface "recognition molecules" communicate with the genes via fine mesh network which has been observed under electron microscopy. The network stretches from the outer cell membrane to the nucleus. It is likely that this molecular trellis serves as a complex communication network whereby a "message" can be transmitted to "shut off" genes whose expression is momentarily undesirable.

First the outer cell membrane "recognizes" another cell that fits it like a lock to a key. Second, it communicates this information back to its nucleus, "shutting off" genes that would interfere with the establishment of communications with the newly recognized cell.

At the moment neuroscientists are engaged in a worldwide effort to understand how cell surface recognition is communicated back into the nucleus, modifying the genes and by this means still permitting DNA to retain effective control of the cells.

CHAPTER 11

Fate Maps

As each neuron ceases to further divide, it begins the mysterious process of assuming an identity. Some cells will be large, others small, some taken up with motor commands, others will be the conveyors of sensory information. In addition to their individual identity, neurons at an early stage gather together into "communities." In general, each cell acquires a definite "address." Based on the cell's "birth date" (the time when it ceases to synthesize new DNA, the first impetus leading to cell multiplication), a prediction can be made where in the brain the cell will finally reside. Cells that reach their "maturity" together and cease further division often wind up occupying similar positions within the mature brain. The converse also holds true: cells that reach maturity at different times wind up occupying different areas of the brain. In addition, it's likely that many nerve cell connections will also be established at this early period of development.

Neuronal "fate maps" can be determined by radioactively labeling the neural plate and studying the distribution of the labeled fetal neurons at their positions within the intact adult brain. From such studies a regularly repeated scenario of brain development can be discerned in creatures as diverse as sea slugs and humans. In general, large cells develop prior to smaller neurons, motor cells take precedence over sensory, and the connecting "interneurons" form next. The supporting and nutritive cells—the glia—are generated last of all.

Again, in general each brain region follows a fairly circumscribed pattern of neuronal organization. Those neurons that are produced first will occupy the deeper cortical areas while the latecomers will be slightly below the cortical surface. In an archaeological dig the deeper one proceeds the older are the artifacts uncovered. In the brain, however, the division of "older and deeper" and "newer and more superficial" is reversed: neurons generated last must make their way to the surface by passing through the area occupied by their predecessors. The logic behind this arrangement has so far resisted attempts at explanation by neuroembryologists. In any case, neural migration is agonizingly slow: somewhere in the range of a tenth of a millimeter per day.

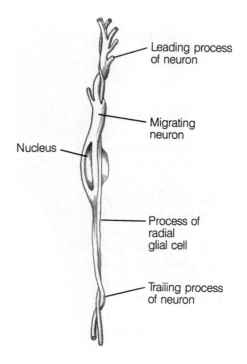

A migrating neuron moves along the "rope ladder" provided by a radial glial fiber.

According to Pasko Rakic, the neuroanatomist at Yale, neurons are directed to their final destination by specialized supporting, or glial, cells. Generated during the early stages of development, these specialized cells possess extended processes that serve as guides. While the cell body of the glial cells is located in the ventricular zone (the area where neurons replicate their DNA and divide), their processes extend in some cases the entire distance to the outer surface of the brain. It is speculated that the glial cell provides the equivalent of a "rope ladder" which the migrating neuron can employ as a means of reaching its final destination. But how does the neuron "know" where it should eventually reside and, as a corollary to this query, how does it determine the best way of getting there?

For a neuron to reach its final destination and make appropriate connections with other neurons, it must first of all orient its axon in the correct direction. In general, the initial outgrowth of an axon is, from the beginning, in the direction required for it to reach its ultimate position within the adult brain.

Upon arrival at their final destination, brain cells from similar regions display an affinity for one another. For instance, after separation and placement within an artificial nutrient medium, brain cells from the same area tend to cluster together, recognizing and preferring the companionship of their own crowd. In this way the fetal brain cells in their migration from the ventricular wall outward form "colonies" from the same "vintage." Along with this tendency to form "cliques," neurons also adopt a preferential alignment. For instance, cells that extend down from the cerebral cortex to, say, the spinal cord assume an alignment that points the axon away from the brain in the direction of the spinal cord. At this point neuroembryologists have no explanation for such "fine tuning" of neuronal identity and position within the brain. The neurons may receive their directions via genetic "program" and may also be influenced by substances secreted by cells other than neurons.

Neural migration, along with other aspects of brain growth, is a contrapuntal melody in which are interwoven themes of destiny and environment, genes and experience. Brain growth and development take place as a result of an incredibly complex interplay of forces, most of which at the present moment are poorly understood. Despite remarkable advances in our ability to visualize the earliest stages of brain development, mystery has so far not been dispelled. In fact, it isn't likely ever to completely disappear. In our feeble attempts to encompass the process, we focus on certain aspects (for example, genetic programming) and ignore other equally important avenues. But most egregiously, it is so easy to lose sight of the fact that brain development is one continuous and interconnected process. Neural crest contains the potential for neural fold which leads to neural tube and brain and spinal cord and eventually thought and what we call mind. From the beginning it's all *simply there*. Our tendency to compartmentalize, limit, and define leads us to believe that our understanding can encompass this marvelous but deeply mysterious process. Modify the genes or chemical environment and early brain development becomes erratic—cells wind up in the wrong place, faulty neuronal connections are formed. But does such tinkering really tell us anything about normal brain development? From our observations of the effects of our own clumsy interferences (experimental manipulations) we are presumptuous enough to declare, "Now we know how brain development proceeds," as if the effects of our intrusions can be so easily dismissed.

CHAPTER 12

The Birth and Death of Neurons

Oscar Wilde once quipped that his most extravagant ambition was to become the best-dressed philosopher in the history of thought. As with many of Wilde's witticisms, this seemingly preposterous hybrid of a single individual combining sartorial perfection with philosophical profundity conceals a subtle truism: philosophy, indeed intellectual endeavors in general, proceeds according to fashions no less mercurial and arbitrary than those existing within haute couture. Take, for instance, the development of our ideas about the formation of connections between nerve cells.

To the architecturally inclined the question breaks down to, How do the cells form the networks they do, why this structure, this scaffolding rather than another? But since the brain is a functioning organ, explanation based on form alone simply won't do. How does it work? How does one nerve cell entice another one to establish a connection with it?

In 1949 a physiologic psychologist Donald Hebb provided a brilliant and inspired proposal: "When an axon of cell A is near enough to excite a cell B and repeatedly and persistently takes part in firing it, *some growth or metabolic change takes place in one or both cells* such that A's efficiency, as one of the cells firing B, is increased." Over the past thirty years research in the neurosciences has been guided by Hebb's intuition.

Consider this experiment carried out by neuroembryologists Viktor Hamburger and Ross Harrison. A chick embryo is deprived of one of its wings early in development (at the stage of the wing bud). A scar forms. As nerve cell axons grow outward toward the area they encounter the scar where ordinarily a wing bud should be. Massive nerve cell death ensues.

Another experiment by Hamburger: a second wing bud is grafted onto one side, resulting in two rather than one wing buds (theoretically

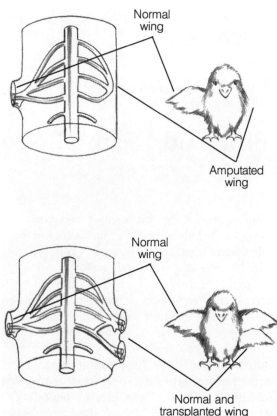

The chick embryo experiment involving a second wing grafted onto one side. More neurons are produced to supply the accessory wing bud.

leading to a chicken with three wings). A great increase in the size and number of neurons supplying the limb buds ensues: twice the number of limb buds calling for twice the number of neurons to serve them.

These two experiments, simple as they may appear, have revolutionized our ideas about the infant brain. Chick embryos inform us on the likely rules and regulations determining the growth of the human brain as well. "Our real teacher has been and still is the embryo—who is, incidentally, the only teacher who is always right," says Hamburger. And what does the embryo teach us?

That during normal development 50 percent of the neurons die off.

That their numbers can be decreased by removing parts of the embryo or increased by transplanting extra body parts so as to create a freak of interest only to the inquisitive scientists (mother hen would have no truck with a chick sprouting an extra wing).

That neurons compete with one another to make contacts, only some of which will endure.

That those endurers will depend for their endurance on their ability to fulfill Hebb's unsightful postulate, "Some growth or metabolic change takes place in one or both cells." Investigation into these cells and these changes have occupied the lifetime of an Italian neuroembryologist named Rita Levi-Montalcini.

A native of Turin, Italy, Rita Levi-Montalcini entered medical school there, was taught by Guiseppe Levi, a professor of anatomy, fled to Brussels in 1938, then returned to Italy just before the war in defiance of Mussolini's "Manifesto per la difensa della razza" which barred academic and professional careers to "non-Aryans." Nonplussed, this tenacious woman, who later untangled the scheme of how one nerve cell influences another, continued her research not in a sophisticated and well-funded laboratory but within the scientifically inauspicious environment of her own home.

In 1942 bombs over Turin forced this experimenter on chick embryos to flee into the countryside where the conditions were even more rudimentary. Despite such deprivations, Rita Levi-Montalcini never wavered, not even on those occasions when her eggs after yielding up their experimental results were consumed to provide the necessary energy to make further experimentation possible.

What signals might one nerve cell be emitting to encourage the survival of a nerve cell with which it is making contact? One nerve cell may link up briefly with several other nerve cells but only one of these linkages is permanent. Why? How is it decided which linkages remain and which disappear? Trying questions, difficult questions, seemingly insoluble questions, these. In order to answer them, Rita Levi-Montalcini refined and improved on the techniques of Ramón y Cajal. She invented a new way of staining nerve fibers with a silver stain, tracing them along their sinuous pathways of delicate Angel Hair. And thanks to this new staining method, Rita Levi-Montalcini was able to carry out an experiment that answered the questions posed a moment ago.

Implanting of tumor cells into a three-day-old chick embryo results in a five- to sixfold increase in the number of nerve cells that innervate that tumor. The increased growth is the result of a diffusable substance, Nerve Growth Factor (NGF), isolated by Rita Levi-Montalcini and other researchers. Although the action of NGF isn't completely understood, it has been discovered, as a result of two decades of research, to act as a trophic substance (from the Greek meaning "to nourish").

Administration of NGFs stimulate neurons to extrude their processes, establish connections, and maintain these connections while other connections lacking NGF are falling by the wayside. It's speculated that NGF sustains the connection, enhances it, establishes it in priority to other connections lacking NGF.

Neurons don't simply grow helter-skelter establishing connections at random, but rather some connections are encouraged, nourished, and abated by "nourishing substances" such as NGF while others are doomed to pass into oblivion. "Targets affect the property of their neurons" as one pundit put it.

Rita Levi-Montalcini's work of genius, persistence, and crystalline brilliance answers one question at the expense of another: granted the importance of NGF and other substances like it, how is it decided which targets will secrete NGF (or something like it) and which targets will be unable or unwilling to produce that same factor? Why does one particular neuron fancy the attentions of one courtier rather than another? At this point an answer to such knotty questions isn't available. Purpose, plans, perhaps providence—three processes neuroscientists aren't comfortable with. One cell links up with another that nourishes it, sustains it, suckles it so that over a lifetime several billion neuronal connections, the protoplasmic kisses of Cajal, can take place. How wondrous is this process of one cell connecting to another to another ad infinitum.

An electrician delegated the task of wiring up a circuit as complex as that of the human brain and capable of soldering connections at a rate of one per second would take over thirty million years to complete the job. Nature performs the same task within much less than a man's three score and ten (assuming that functional connections may continue to form until our last gasp).

No new brain cells after birth—all cells out on the table before our first birthday—but perhaps new connections between cells continuing as long as we continue. In the process neurons exhibit the fickleness of overly comely suitors—they may change shape, alter identity, neurotransmit with one chemical at one time and favor different "messengers" on other occasions. The purpose of this preordained but nonetheless inscrutable plan whereby like winds up in continuity with like? A difficult but vital question summed up by Dale Purves and Jeff Lichtman in their scholarly textbook, *Principles of Neural Development:* "Neurons affect the properties of their targets . . . targets affect the properties of the nerve cells that innervate them. This kind of interdependence is presumably a means of ensuring that every nerve cell in the adult has a useful function."

But function and purpose are derivative terms. From our observations of the brain we detect, or believe we detect, patterns and from those patterns we project our sense of purpose. The brain, meanwhile, grows the way it must, knowing nothing of our purpose or the functions we impose upon it.

CHAPTER 13

Nerve Fiber

Sinuous and labyrinthine, the nerve fibers interweave in a marvelous complexity of dendrites and axons. Nerve fibers are more stable, easily locatable, much less dependent than the nerve cell body on the whimsicalities of chemical stains. For this reason the nerve fiber is always easier to locate than the nerve cell body.

The first to describe the nerve fiber was Anton van Leeuwenhoek, clothier, haberdasher, deft politician from Delft, grinder of lenses, a man reputed in 1683 to possess acute visual powers. All records indicate that he was also in the grip of an obsession: to see everything in God's created universe, living and nonliving. This obsession occupied his mind day in and day out. Grind a lens, peer through it, describe what was seen, make a picture of it, grind another lens so as to see more—that was Leeuwenhoek's obsession.

Like most obsessives, Leeuwenhoek was a private man, revealing little about how he shaped his lenses, not even the exact magnification that he employed in his experiments. A writer of letters rather than a giver of speeches, Leeuwenhoek preferred the anonymity of communicating what he had seen by means of a series of epistles to the Royal Society. "Microscopical observations of Mr. Leeuwenhoek concerning the optic nerve" was the title of one of them—nothing exciting, nothing likely to make a bestseller list or throw the populace into a frenzy.

But Leeuwenhoek's observations today are recognized as a stroke of genius. While others only speculated, Leeuwenhoek simply looked—the essence of a scientific method. Unfortunately, however, he also speculated a bit, saw in his "mind's eye" things that his mortal eyes didn't and couldn't.

Leeuwenhoek, like every other scientist in the seventeenth and eighteenth centuries, was enamored of everything Greek and believed in the existence of a "spiritus substance" that passed along hollow nerve fibers. Leeuwenhoek, therefore, looked for hollow passageways within nerve fibers that could act as a pathway for the spirit. When he failed to discover these hollow passageways that haunted him, he was able, most unscientifically and unwisely, to convince himself that he had. "What the material is that is enclosed in the [spinal cord, fibers or tubes] I was never able to determine with certainty, although I believe that it was a very fluid humor which passed off as a vapor."

Despite Leeuwenhoek's obsessions and his tendency to leap to conclusions unsupported by evidence, he was nonetheless the first person in history to see nerve fibers. He drew them; the drawings still exist today, recognizable in their essential correctness. Most marvelous of all was Leeuwenhoek's confidence in the reality of what he saw (others hadn't the opportunity). "I regret that in this matter I have been unable to display these visible canals to anyone, for no sooner did I move them to my eyes for examination than almost immediately, in less than a minute, they dried out and contracted so that this astonishing site wholly vanished beyond recall."

Leeuwenhoek was a mechanist, successor of Descartes who half a century earlier modernized the classic theory of animal spirits which were manufactured in the brain, stored in the ventricles, and passed via hollow tubes (the nerve fibers) to initiate voluntary movements. Since Leeuwenhoek believed he could see these hollow tubes, believed the nerve fiber was no less than the passageway for the conveyance of spirit, Leeuwenhoek today is looked upon as a strange blend of the materialist and the vitalist, indeed, like Descartes before him. Both men were part scientists, part believers in "spiritus substance."

After Leeuwenhoek, nature went into hiding for fifty years. No one had Leeuwenhoek's patience, his cunning, his control. The microscopic examination of the nerve fiber languished, therefore, for want of proper constraints on the imagination of the microscope peerer. Frequent "artifacts" were described—a polite way of stating that microscopists didn't know what they were doing and mistook pieces of fat or tiny bits of tissue debris for the real thing.

Even Leeuwenhoek spent his final days muttering about globules: optical artifacts, aberrations, produced by the primitive microscopes then in use. A speck of tissue, smaller than the nerve cell, took on a halo and a globular appearance. As a result there was a "globule theory," whereby the artifacts were elevated to a position mightier than the neurons themselves.

Such foolishness was possible only until the invention of the achromatic lens: the light that emerges from this forms images free from extraneous colors. With this invention, knowledge of the nerve cells advanced at a comparatively rapid pace, although some people would have difficulty equating fifty years with rapidity. But, pace, we speak now of more leisurely times when science, dependent as it was (and still is) on technology progressed slowly . . . slowly . . . slow . . . ly.

Nerve tissue is soft and delicate and diaphanous. In its natural state it cannot be cut or sectioned but must be teased apart between two needles (Leeuwenhoek had need of his astute vision). Seventy-five years after Leeuwenhoek it was discovered (rediscovered, actually, since the Egyptians discovered this first) that body cells, nerve cells especially, can be hardened without loss of structure via "fixation" with alcohol, formalin, chromic acid, or "wood vinegar." That done, the tissue can be stained, embedded in paraffin or wax, and then sliced. Subsequent developments depended on the imagination of the microscopist and the inventiveness of his dye manufacturer. Carmine in 1858, Indigo in 1859, Aniline in 1862—with each new stain more and more of the complexities of the nerve cells stood revealed. All that was needed was someone with the intuitive wisdom to put it all together. Otto Friedrich Karl Deiters did that in 1863. He described the nerve cell body, the axon, the dendrites, recognizing that these elements were joined. He was less sure of how individual nerve cells connected up. That would come later but not, unfortunately, for Otto Friedrich Karl Deiters (not unless you believe scientists are rewarded for their good deeds by the opportunity to look down from above and observe the good deeds of those who come after them and improve on their work). Deiters was dead at thirty, his intellectual edifice done in by a specimen of the lowly *Rickettsia prowazekii* transmitted via the bite of the still more lowly body louse. For those given to shaking their heads and sighing on the topic, "My, how the mighty have fallen," Otto Friedrich Karl Deiters is worthy of special attention. He was at once genius, neuromicroscopist, synthesizer, the first person ever to look upon the nerve cell in its nakedness and recognize what he was seeing without feeling the compunction, like Leeuwenhoek, to elaborate on what was seen and thus ruin it all by wrongheaded speculation.

Deiters made things easy. Put everything in its place. Slice the brain, harden it with preservatives, cut the tissue, stain the tissue, cut the tissue again into finer and finer slices, place the final product of the staining and the cutting under the microscope and, finally, but most importantly, *simply look.*

Over the next fifty years A.D. (After Deiters) neuroscientists competed with one another for the privilege of achieving some measure of immortality: they bestowed their names on parts of the neuron. Louis-Antoine Ranvier, Augustus Volney Waller, Willy Kühne, Franz Nissl, Rudolph Virchow. In their time these men were legends, enjoying recognition among their peers that most scientists only dream of achieving. Today they live on only because they were bold enough or insecure enough or sufficiently megalomaniacal to tack their names to the specific observations they made of the neuron. Franz Nissl, for instance, developed his own staining method whereby he catalogued the death of neurons, the cascade of events that occurred whenever a neuron finally gave up the ghost. "Primary irritation" he called it; chromatolysis it's called today. All of the contributions of these men were important, but still only footnotes.

After the nerve cell body and its processes had been identified and their relationship universally accepted, a more engaging problem remained: How does one neuron make contact with its neighbor? To answer this, it was necessary to stain nerve cell bodies along with all the nerve cell fibers coming off them (single axon and multiple dendrites). When this had been accomplished (only partially accomplished, really, since no one can ever be certain he has stained and seen *absolutely everything*), two opposing groups arose and squared off with each other. The first group comprised those who believed that the nerve cells and their processes existed like trees in a forest: a lot of interlacing and intertangling of branches but still, when you get right down to it, individual trees nevertheless. They developed and embroidered the concept of the neuron, appropriated it as a sobriquet ("neuronists" they called themselves), spoke at international meetings on the "neuron theory," and in moments of reverie no doubt repeated to themselves as a mantra, "Neuron, neuron, neuron."

Their opponents, emphasizing the same technique and staining, came to a different conclusion: all cells and fibers are in direct contact, the brain exists like a spiderweb in which everything is ultimately connected with everything else. Their sobriquet was "reticularists." Today they're much out of fashion with those who study structure (neuroanatomists) but enjoy a renewed credibility among those who ask, "How does the brain work?" rather than simply, "How is it constructed?" A nerve cell may influence another nerve cell three hundred synapses away. How else could one explain the newborn infant turning its eyes toward the source of a sound? Only transmission over many neurons could explain that. The brain acts as a whole and not as a group of isolated cells: Baby looks to see what Baby has heard. But does this integration of sight and sound imply a spiderweb arrangement? The reticularists said yes, but the neuronists who said no turned out to be right.

CHAPTER 14

Synapse

Controversy, argumentation, the thrill of proving oneself right and everyone else wrong, hurt feelings, a bit of grandiosity—such were the ingredients out of which was constructed our present-day understanding of the brain.

By 1891 the German anatomist, Heinrich Wilhelm Gottfried von Waldeyer-Hartz, had coined the term "neuron" and established a reality: give something a name and you've created a concept, molded the world to your wishes. "The nervous system consists of numerous nerve units (neurons) connected with one another neither anatomically nor genetically. Each nerve unit is composed of three parts: the nerve cell, the nerve fiber, and the terminal arborization." German compression. Lucidity. How could anyone say it better?

"All Waldeyer did was to publish in a weekly newspaper a resume of my research and to invent the term 'neuron,' " recalled Ramón y Cajal years later in some bitterness and, I would proffer, the hurt feelings and touch of grandiosity I mentioned a moment ago. But I prefer to imagine Cajal in his more serene moments, those occasions when he claimed that to look into the microscope at the neuron was to stare without intermediary into the very face of God. The seeker after truth, Cajal wrote, has "the inevitable duty of distinguishing the apparent from the real, the fortuitous technical fact from the preexisting and general fact. And at the hour of judgment, we must depersonalize ourselves, forget the seductive prejudices, those both of ourselves and others and see things as if they were contemplated for the first time."

To "see things as if they were contemplated for the first time"—Cajal's was a religious vision, an eschatology born in the hills of Navarre (northeastern Spain) and nurtured throughout a lifetime of peering through microscopes in order to catch a glimpse of Truth (writ large).

Today Ramón y Cajal's vision of truth has endured. "Reticularists" is only a quaint term appropriate perhaps for a challenging crossword puzzle. Ramón y Cajal, on the other hand, is recognized as a seer, a discoverer of truth instead of just one of many seekers after truth. He's also a national treasure. Any Spaniard raised and educated in his country will recognize the name even though he may not be able to tell you much about Ramón y Cajal's contribution to our understanding of the brain.

If neurons are not continuous with one another, how then do they communicate? Investigation into this matter involved leeches, squid, mammals, crayfish, torpedo fish and, on occasion, humans as well. Picking up where Ramón y Cajal left off, a British neurophysiologist Sir Charles Sherrington wrote in 1892 on the "state of present knowledge: the tip of a twig of the [axonal] arborescence is not continuous with, but merely in contact with the substance of the dendrite or cell body on which it impinges." At this point, it was necessary to come up with a word, a fitting, proper, and preferably elegant word for the "special connection." Sir Charles went about the task with perspicacity; he made inquiry of a Greek scholar at Cambridge named Verrall. *Synapsis,* "clasp" in Greek, was modified to simply "synapse." Another concept finally became fully established in the lexicon of things neuronal.

Synapses, it's fair to say, dominate present-day neuroscience. Connections between cells and groups of cells are believed to be the basis for the incredibly complex performances of computation, information storage, creativity and, most important, learning. And our ability to learn new information continues until the day we die. Our brains must therefore be capable of modification. It is believed synapse formation underlines this modification. If you stimulate the nerves to the abdominal ganglia of the sea hare, *Aplysia californica,* the creature will retract its gill. This reflex can be manipulated by changing the concentration of calcium and other substances in the environment. Synapses, therefore, operate in a context: chemical events in the immediate environment determine whether the animal will pull back the gill or leave it in place. It's probable that our brain cells operate according to similar context-dependent rules.

Electrically stimulate the hippocampus of a rat and the relevant neurons establish more synaptic contacts, sprout, expand, "reach out and touch someone." Gary Lynch and his collaborators have reported that these changes are the result of alterations in synapses. Courageously, cautiously, they have suggested to their peers that the brain modifies itself and is modified by events impinging upon it. The title of their ground-breaking paper says it all: "Brief bursts of high frequency stimulation produced two types of structural changes in rat hippocampus." Change the environment, alter the stimulus, change the synapse, change the brain—former dumb rat becomes currently smarter rat. All this done by altering the quality or quantity of synapses.

From the indisputable fact that we are born with all the neurons we're ever going to possess, some pundits in the past have jumped to the disputable conclusion that synapses, too, exhibit similar disinclinations to alter in number or form. Nobody believes that now. When one neuron connects with another, the likelihood that that connection will endure can only be gauged via the gambler's art. Probabilities, statistics, Lady Luck—pick your favorite term for the inscrutable and improbable.

"The pattern of connectivity achieved during development is a balance between forces that induce synapse formation and forces that promote synapse withdrawal" is how the process is described in a textbook. "Patterns," "forces," a "balance"—fluff words that translate less pedantically into "Nobody knows exactly why one synapse is formed and endures while another merely forms and remains for a while but then fails to endure."

Cut the nerve supply to a muscle (denervate it) and after a while the nerve fiber will put out sprouts like a flower. These sprouting nerve fibers will cozy up to the muscle fiber that has lost its nerve connections and establish new ones. Soon nobody will be able to tell there was ever anything amiss. The same sleight of hand can be done employing the venom of the cobra snake which acts like the curare employed by the Indians of the Amazon in order to paralyze the respiratory muscles of their prey. In this experiment, which most thoughtful scientists conduct *very, very carefully,* the toxin blocks the synapse: the poison paralyzes the muscle, especially the respiratory muscles. Within a few days of introducing such a troublesome agent, motor nerve fibers will begin to sprout. This makes a good deal of difference in a laboratory experiment but little in the Amazon—no recipient of an arrow dipped in curare has yet managed the feat of holding his breath the few days it takes for nerves to sprout new connections.

Change the environment, change the synapse, change the brain. It's likely that as I write these words and you read them synapses are affected in your brain, a certain "modifiability" is taking place that someday neuroscientists may be able to demonstrate to your satisfaction. It is likely, too, that this demonstration itself will modify other synapses in other ways. The brain is a dynamic organ and, platitudinous as it may sound, not only are no two brains exactly alike but, even more eerie, the same brain is never exactly the same from one moment to another.

"The possibility that synapses turn over continually at some steady rate in the absence of any experimental manipulation has been raised

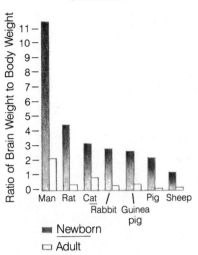

The ratio of brain weight to body weight in selected newborn and adult mammals.

several times over the years but this idea has not been widely accepted," wrote Doctors Purves and Lichtman. But they add an important coda: "As techniques have improved, however, evidence for normal turnover has gradually grown."

Translation: as our technology grows more sophisticated we learn in more detail how the material brain is material in ways that most of us don't think about when we speak of "matter" or "materiality." At the present moment our technology forces us to deal with extremes, best-case and worst-case scenarios such as the fetal brain and the aged brain.

Peer at a slice of the brain of a fetus under a microscope and that moment of frozen time beneath your lens reveals a reaching and striving for more synapses, "increased connectivity." Peer through that same lens (you'll need an electron microscope for this determination, but that's incidental to my point) at a chunk of the brain of an octogenarian and you see fewer neurons and fewer synapses. Over a lifetime, nerves die off, synapses decrease in numbers: there are fewer nerve cell processes on which synapses can form. The fetal brain is an infinite possibility for synaptic organization yet to come. Old age is the muting of that possibility; there are fewer neurons available to discover one another and snuggle together. With every thought that's thought, the brain changes. Synapses form, are maintained, and endure a while or

A Young   **B** Old

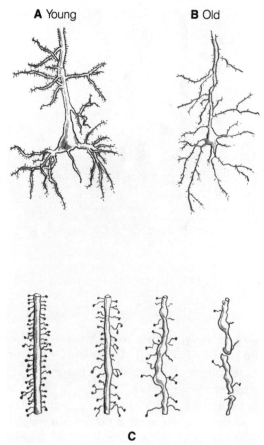

C

Neurons change with aging. Depicted in A is a neuron of a three-month-old rat. B shows a neuron from an aged rat. The aged neuron is smaller and has a diminished number of synaptic spines on its surface. C demonstrates progressive changes in the appearance of dendritic spines in aging humans.

form a "dead end" and pass away like October leaves. How does one analogize such a process? It would take a poet. Better yet a poet who knows the neuronal terrain. There was one such man, Sir Charles Sherrington. Here's his analogy. No one has ever said it better. "It's as if the Milky Way entered upon some cosmic dance. Swiftly the brain becomes an enchanted loom where millions of flashing shuttles weave a dissolving pattern, always a meaningful pattern though never an abiding one; a shifting harmony of subpatterns."

CHAPTER 15

Genes

Two primates stare at each other from across a set of bars. One primate is in a cage; the other is standing outside the cage while holding a briefcase. Primate number one, a lowland gorilla, has nothing much to do but stare. Primate number two, a corporate lawyer, has only a few more minutes before he must scamper back to his office to tend to matters primate number one could never learn anything about (and probably wouldn't want to in any case). Whence comes this huge difference in "brain power"? How is it decided which primate carries the briefcase and which remains behind to pass away the time picking fleas from its coat? A purely scientific answer to such a question isn't as easy to come by as one anticipates (putting aside for the moment such responses as, "Primate number two is endowed with an immortal soul," which, however true that proposition may be gets us into problems of a far different sort). Certainly the answer to the dilemma of who winds up on which side of the cage can't be answered by reference to genes since the total DNA content from bacteria to man varies unevenly.

From bacteria to fruit fly—twenty-five times more DNA. From fruit fly to mouse—twenty-five times again. From mouse to man—no significant difference. In essence, within mouse and mouse chaser the total amount of DNA in the nucleus of the original fertilized egg doesn't differ by more than 10 percent. Now contrast this similarity with a quantum jump in cell numbers and overall brain complexity.

The nervous system of the fruit fly contains about a hundred thousand neurons, that of the mouse fifty to sixty times more. When we pass from mouse to mouse chaser the numbers boggle the mind: five or six million in the mouse, several tens of billions in our own brain. The number of cells, organizational complexity, performance—all increase spectacularly while the total DNA remains constant within 10 percent.

Next, consider the nature of genes compared to synapses in the human brain. Two hundred thousand to perhaps a million genes compared to untold billions, perhaps even trillions, of synaptic connections (it's not unusual for a single neuron to be involved in a thousand or more synapses). Neuroscientists, paradox-prone, are thus faced with a seemingly Inexplicable Paradox: the complexity of the brain is built up from a comparatively small number of humble genetic components and yet there's simply no way one gene could ever control the development of one brain cell (there are too many brain cells compared to genes) nor the number of synaptic connections.

A solution to this paradoxical situation has been suggested recently by Dr. Jean-Pierre Changeux, a neuroscientist in Paris.

Imagine a decision tree based on a simple yes-no or right-left or up-down dichotomy. We encounter such situations on a daily basis but rarely appreciate their inherent complexity. For instance, each time during a drive that you come to a fork in the road, your decision to go to the right or to the left results in a unique pathway. Multiply the number of forks in the road sufficiently and soon the possible combinations become almost infinite. Twenty forks in the road provide 2^{20} or over a million completely different pathways. The simple decision to turn to the right rather than to the left or vice versa when carried out twenty different times is a determinant leading to incredible variation. Applying this to the human gene pool, 1,000 available genes—a small number when compared to the total of 200,000 potentially available genes—provides for a genetic variability which approaches infinity: 10^{2700}.

For years neuroscientists have pondered this matter of "evolutive nonlinearity" (who is on which side of the cage) and, in explanation, have woven theories of varying fancifulness.

How might one explain the striking stability of the genome (the sum total of genes) for our two primates coexisting with an increasing behavioral diversity and anatomical complexity within the brain? One theory, that of the very same Dr. Jean-Pierre Changeux of Paris, suggests that the whole matter of brain complexity depends upon synaptic activity patterns. Here's how it works. At a critical stage of development, referred to by Changeux as "structural redundancy," larger numbers of synaptic contacts are established than are necessary. Which connections endure depend upon how often they are utilized. This process is a familiar one in the brain: large numbers of cells are culled down to a smaller, more compact number by means of a "Darwinian" selection; depending on the state of activity of the synapse, the neuron and its connections may stabilize or regress.

Such a theory—it is, indeed, only a theory which so far hasn't been proven—would explain differences in behavioral complexity between two organisms coexisting with striking genetic similarities. Such a theory also relies on functional rather than anatomical considerations: Which cells are "operative," which synaptic connections are maintained, which ones are left to regress? Two brains may thus look alike but vary a thousandfold from the point of view of performance.

"What was so special about Shakespeare's brain that made him so intelligent? Did he have more brain cells?" asks Emily of her high school biology teacher who, embarrassed and uncertain, may at that moment wish to remind everyone present that when it comes to the brain the biggest fool may ask questions that the smartest person can't answer. "Sorry, Emily, it's not that easy."

When designing the human brain, nature was part architect, part ethereal chemist, part logician, part cartographer, part electrical engineer, part light-show illusionist, part knave, part miracle worker. "How many brain cells" isn't all of it, isn't even the most important part of it. A whole slab of brain can be removed from the infant secondary to bad luck, an accident, or a tumor. That infant can grow up to work at NASA, be a Rhodes scholar, may not even know himself (if his parents don't choose to tell him) that a large portion of brain was once removed. These things are possible only because somehow that infant's remaining neurons fancied other pathways, linked up with second-best and third-best choices, and made the most of the situation. "Street smart" is the infant brain; it can up to a point make the most of impropitious circumstances. That qualifier, "up to a point," translates into this: if Johnny's brain tumor develops before six or eight (some neuroscientists would accept ten), Johnny will grow up walking and talking and thinking much like the rest of us. But if that violation occurs during Johnny's teens, he'll walk with a limp, may have difficulty with language (if the tumor is in Johnny's left hemisphere and he's right-handed), or may not do so well at drawing or sculpting (if that tumor decides to take up residence in the right hemisphere).

The infant brain has an ability to set things right, to establish connections, break them, reestablish them somewhere else so that not even a professor of neurology can examine a particular baby and know for certain that there's anything wrong. The adult brain doesn't possess that capacity anymore. It lost it somewhere between the playpen and the bull pen. If only neuroscientists could discover how to make the adult brain like the infant brain once again, imagine what it would be like: old men and old women tossing aside wheelchairs and walkers, strutting, skipping, startling those around them, recovering once again their self-respect, ridding themselves forever of those half-formed fantasies everyone develops who has ever suffered a brain injury. So far though, no one has discovered a way of making the infant brain retain its capacity for self-repair. At some point the music stops and no one can start it up again. Not till the brain understands itself (a paradox if there ever was one) will the wisdom of the infant be transferred to anxiously expecting adults who have been taught to believe over a lifetime that science can accomplish anything.

CHAPTER 16

Culture

A pig's brain is fully developed at birth and Mr. Pig displays a corresponding finality and inflexibility in his responsiveness, one of the reasons that on the average we're eating him rather than the other way around.

With apes, there is a bit more flexibility—some scientists even claiming that certain specimens can be taught to "talk." No scientist so far though has advanced for our consideration a specimen capable of fathoming the meaning of the proverb "The tongue is the enemy of the neck."

At birth, the human infant brain is smaller and less developed as compared to, say, the brains of monkeys and apes. The advantage of an immature brain at birth? Infants are more open to the influence of environment and culture . . . less "hard-wired." This is only a supposition, however. There are no data on the evolution of the structural and functional complexities of the human brain. Of course, if we go back far enough, the endocasts of human skulls suggest informative differences between our Wall Street stockbroker and his ancestor who stalked his clients by less subtle means.

When we enter recorded history there isn't much to be said regarding differences in the complexity of brains of people drawn from different ages. No increase in brain size has occurred in the last three thousand years of human evolution. No doubt Charlemagne had a bigger brain than Voltaire but Charlemagne was bigger and it's the brain/body ratio that's important, not simply putting two brains on scales like pugilists weighing in for a championship fight.

A plot of brain size in relation to body weight of the human infant as compared to the adult mammals of several species, shows that in humans the infant brain is proportionately about six times as large as it is in the adult. This ratio is even greater in the premature infant (Newton was remarkably premature). The importance of the brain wasn't fully appreciated, however, until the development of methods for measuring the total oxygen consumption.

In the adult the brain consumes 18 percent of the body's total oxygen consumption at rest. This figure becomes more meaningful when you realize that in the adult the brain is only 2 percent of the total body weight. While comparing the adult to the infant brain it is also illuminating to include other body organs as well. For instance, in the newborn infant the brain is more than twice the weight of the liver. In the adult the liver is heavier than the brain and warmer, with the ratio closer to one. In short, it's likely that the brain is the warmest organ that the infant possesses. This matter of warmth, incidentally, has occupied some of the best scientific minds throughout the ages. William Harvey, discoverer of the circulation of the blood, thought that body heat arose from the heart. Priestley, Lavoisier, and others favored the lungs. It was Lavoisier who formulated the procedures by which body heat can be measured (the concept of the calorie). This is all the more remarkable when it's considered that Lavoisier's interest in chemistry and heat production wasn't his life's work but only a hobby. (Unfortunately, while his hobby made him a scientific immortal, his life's work did him in. As part of Louis XIV's corrupt taxation system, Lavoisier was sent to the guillotine in 1794. "The Republic has no need for Savants" were the final words of the sentencing judge.) Today infant researchers employ Lavoisier's concepts to demonstrate thus far unexplained forms of savantry in the newborn. By the age of six days a baby can choose a pad soaked in the milk of its mother's breast rather than a similar pad soaked in the milk of another mother. Which only goes to prove that at six days of age the infant brain is capable of an olfactory performance beyond the ability of his or her investigators.

One seventh of the newborn's weight is brain. From then on the absolute brain weight increases while the percentage of brain-to-body weight decreases. We're talking now of complexity, not just a further increase in bigness. These changes are wrought by infolding—the shift from an ivory-knobbed smoothness to that wrinkled, crinkled look that every medical student encounters when his instructor holds up that first brain. There are two reasons, therefore, why the brain at birth can be only so big and not bigger: the increase in complexity requires an environment to stimulate it, and the brain must imbibe that environment along with its mother's milk. "The slow maturation of human infants is ideally adapted to the molding of species' specific behaviors by social input," as one neuroscientist put it more stuffily.

Second, Mother's pelvis is narrowed as an adaptation to walking on two legs rather than crawling on all fours. Restriction in the birth canal was a consequence of that pelvic narrowing. With Caesarian sections babies with bigger heads were given a chance to make it. Formerly these big heads meant death for Baby or Mother or, if the doctor was foolhardy or incompetent enough, for both. The development of embryo transfer techniques may enable our species to circumvent the female pelvis entirely—Nancy or Johnny staying the course in a temperature/nutrient-controlled artificial environment. Will this mean infant brains will be bigger at birth? We'll have to wait and see, won't we?

Because the complexity of the mammalian brain has increased from pig to monkey to ape to man, there's been a change from a specific to a generalized responsiveness. More has become possible than simply fifty different ways to crawl out of a nest or cave. Instead have come new ways of outwitting, outcunning, outkilling, outliving the competition in the environment.

"Adaptability for problem solving" (our stuffy psychologist again) has been overlaid on reflex responses just as—and in direct proportion to—the cerebral hemispheres have covered the older cortex and midbrain. The evolution of the human mind (translation: all the things done by the brain) has tended toward greater flexibility and responsiveness to the environment. But a price is paid for this flexibility: helplessness.

The human infant is the most helpless creature in existence. If you don't feed it, it doesn't eat. If you don't pick it up, it doesn't travel. What is the basis for this helplessness in the infant brain? Nature has prepared it for the future at the expense of the present. Culture, rather than the physical environment, is now the Great Imprinter. The newborn needn't grow fur in order to keep warm in a cold climate. He or she needs only the good fortune to be endowed with a warm blanket. The infant needn't worry about developing more rods in the retina in order to see better in the dark. Illumination can do it all. Cultural invention has, in fact, reduced the need for special adaptiveness. What's needed, instead, is the flexibility to adapt to almost any conceivable environment. And while pondering this flexibility, ponder also the following questions: What brain changes are responsible for the behavioral differences between us and our primate relatives? When we do something foolish, something socially ridiculous and nonadaptable to our environment, why do we later confess we've "made a monkey" of ourselves?

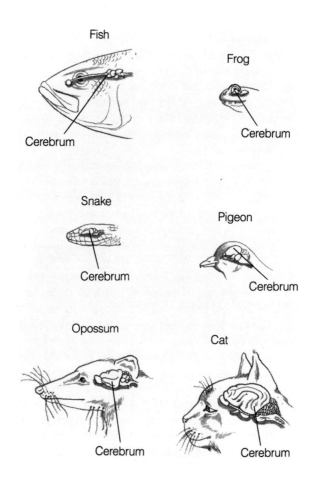

The cerebrum increases in size as one goes upward on the vertebrate scale from fish, frogs, and snakes to monkeys, chimps, and man. The increase in size in primates is accompanied by a corresponding increase in complexity.

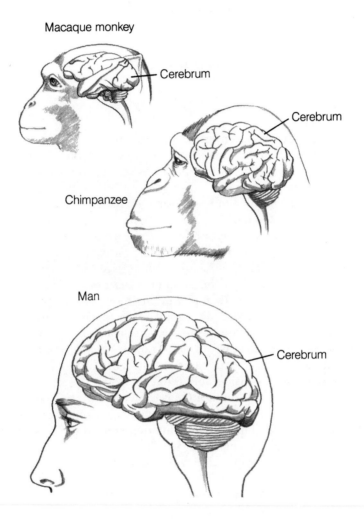

Macaque monkey

Cerebrum

Cerebrum

Chimpanzee

Man

Cerebrum

CHAPTER 17

Variation

Before thirteen weeks after fertilization that part of the brain destined to evolve into the cerebral hemispheres appears as smooth as the head of an ivory walking cane. A month later that cane has started to look more like a gnarled walnut.

By eighteen weeks the brain is divided top from bottom by an elliptical wedge. On the top half are the frontal, parietal, and occipital lobes. Below the wedge is the temporal lobe. The surface of the hemispheres continues to grow and evolve a complex pattern of wrinkles, sulci, separating an interlocking network of brain tissue, gyri. These surface landmarks are the result of the brain growing inward and downward, turning in on itself rather than continuing to expand outward against the confines of the surrounding skull. This ingenious arrangement allows for an increase in the surface area of the cerebral cortex without any corresponding increase in the cranial size. A wrinkled tissue stuffed into a purse serves the same purpose: the surface area enlarges while the volume is considerably reduced.

The initial patterns of unfolding occur in an invariant order regardless of race, color, or creed. Later, things become more complicated, more individualized. This individuality depends on the peregrination of cerebral tissue as it inches every which way in order to maximize the amount of brain that will reside within that skull over the next three quarters of a century.

A graph measuring increases in the volume of cortex displays a sharp deflection upward at the time of the appearance of the brain convolutions. At this moment the brain is altering itself to accommodate lifestyle. The raccoon's paw, the rabbit's whiskers, the pianist's hands, the pig's snout—large areas of the brain are assigned to these structures. For instance, a raccoon brain will hypertrophy in areas that represent the skin of the front paw. Electrical stimulation in the laboratory of this part of the brain leads to movement or sensations in that

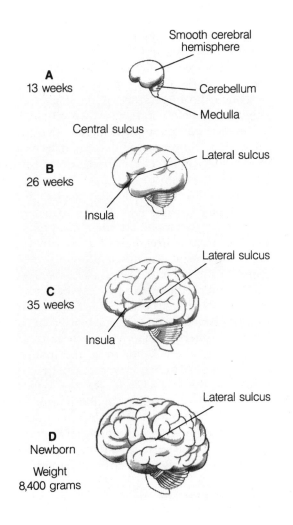

A
13 weeks

Smooth cerebral
hemisphere

Cerebellum

Medulla

Central sulcus

B
26 weeks

Lateral sulcus

Insula

C
35 weeks

Lateral sulcus

Insula

D
Newborn

Weight
8,400 grams

Lateral sulcus

The left cerebral hemisphere seen from the side and depicting successive stages in the development of sulci and gyri. Half actual size.

paw. Exploration by the raccoon of the wild leads to enhanced activation of the brain tissue, the gyri, which correspond to the paw area of the brain. A similar situation exists in our brain as well. Our hands, particularly our thumb and first finger, occupy volumes of brain tissue out of proportion to the size of the thumb or first finger. The brain is built for function, is "user-friendly."

A monkey climbing a tree in the jungle uses all its five fingers for balance and support. Each of the fingers can be "mapped" in the monkey brain. Touch the fingers and a small part of the brain is activated. Touch another finger and a nearby but nonetheless distinct area "lights up" within the brain. Each finger, it seems, has its own exclusive brain region. Impressed with this observation, scientists working under the auspices of The Neurosciences Institute of New York decided several years ago to investigate what happens when a monkey loses one of its fingers. Specifically what happens to the brain area that served the missing finger?

To find out, the scientists lopped off one of a monkey's fingers (the third, the middle finger). Measurements of brain activity several weeks later revealed a curious result: the missing finger's hitherto exclusive brain region was incorporated into the brain areas representing fingers two and four. At the completion of this process there was an expansion of the brain areas representing the still intact fingers. Indeed, fingers two and four exhibited enhanced sensitivity to touch, could detect fine surface contact that, formerly, would have gone unnoticed. A similar result could be brought about by opening the monkey's skull and deliberately injuring the brain area serving a finger rather than directing the damage at the finger itself. For the next several weeks adjacent brain areas start substituting for the injured brain area.

The brain is dynamic, altering under the influence of time and shifting circumstances. More important, the brain organizes itself. No genetic program exists, or could exist, telling the brain how to rearrange itself and coordinate brain cells, how to coalesce into a cooperating group.

"Our hypothesis is that at any one time neurons respond to only a small fraction of anatomically delivered inputs," says Dr. Michael M. Merzenich, director of the Coleman Laboratory at the University of California at San Francisco, who carried out the experiments described above.

Over time the brain changes its functional connections on the basis of experience. Thus, the "brain map" of a monkey can be altered by altering the brain's input (cutting off one of the monkey's fingers). These "map changes," as Merzenich refers to them, are due to alterations in synaptic effectiveness rather than to the growth or movement of axons or dendrites. The whole process is much like an electric system in which different effects are brought about by directing a passage of electricity along certain channels rather than others: turn one light switch and the lights go on in the living room, turn on another and there is illumination in the hallway.

"The first stage of map development is the establishment of anatomical inputs and cortical architecture in the very young animal. The second stage is the establishment, adjustment and maintenance of the details of the cortical maps by experience. The second stage appears to be operational . . . throughout life," remarks Merzenich.

Even more exciting than the existence of this "brain map" is the fact that the map can be altered and rearranged throughout a person's life. Merzenich provides, as an example, the mechanical parallel of learning to smoke a cigarette. The representation of finger and thumb used to hold the cigarette alter dramatically. Motor and sensory factors are altered in tandem as the act of holding the cigarette becomes functionally "mapped" onto the brain. Such a dynamic view of brain processing also provides an explanation why relearning is always easier than learning for the first time. "Take relearning to smoke a cigarette. At first the cigarette is extremely foreign and you handle it clumsily. But with each relearning you are a little sooner back to a smooth performance of the task. Now does that relearning constitute a remapping? We think so."

If Merzenich is correct, studies of "brain mapping" may provide the neuronal explanation for habit. Using his own example, one of the hardest aspects of breaking the smoking habit is the comfort produced by repetitively going through the same motions: taking out the cigarette, holding it, putting it into the mouth (an area of large cerebral representation on the brain map), lighting it, repetitively bringing the cigarette from mouth back to fingers. During a period of abstinence from smoking the motor patterns are less facilitated and, after a while, almost disappear. They don't entirely disappear, however (witness the difficulty heavy smokers have in breaking the habit). Habit, therefore, can be explained as a modification of the brain's functional organization. It's always easier to do the same thing again and again rather than do something new. This is how we define a habit. Now thanks to Merzenich's research, habit can be understood in terms of brain function. Create a habit and you map onto the brain a specific pattern of sensory and motor connections. To break the habit this pattern must be disrupted and replaced by new ones. Without waxing too philosophically on the matter, Merzenich's research on functional maps supports the view more commonly enunciated by Eastern than Western thinkers that the mind and brain are a unity.

While Descartes was writing "I think, therefore I am," the movement of his hand and the positioning of his fingers on the pen were being mapped onto Descartes's brain. Equally likely, the process of "thinking" was represented by other alterations in mapping within Descartes's brain. It's possible if Descartes had changed his habits and his interests his brain would have altered accordingly. Starting in the womb, proceeding to the nursery, school, university, office, and deathbed, the brain's functional organization never ceases to change but varies according to its experiences.

Dr. Gerald Edelman of Rockefeller University in New York explains how the brain reorganizes itself minus anyone or anything telling it how. Natural selection works within the brain as well as in the jungle, Edelman believes. He speaks of a "Darwinian competition" and struggle wherein selection is not neuron by neuron but by groups of neurons. This process operates within the aging monkey as well as in a monkey taking his first brief sojourn away from Mother Monkey. A competitive process is present, with any portion of the brain containing many more neurons than it actually needs. With injury, adjacent neurons take over, the shift occurring within groups of neurons, and dynamic patterning carries the day. Do not ask, therefore, "What does *this* neuron do?" but rather, "What is the neuron's history, what kinds of actions in the past has it been involved in?" Neurons exist as pieces in a fantastic jigsaw puzzle that can change its pattern from moment to moment.

Imagine a jigsaw puzzle of, say, an ocean scene. Certainly some of the puzzle pieces will correspond to the beach. Now suddenly, miraculously, this overall scene changes to the Alps in winter. Now the same pieces will be incorporated so as to represent snow. The jigsaw piece hasn't a solid identity of its own, instead it takes its identity from the overall scene of which it is a part. Learning, too, may depend on such shifts in neuronal identity. Infants (and adults too) learn quickly under some circumstances and more slowly at other times. Learning requires awareness (extravagant advertising claims aside, you cannot learn a foreign language by playing tape recordings during sleep. It's been tested—it can't be done.).

"Dynamic self-organizing properties"—these are the current buzzwords of neuroscience research. The brain is a living, changing, ephemeral even fickle organ from which everything else proceeds: doubt, Linda's first steps, the businessman's cunning, *Cats*, criminality, Einstein's theories of relativity. The brain is responsible for all of these; somehow it constructs the myriad of creations from the interplay of neurons, often the same neurons at different times and in different ways.

"If we study the brain we'll find out the basis of genius," a neuroscientist once boasted. Others have looked at the brains of geniuses and haven't found anything remarkable; genius is not explainable simply by studying numbers of neurons or connections between neurons— the task is not only daunting but wrongheaded in its insistence on literalness.

Neurons remain "functionally fluid" throughout the lifetime of the orangutan or the Harvard professor. The experiences and interests of the orangutan and the professor will influence how and what patterns and circuits neurons will find themselves an integral part of. But neuroscientists are a long way from looking at a brain and thereby divining the interests and experiences of that brain's owner. Perhaps that day will come, but it is not likely that any of us will be around to serve as its herald. More humble correlations of brain and behavior are possible, however.

Looking at the size and convolutions of the brain, its dippings and windings and twistings, an anatomist can glean enough information to make shrewd guesses about the kind of world encountered by the brain's owner.

But the uniqueness of each individual environment (no two creatures ever encounter exactly the same reality) results in a corresponding uniqueness in brain organization. For this reason if looked at closely enough no two brains are ever exactly alike. Even identical twins don't have identical brains. In the 1820s Franz Joseph Gall intuitively grasped this, suggesting that the palpation of the skull could reveal important information about the brain underneath, could provide hints about a person's so-called intellectual and moral functioning. But Gall's phrenological theory eventually came a cropper: amativeness and republicanism (two attributes assigned by phrenologists to specific brain areas) can't be located in a specific mass of brain tissue. Gall went too far and insisted on a literalness nature never intended. Despite his foolishness, however, Gall had a point: the growth of a particular area of the brain is never serendipitous, never just chancy.

There are always small variations among brains. These variations must be taken into account by the neurosurgeon who probes two brains. For him these two brains must be acknowledged in all their uniqueness. There's no anonymity within the brain. Treat one brain like another, thrust forward the scalpel at one point simply because it would be the proper thing to do at one point in another brain—this is the prescription for a funeral and later, a lawsuit.

Individual variability is most easily appreciated in the folds, gyri, and crevices, sulci, of the human cerebral hemispheres. What is the functional significance of this individual variation in human brain structure? Nobody knows.

If large blocks of tissue are taken into account, answers can be found to "Why is the left hemisphere slightly larger than the right in right-handers?"

"Because the left hemisphere is specialized for language," answers the neuroanatomist, although that answer misses the point, why the left rather than the right? He has no answer for that one. Any satisfactory answer would have to tackle several questions that come first, for example, Why is the left half of the brain concerned with a business carried out by the right half of the body and vice versa? No neuron ponderer has yet divined why the Grand Anatomist built us criss-crossed. How much easier it would be, how much more intuitive and commonsensical, if the right brain did business with the right side of the body and the left brain parlayed with the body on the left. But the brain defies our simplistic notions; it grows at its own rate and according to the unique environment that it encounters. This process, very much a matter of what's possible under the circumstances, occasionally goes awry but with a normal brain resulting nonetheless.

"One occasionally sees atypical and accidental arrangements with regard to the path and orientation of axons," wrote Ramón y Cajal during a lunch break in 1929. "All these aberrations are produced during fetal development and can be explained by obstacles which the neurons must surmount during their migration."

In surmounting these obstacles the neurons sometimes go awry, another explanation of why two brains are never precisely alike. Like travelers who stop at a medieval inn, take a fancy to their new environment, agonize a while, give up their pilgrimage, and settle, the neurons, on occasion, end up in anomalous locations. "Ectopic neurons," as our neuroanatomist describes them, are found in perfectly normal brains (all men and all women have a bit of the maverick in them, at least when it comes to their brain anatomy).

But if too many neurons elect to go their own way, the brain's organization breaks down irretrievably. Only the occasional pilgrim can reconsider. The majority must continue along their chosen path lest meaning be lost and chaos ensue. Another way of looking at the same thing: wandering neurons like wandering pilgrims may give rise to novel forms of organization, new societies, new brains. In the embryo, misplaced neurons, on occasion, give rise to new forms of neuronal organization. Novelty and variety may result from the pausings of neurons during their travels. But, on the whole, these variations from the Path are unfavorable.

"Novelty for novelty's sake" is a bumper sticker encountered only rarely as neurons travel along paths to their final destination.

CHAPTER 18

The Neuron in Place

The daunting complexity of the human brain has stimulated researchers to seek "simpler" nervous systems. While fewer numbers and larger neurons may be found in some worms, the complexity of the resulting neuronal network remains no less daunting. The brain, whether it be of a worm or of a man, derives its complexity from the number of interconnections rather than, simply, the number and variety of nerve cells. In the entire human brain there are no more than a few hundred different types of cells. Each portion of the brain can be parceled into neuronal "sets" containing perhaps five different types of neurons. It's not the variety of cells, therefore, that renders the brain more complex than, say, the kidney. Instead, complexity depends upon interconnections between different cell types included within a neuronal set. The neuroscientist seeks to discover the pattern of connectivity between cells. And this is no easy task since cells develop at different times, in different places, migrate to different shores within the brain, and enter into synaptic associations that never could have been predicted on the basis of the cell's origin.

The task of establishing patterns of connectivity is also complicated by the fact that the human brain is so uniquely precocious. Synapses begin to form in the brain at about the second month of gestation and the process is well advanced at birth. (In other mammals few synapses are present in the cortex before birth.) The neuroscientist intent on tracing pathways of connectivity, therefore, must get an early start: in fetal brains older than two months many connections have already been laid down. Other cells may not establish connections for many months, simply lying "dormant" awaiting the arrival of axons from other cells with which they will form neuronal circuits.

Looking at a neuron "in place," knowing its cell of origin, observing the cells in its immediate vicinity—all these are helpful, but nonetheless mystery and wonder remain. Why does the cell establish connec tions with one cell rather than another? Why do synapses form here rather than there, now instead of earlier or later? To him who would divine the process of brain development, nature has readied an awesome challenge. Necessity and chance, freedom and determination—the infant brain is the product of these mysterious forces, is shaped by them, can only be defined by some undiscovered and, one suspects, most likely undiscoverable blend of these forces.

Neurons are born, change their position, their shape, migrate to areas far distant from their sites of origin, and establish contact with unpredictable cells from other parts of the topography. Some of the earliest cells further compound this complexity by engaging in only a "cameo appearance" and then disappear forever. Ramón y Cajal noted such a cell in 1891 and never bothered to name it, merely noting its existence. Later the cell was seen again by another gazer into microscopes. Retzius, a self-effacing man, called them "Cajal cells." Ramón y Cajal, secure within himself, already confident of his own genius and place in history, insisted that Retzius be given his due. Cajal laughingly christened the cells, "Cajal's cells of Retzius." Cajal was a humorous man, he could afford to be, and was willing and able to share the wealth since he was already in his own lifetime an immortal, a legend. Both Cajal and Retzius shared a laugh regarding these cells: in humans the cells disappear before birth; they are transformed from the first and most important cells in the cerebral cortex into, simply, nothing. Other neuroscientists disagree. They think they can trace the Cajal-Retzius cells and have indubitably done so in the brains of dogs, but they have provided a less convincing demonstration when it comes to the brain of a man.

Brain cells are born, migrate, interconnect. In many cases they don't connect but disappear instead. This mix of the observable and unpredictable engages the attention of the neuroscientist, keeps him challenged—and hopefully humble as well.

To him who cannot predict or define the fate of a single brain cell is given the task of explaining the whole tapestry. That should keep him humble just as it did Cajal. The task is no different now than in Cajal's time: How does one cultivate the spirit of inquiry and keep it tethered by an equally vigorous humility?

CHAPTER 19

Uniqueness

Nature as well as art provides innumerable examples of complexity arising from tiny variations expressed via the employment of a modest number of components: fugues, origami, chess.

From only twenty-six letters Shakespeare composed his sonnets and Spengler mused on *The Decline of the West.* It's unlikely that additional letters—however they would be arrived at—would enhance our poetry or our history.

We must be equally cautious in assuming that because the human brain contains more neurons than those of other living creatures, it must for that reason be more complex in every way compared to the brains of "lower animals."

"Apart from the concept that complex functions require a large number of neurons, we have no definite understanding of the relationship between a particular function of the nervous system and the number of neurons required to perform that function," remarks neuroembryologist Marcus Jacobson.

For years neuroscientists have applied the components/complexity theory and assume that we must be "smarter" and "more advanced" because we possess the greatest number of neurons. In worms, for instance, there are about ten thousand brain cells. Crayfish contain between seventy and eighty thousand. Insects contain between 10^6 and 10^7 neurons. When talking about mammals, increase this number by two orders of magnitude until we arrive at our own brain which contains, by cautious estimate, between 10^8 and 10^{12} cells.

A closer look reveals the limitations of such comparisons: many "lower" animals possess brains of daunting complexity. Many parts of the nervous system of the octopus, for example, are complex beyond anything found within our own nervous system.

Cajal took a measure of our visual system and found it wanting in comparison to the lowly insect. "The complexity of the insect retina is something stupendous, disconcerting and without precedent in other animals . . . Compared with the retina of these apparently humble representatives of life . . . the retina of the bird or the higher mammal appears as something coarse, rude and deplorably elementary."

Claims that the powers of the human brain arise purely from the number of neurons resident within our skulls should be labeled, therefore, for what they are: pure chauvinism. And there are several reasons why we should not be chauvinistic in our attempts to understand the infant brain. The development of the human brain has undoubtedly more to do with the amount of synapses (connections) among brain cells rather than the sheer number of brain cells alone. Although there are a few synapses present in the cerebral cortex before birth in the brains of many "lower animals," synapses start forming in humans during the second month of fetal life and many are already formed by birth.

The size and complexity of the human brain frustrates any attempts at precise enumeration of neurons. No simple rule exists correlating body size and weight with neuronal size or numbers. For instance, a four-ton elephant is a million times larger than a four-gram shrew and has a brain ten thousand times larger than the brain of the shrew. The neurons, however, vary only slightly in size. Growth of the elephant and shrew brains is also strikingly similar.

Of all the organs in the human body before birth the brain's rate of growth is the smallest. If the brain developed more quickly, other factors aside, pregnancy would undoubtedly be shorter. The slowness of brain growth as well as its nutritional demands limit the number of infants born at one time. Brain size is also related to longevity. Among mammals, the greater the absolute weight of the brain, the longer-lived the animal.

When brain size is compared to the size of the rest of the body (brain-to-body ratio), it becomes obvious that the brain decreases in comparative size as pregnancy advances. Brain weight is 18 percent of body weight at three months after conception, 16 percent at four months, 14 percent at five months, and about 12 percent at birth. This shrinking of the brain in comparison to the rest of the body continues up until adulthood. The brain of a twenty-year-old father is 2.5 percent of his body weight compared to the brain of his one-year-old son which is 10 percent of his body weight.

Science fiction scenarios often contain suggestions that the human brain could be much larger and, by implication, confer on its owner enhanced intellectual capabilities. The two main obstacles to such a brain-growth explosion are the size of the female pelvis and the inability of the fetal heart and circulatory system to provide sufficient oxygen and nutrients to serve additional brain cells. While the first impediment could conceivably be overcome by some form of artificial support system, "a test-tube baby," no science fiction creator has as yet suggested a means whereby the fetal heart could be boosted to supply a brain greater than 12 percent of the body weight.

When the heroine of *Alice's Adventures in Wonderland* tasted the contents of the bottle in an attempt to "telescope" herself to a size small enough to be accommodated through the little door leading to the lovely garden, Lewis Carroll glossed over one important implication: if Alice's body weight was reduced to one tenth of what it was, her body could not have accommodated a brain much bigger than that of a cat or perhaps, appropriately, a rabbit. Unfortunately for Alice lovers everywhere her intelligence and responses would have also resembled those of a rabbit or at best her cat, Dinah, rather than those of a precocious Victorian child. Nutritional requirements vary according to the cube of the body's linear dimensions.

When Alice, at a later point, ate from the cake and soared to more than nine feet in height, she couldn't possibly have looked just like Alice-of-ten-inches-only-grown-bigger any more than an adult looks identical to the way he looked as a toddler. A tenfold increase in size is attended by a corresponding change in form, indeed, the same changes that befell Alice Liddell as she underwent the metamorphosis from a child to a charming young lady. Bodily organs including the brain undergo changes in form (increase of the body mass by the cube) rather than simply alterations in linear dimensions. For this reason comparisons of the brains of a child and an adult must take into account more than a simple increase in size. Brain size must *decrease* in comparison to body size if life is to go on. Twelve percent—the brain-body ratio at birth—is the upper limit.

CHAPTER 20

Wild Brain-Tame Brain

We can train a dog to go out and fetch our morning paper but the world is still waiting for the first dog who can read it to us while we sip our coffee. Obviously the dog's brain imposes certain limitations on its present and future behavior: its brain isn't capable of the complex performance of reading.

If you study brains from different species, starting with reptiles and proceeding up to our newspaper-fetching dog and then on to primates and finally man, the most impressive finding is an enlargement of the cerebral hemispheres. On the basis of this progressive and readily demonstrable enlargement, most students of the human brain have confidently concluded that the cerebral hemispheres are responsible for those behavioral repertoires that are unique to human beings. This "canonization" of the cerebral hemispheres rests on the following logical format: we can do many things that other creatures can't and, in addition, we possess more highly developed cerebral hemispheres. Ergo, it must be the cerebral hemispheres that enable us to do these marvelous things. As any logician can tell you, that premise rests on some pretty shaky reasoning. For instance, perhaps our ability to read and not merely fetch our newspapers depends on other areas operating in addition to the cerebral hemispheres. The resolution of such a question required an experiment sophisticated enough to make the necessary distinctions as to what areas of the brain are capable of doing what. In the late 1970s such an experiment was carried out.

Investigators at the department of neurology and pediatrics at Ohio State University reported in the journal *Science* a most unusual observation. A pair of twins, two months premature, were investigated. One of them, a boy, was perfectly normal. The girl, in contrast, was totally lacking cerebral hemispheres. Such a child cannot long survive and is thought by many not to be truly human (an opinion not held by the experimenters who took "ethical considerations" into consideration in the planning of their experiment).

These immature infants were tested for their ability to learn. Two stimuli (a flashing light and an emitted sound) were paired with each other and presented repeatedly to the subjects. Intermixed with these paired stimuli were test trials when only one, the first stimulus, was presented.

In this technique (a classic association experiment) learning can be inferred when a subject displays some kind of "surprise" response. The heart rate, for example, may accelerate when only one stimulus occurs instead of the expected pair of stimuli. The results of the experiment are almost too startling to believe: both infants demonstrated by their responses that they had learned that the stimuli usually occur in pairs. In the investigators' words, such a finding "clearly documents the existence in the premature human infant of associative processes relatively independent of the cerebral hemispheres." Their conclusions are even more provocative. "Complex psychological processes such as learning do not appear to be exclusively within the domain of the cerebral hemispheres." Thus, contemporary research on the infant brain is suggesting that our human capabilities are not "locked into" the cerebral hemispheres like precious jewels within a safe at the Plaza Hotel but, rather, our behavioral repertoire is very much dependent upon the *whole* brain. Our subcortical centers (those we share with "lower" animals) are capable of doing a lot more than we usually give them credit for. Indeed, learning can occur in the absence of both cerebral hemispheres.

The brain weight of a domesticated animal is between 15 and 30 percent less than the brain weight of an animal of the same species raised in the wild—a curious phenomenon with important consequences. The petted and pampered Pekingese who accompanies its owner to a fashion show isn't likely to endure for long if let loose in the woods. This is the price that must be paid by those animals "fortunate enough" to get on with their human benefactors.

This reduction in brain size varies according to which part of the brain the neuroscientist studies. The most severely affected is the visual cortex: 35 percent fewer cells are in the dog sprawled in the living room compared to its counterpart running with a pack in the woods. Cerebellum: 15 percent fewer cells.

Nor is the matter of brain weight easily separated into a neat dichotomy of nature-nurture. The brain weight in the first generation of animals born in captivity is 10 to 20 percent less than that of their parents. But if an animal is born in the wild, captured, and raised in captivity, it has the same brain size as those siblings lucky enough not to be captured.

A lion escaped from a circus sets off a panic; there is a rush for firemen, nets, tranquilizer guns. The "king of the beasts" hasn't lost his ferocity or his cunning. His brain is still a respectable functionary that can teach a lesson in jungle logic to anyone who gets close enough. Our neuroscientists tell us that perhaps an escaped lion raised from birth in the enforced domestication of a circus wouldn't be so fearsome. Maybe so. It's not likely, however, that the fireman or trapeze-gun marksman would find that an argument convincing enough to cause him to cozy up to Brother Lion.

If you take domesticated pigs and set them loose in the wild, those who survive to breed produce little pigs with no increase in brain size over the next several generations. Domestication, it seems, exacts a price. From afternoon siestas, free corn, and "nothing in the world to do" pigs can't suddenly revert back in one generation to pushing and shoving around in the underbrush looking for food and avoiding the unfriendly.

Underlying these changes in brain weight are equally dramatic alterations in the complexity of the branching of individual neurons. Long-lasting effects occur as a result of experience. The more complex the experience, "the richer" the environment, the more complex the brain. Rats provided with playthings, mazes to run through, and just the right amount of stimulating companionship wind up as the proud owners of brains weighing more. Their cerebral cortex is thicker; there's an increased number of nerve cells. Whether or not any of these changes contribute to the happiness and well-being of a rat remains an impenetrable mystery. What isn't mysterious, however, are the claims that some neuroscientists have made about the effect of experience on brain growth: the greater the diversity and challenge of the environment, the greater the complexity of the brain, they tell us.

In the laboratory of William T. Greenough, professor of psychology and anatomical sciences at the University of Illinois, rats reared in enriched environments (toys, plenty of room to run around, companionship) displayed more extensive dendritic connections than did rats raised in more "deprived" conditions.

"These results suggest the number of synapses per neuron in a variety of brain regions (maybe most) is determined to a significant extent by the circumstances under which the organism develops," says Dr. Greenough. "We speculate that these changes are involved in storing information arising from experience."

By altering the number (or pattern of synapses) it's believed possible to alter the functional circuitry in the developing brain. Couple this with the theory of "selective stabilization of synapses" propounded by Jean-Pierre Changeux mentioned earlier. Not only are more connections made on the basis of experience but, in addition, experience leads to a selective alteration of the strength of the individual synaptic connections.

On the basis of rats raised in enriched environments and enriching their neuronal connections thereby, human parents have been encouraged to hang mobiles over cribs and hover over their infants while making funny faces and uttering cooing sounds. While these procedures may be recommended for the fun they provide for the infant, brain growth studies allow only very cautious and ambiguous conclusions. While it's true that as a result of the enriched environment neurons may grow bigger or more of them appear in given parts of the brain, these changes often occur in areas that at present lack a clearly defined function.

In addition, bigger brains aren't necessarily correlated with greater intelligence. These reservations aside, however, it remains an appealing argument that the increased complexity of brain growth mirrors environmental enrichment. Darwin had something to say on this point as he did also on the subject of brain size in domesticated animals. But Darwin was a one-track thinker; he encountered evolutionary principles wherever he looked, even in the developing brain. "Every cell which best performs its function is, in consequence, at the same time best nourished and best propagates its kind."

The idea of a "cellular struggle for survival" with each cell fiercely competing with its neighbors for life and space appealed to the mercantile mentality of the late nineteenth century. Only the best survive, only the most hearty brain cells establish enduring connections. All very neat, economical—a truly parsimonious explanation. But Ramón y Cajal, the artist, bid his illustrious contemporary to temper his enthusiasm and wait a bit . . . willingly suspend belief . . . forgo the impulse to evolutionize all of creation.

"We must, therefore, acknowledge that during neurogenesis there is a kind of competitive struggle among the outgrowth (and perhaps even among the nerve cells) for space and nutrition," Ramón y Cajal wrote. "However, it is important not to exaggerate . . . the extent and importance of the cellular competition to the point of likening it to the Darwinian struggle."

If there is a purpose behind the "natural selection" of neurons, it is *uniqueness*. To the evolutionist, of course, "purpose" is a heresy: nature has no purpose. But when the statements of evolutionists are looked at closely enough there is always room left for purpose to be slyly introduced in the discussion.

"The selection of the survivors that form the final set [of neurons] must be determined on the basis of some type of benefit or functional effectiveness . . . There is a competition between neurons which results in the elimination of some neurons and the survival of others contingent on their fitness to survive." But what determines the fitness to survive?

If a group of neurons is provided with additional target cells upon which the individual neurons can establish connections, more of the group survives than usual. Thus, cellular death isn't written into the gene script but can be altered by the environment. The life-or-death struggle ultimately involves how many of the neurons are able to establish connections. Indeed, neurons endure in direct proportion to their capacity to connect with other neurons. Sociability is rewarded— the loner winds up "naturally selected" out of existence. It's speculated that slight differences in presynaptic neurons set up a "struggle" for space on the postsynaptic cells. The "best cell" or "most fit cell" wins out. This argument is very appealing. It fails to account, however, for the uniqueness of each brain.

I've said here that no two human brains are exactly alike. Neuroembryologists tell us that major variations occur in the brains of locusts. Even among organisms with exactly the same number and positions of neurons, differences persist in the fine patterns of axonal and dendritic branches. Axons within the brain of the common housefly aren't precisely the same from one fly to another. No two leeches, sparrows, or Alaskan bears have brains that are exactly alike. Indeed, "no two brains of individuals of the same species are exactly alike. There are always individual variations," our neuroembryologist tells us.

CHAPTER 21

Earliest Movement

What does the fetus do during the nine months preceding its Grand Exit? Does it sleep? Does it move? (More easily answered that one, we have the testimony of mothers everywhere.) What kinds of movement? What organization prevails within the womb? In the past decade technology has provided answers for such formerly unanswerable questions.

A pulse of sound is beeped into the womb. It bounces back. The ultrasound machine sorts out the reflections and codes them as an image; sound waves provide the image instead of X rays. A safer procedure. More dynamic. There are none of the dangers inherent in introducing a camera into the womb which inadvertently may serve to document the fetus's final gasp.

Ultrasound provides the doctor with information on, Who is there? What does it look like? Boy or girl? Anything wrong? ("Anomalies" is the euphemism employed to describe deviations from normal.) How far along is Beth? Is she ready to come out? Is she healthy or sick? Finally, should the doctor deliver her now or later? These are the practical questions the ultrasonographer must answer in order to justify his existence. That done, the really fascinating details can be entered into.

The fetus's earliest movements occur at seven and a half weeks of age. At this early moment the fetus is about two centimeters in size and its movements consist of a slight shifting of the fetal contours. The whole sequence occurs within a time frame between the blink of an eye and speaking out loud the word "life"—about half a second.

Within another week the tiny body moves in its entirety but minus a distinctive pattern or sequencing of body parts. The movements are delicate, slow, and limited in range. Less than a week later these same movements are more forceful and rapid but still as delicately smooth as befits a creature moving in liquid rather than air. One should recall that the force of gravity is also diminished in such an environment. "The reduced effect of the force of gravity in utero makes many movements more fluid and elegant than after birth," says Dr. Johanna I. P. deVries, the obstetrician who recorded these very early fetal movements.

Try lifting and then gracefully dropping your arms to your side starting from a horizontal position. Try the same thing in a swimming pool. Unless you've been trained in tai chi or dance it's unlikely that your movements will be as delicate and as graceful in air as they are in water. A similar situation persists in the womb: tiny fetal movements are prolonged, graceful, a kind of ballet. Sudden relaxation of the arms, for instance, doesn't produce a rapid drop of the elevated arms. Instead they fall like autumn leaves, gracefully, artlessly.

By fifteen weeks, sixteen distinct movement patterns occur with varying regularity: just discernible movements; startle; general movements involving the whole body; hiccuping; breathing; isolated arm or leg movements; isolated movements of the head backward, to the side, and forward; jaw movements; sucking and swallowing; hand-to-face movements; stretching, yawning; body rotation. All of these carry over from womb to bassinet and whether in the fetus or the newborn the movements remain specific and recognizable, light years away from the uncoordinated random efforts previous investigators had speculated about wrongly. Further, the movements follow a sequence starting with "just discernible" movements and proceeding up to "yawning" and "sucking and swallowing." There is even some indication that the movements proceed in tandem with developments within specific parts of the nervous system. For example, synaptic connections can be found at six weeks within the cervical spinal cord. And this period coincides with the beginning of hiccups and arm movements, two activities requiring a functioning cervical spinal cord. The baby brain reaches a certain developmental stage and behavior ensues: the arms flex, hiccups occur. But not until the baby brain reaches a sufficient degree of synaptic organization does anything occur. And then at seven and a half weeks appear those "slow, small shiftings of the fetal contour," as Dr. deVries and her colleagues describe the matter.

By sixteen weeks the fetus moves its hands in jerky, sporadic motions. Several weeks later these movements smooth out, coordination enters, and intention appears. The hand reaches, touches the face, may remain for a few seconds on the face as if feeling it, exploring it. "As the nervous system develops there are little stages when things happen . . . little spurts of development. That development is toward aggregation, association, smoothness, coordination," according to ultrasonographer Jason Birnholz of Harvard University.

Nearly a century ago in 1888 a German observed that the fetus "breathes." He did so by inference based on the observation of forceful diaphragmatic movements thought to have been visible through the mother-to-be's abdominal wall. Not until 1970, however, was this issue finally confirmed, and that confirmation held only for lambs. "Respiratory Movements and Rapid Eye Movement Sleep in the Fetal Lamb" was the title of the paper that established to everyone's satisfaction that which formerly had been established only in the minds of the unusually observant and perspicacious. From that moment onward, observations accumulated rapidly: not only the fetal lamb but the fetal human as well breathed regularly, measurably.

Short segments of fairly regular movements of the diaphragm appear between sixteen and twenty weeks. At fifteen or sixteen weeks the fetus can breathe. But the lungs don't work. The fetus doesn't breathe for very long at a time. At this early point in life's journey, breathing takes place in the "technical sense" only. Eight or nine weeks later breathing movements are less frequent. More weeks later breathing speeds up once again, at first irregularly and then with a regular rhythm. During the last three months breathing becomes organized and predictable; you could mark time by it.

If the fetus is oxygen-deprived, breathing movements change in their character: they decrease in frequency. Breathing waxes and wanes with a periodicity that is affected by numerous factors: mother's sedation; how much she fancies alcohol and cigarettes; even the time since her last meal.

In order to get a fix on fetal breathing patterns, it is necessary to make more than casual observations. In the last three months of the pregnancy more than an hour of monitoring must be expended before the obstetrician can make comments on the fetus's condition that deserve to be taken seriously.

"The simple occurrence of breathing can be informative regarding the state of the fetus," states Dr. Jason Birnholz who has observed via ultrasound the breathing patterns of thousands of fetuses. On occasion Birnholz's observations have also included, sadly, fetal gasps—often signs of distress. When Birnholz observes the prolonged inspiratory gasping he is aware of the dire consequences of what he is seeing: gasping is a "terminal event in fetal lambs," as one observer put it. And it can also be a "preterminal event" for somebody's baby if the obstetrician doesn't act decisively enough.

In addition to breathing, the ultrasonogram reveals fetal eye movements. By fifteen weeks the eyes can be seen ultrasonically (the eye appears on the ultrasound screen as a bright white circle—the lens of the eye actually). Eye movements follow a developmental sequence:

isolated brief slow excursions, more brisk movements (twenty to twenty-four weeks); a series of three or more darting movements irregular in direction and duration (twenty-three to twenty-four weeks). Over the next ten weeks rapid eye movement (REM) increases. The importance of all this? Rapid eye movements peter out if the infant is deprived of its oxygen. If mother is too sedated, rapid eye movements are also observed to disappear.

Six months into the pregnancy, eye movements and breathing are linked: rapid eye movements, combined with irregular, jagged breathing. Later in pregnancy, in Beth, who's almost ready for her Coming Out, regularity in breathing becomes associated with smooth, slow eye movements. This pattern will persist throughout childhood; during periods of rapid eye movements the breathing becomes irregular and jerky. Dreams disturb the sleep, disturb the breathing, disturb the sleeping—this is our explanation in children and adults. But what can we say of the fetus? Does it dream as well? It is hardly necessary to point out, I expect, that dreaming must imply something to dream about. Indeed, what could the fetus be dreaming of? No neuroscientist, unaided by input from some Higher Authority, could ever begin to answer that question.

Based on ultrasound recordings, judgments can be made about the fetus and the parents told more than perhaps they wish to know about their baby. Mentally retarded infants, for instance, spend less time in REM sleep than do normal babies. Babies can be tested in the womb for hearing, movements, breathing, and eye movement patterns. There are no grades in this super elementary school—it's Pass or Fail.

A buzzer is placed against the abdomen of the mother-to-be at the point where, a moment before, the ultrasound has demonstrated the infant's ear to be lying. Buzz! The infant startles, jumps. The buzz is repeated, one . . . two . . . three . . . ten buzzes in all. Each time, the infant's eye blinks. Bodily startling, however, ceases after the first few stimuli. This is normal habituation: the brain "turns off" to a repeated stimuli and seeks novelty.

If the experiment is repeated a day or so later the sequence occurs again: a startled response to buzzer one . . . only eye blinking to buzzer seven or eight . . . not much of anything to buzzer ten. Novelty produces a response; monotony reduces that response. This pattern can be demonstrated and has been demonstrated in the aplysia. *Primitive memory:* the aplysia withdraws its gill when its siphon is stimulated. But with each stimulus the gill withdrawal lessens and finally ceases all together: *Habituation.* The fetus, too, withdraws or otherwise responds when prodded or poked or otherwise assaulted. (The ultimate assault is the abortionist's curette prodding that fetus into a frenzy. This has been photographed and that film shown in the White House to mixed reviews: to some viewers discomfort, anguish, or pain exists only for that creature that can speak.)

A unity exists between that aplysia, that fetus, that infant lying in its mother's arms—the unity of the brain. Stimulate the brain of any of that trio and if your stimulation is well chosen you will get a response. Repeat that stimulus too many times and the response will cease. Conditioning followed by habituation: a rhythm basic to every brain or, in the case of the aplysia, primitive nervous system ever investigated. Indeed, this process could be taken as a prerequisite for inferring the existence of a functioning brain. Only the dead brain can't be conditioned, habituated, or taught anything.

Can the unborn infant think? Does it dream? Does it have a personality? These questions were put to the pioneering ultrasonographer, Dr. Jason Birnholz. He reflected a moment and then answered a question with a question.

"Do these things we're seeing with the sonogram reflect the personality of the fetus? Does the fetus have a personality? These are things that I think you have to leave for the future." After further reflection he explained: "I think you have to recognize that our ability to use ultrasound to look inside is a new one. In fact, to look at things like eye movements has just come about in the last few years. And that's not very long in the scheme of things. Looking at responses to sound, to light, to pressure or whatever—these are brand-new things and it's just a bit early. We've got to get our technology straight before we start confronting the philosophy."

No doubt the good doctor is correct: observation and then philosophy rather than the other way around. But philosophy has a way of creeping up on us. Indeed, we are all natural philosophers. Further, fetal research provides anyone philosophically inclined with more than enough curious facts to philosophize about.

CHAPTER 22

Mind

A fussy infant only a few hours old can be calmed if a tape is played of the pulsatile events that form the background sounds within the uterus. Each pulsation that reaches a peak of about ninety-five decibels results from blood being driven through the uterine vessels by the action of the heart. Playing recordings of these sounds soothes cranky infants. The sound of the mother's heartbeat won't do it; nor will a metronome or other ingeniously designed gadgetry. According to the University of Pennsylvania psychologist Burton S. Rosner, who carried out this experiment, "Intrauterine and other sounds are soothing (to fussy infants) only when presented at levels comparable to those found in utero." Based on such findings neuroscientists have speculated on such questions as "When does the fetus begin to think?" "Does the fetus have a mind?" (as if anyone has satisfactorily resolved the nature of the adult mind).

If you place a vibrating tuning fork on the abdomen of the pregnant woman, the fetus (if over twenty-nine weeks) will respond to the stimulus with an acceleration of heart rate and an increase in kicking movements. While this may represent a response to vibration rather than to sound in the strict sense, it does suggest that the fetus is not as hermetically sealed off from the outside world as we have been led to believe.

In 1982 two physicians, one from Mount Sinai School of Medicine in New York and the other from Hahnemann Medical College in Philadelphia, decided to explore a bit further this question of whether the fetus may be capable of exhibiting "mind."

By carefully monitoring fetal heart rate patterns these investigators came upon an extraordinary discovery. Under ordinary conditions, if stimulation is applied to the mother's abdomen, the fetal heart rate accelerates by about fifteen beats per minute. Instead of occurring after the fetal movements, however, the heart rate begins to accelerate approximately six to ten seconds before the fetus starts moving. According to these two investigators this anticipatory heart rate increase parallels the situation that exists in adults: heart rate increases during the contemplation of action and several seconds before any detectable movement takes place.

"Whether this indicates conscious thought and planning on the part of either the fetus or the adult or is merely a reflex action is a moot question," wrote these investigators, "nonetheless an intriguing one that merits further exploration." But the question concerning whether or not "mind" exists in the fetus is not likely to be decided by neuroanatomists (the cell counters and nerve cell tracers) but by neuroscientists who utilize technological devices that monitor function. For example, cortical neurons exist within the prefrontal cortex and are formed before birth. These same neurons remain without a task ("nonfunctional") until about the third year of life. For the moment let's put aside the question of when or whether the fetus possesses a mind (it's too "controversial"—who could possibly be sure about such a thing) and take up a more manageable inquiry. Are there any indications that events during fetal life may affect the quality of life at a later point? For every arcane question there inevitably arises an arcane specialty that attempts to provide an answer. Behavioral teratology is taken up with the effects during fetal life of changes in the internal and external environment on subsequent brain development. In general (the "bottom line" as a bureaucrat might phrase it), damage done to the developing brain depends principally on when the "insult" occurs.

In laboratory rats and mice the structural damage to the developing brain can be predicted from the timetable of neuronal production. Just as one can construct a schedule of when certain neurons can be expected to appear, it's also possible to construct a scenario in which neuron damage at a certain point will inevitably lead to a particular behavioral consequence. For instance, hyperactivity in mice seems to be indicative of brain damage occurring during the middle part of neural production. In contrast, an "insult" before or after this critical period often leads to hypoactivity. And it's useful to be reminded that these behavioral deficits often—in fact, usually—occur in the absence of other easily identifiable alterations in appearance or behavior.

"Many systemic insults during brain development do result in lasting behavioral alterations, while leaving the affected animals normal in appearance," comments Dr. Patricia M. Rodier, a professor and anatomist at the University of Virginia in Charlottesville.

Imagine a rat or a mouse or, we mustn't shrink from the possibility, a human with an outwardly normal appearance but with the potential for profound alterations in feelings and behavior. This is the stuff of horror films, science fiction scenarios of "aliens" from outer space

("How can you be certain that your next-door neighbor isn't *one of them?*). But one doesn't have to let his imagination run wild in order to discover some real and equally disturbing influences on normal brain/behavior development. For instance, agents that are known to be useful in modifying the adult brain (certain powerful tranquilizers) may be teratogenic (literally, "monster-producing") when they come into contact with the fetal brain. This is the principal reason why pregnant women are encouraged to do without tranquilizers during their pregnancy. While tranquilizers might be helpful to their brains via anxiety reduction they may, at the same time, be wreaking havoc within the brains of their concepti.

Multiple areas can be involved when a rat brain is exposed to harmful substance within the midperiod of neuronal production. During this short span dozens of structures and systems are in active growth and, therefore, adversely affected. As a result, each brain area developing then may wind up harmed in some way. A harmful agent encountered at the appropriate time has the potential to interfere with vision, learning, and balance. Subtler behavioral repertoires can also be affected such as general motor activity, curiosity, and exploration of the environment. The variety of impairments that can result is extensive, even if only a few harmful agents are administered. Such findings have spurred neuroscientists to redirect their efforts away from a one-agent-causes-one-disability orientation. Instead, it is now believed that the same brain injury can result from many agents as long as they're encountered at the same "critical period." Further, the same agent may exert a different effect if it is introduced at an earlier or later time of development.

The timing of major developmental processes in the formation of the human brain are a function of age in fetal weeks. For example, neuronal proliferation begins within the first four weeks of development and is nearly complete by twenty-four weeks. Neuronal differentiation, in contrast, begins at about fourteen weeks and continues, reaching a peak at birth.

Investigation of the thalidomide tragedy revealed that no malformations occurred when the drug was taken less than thirty-four or more than fifty days after the mother's last menstrual period—an extraordinarily restricted period of vulnerability. If the exposure took place in the thirty-nine-to-forty-four-day period, the infant was born without arms or with severely stunted arm growth. If exposure occurred within forty-two to forty-eight days, the lower limbs were shortened or absent altogether. Between forty-one and forty-three days the heart as well as the limbs could have been affected.

Exposure to thalidomide preceded by about two weeks the comple-

Timing of Developmental Processes

Developmental Process	Gestational Age					
	0	10	20	Birth	20	40
Neuronal Proliferation						
Glial Proliferation						
Neuronal Migration						
Neuronal Differentiation						
Axonal Growth						
Synapse Formation						
Process Elimination						
Myelination						

Formation of the brain can be plotted as a function of age in weeks. For example, at ten weeks neuronal proliferation is active whereas synapse formation has hardly begun. At twenty weeks just the opposite situation prevails: neuronal proliferation is well on the way to completion whereas synapse formation will continue at a hectic pace until birth and beyond. Many developmental processes overlap and therefore injury to the brain at any time is apt to interfere with concurrent processes. The diagram is only approximate since the timing often differs between components of the nervous system. In other instances the details are not available concerning the precise timing for all events.

tion of the normal developmental sequence (the development of an upper or lower limb, closure of the heart, and so on). Thus, the final "teratogenic effect" depended principally on the time of exposure. Innumerable mothers took thalidomide during noncritical periods of their infant's development and, by currently available criteria, their infants didn't suffer any disability. What could account for such a seemingly erratic course of events? One explanation involves differences in activity of crucial enzymes involved in metabolizing thalidomide. It is speculated that these enzymes may be available to the fetus for only limited periods. Since these variations can wax and wane in ways that cannot always be predicted, the possibility of fetal damage must be considered to extend throughout pregnancy. Particularly vulnerable are those infants born before their time.

It has been known for years that prematurity is associated with a subsequent development of learning disabilities and the minimal brain damage syndrome: mild problems in coordination associated with the presence of subtle but nonetheless consistently demonstrable abnormalities in the neurological exam. A team of neuropathologists at the University of Washington School of Medicine in Seattle discovered extensive brain lesions in premature infants who died during the first month of life. They discovered brain lesions spread widely throughout the cerebral cortex as well as in areas deeper within the brain. The investigators speculate that the abnormal brain structures (strongly associated with prematurity) are responsible for the learning and behavioral disorders that occur later in childhood. Further, the brain abnormalities were noted to occur across a wide spectrum: some brains were extensively damaged while others had only minimal degrees of damage. In milder cases it would not be possible to predict what problems, if any, might occur in later years. Perhaps no problems at all would surface. More likely, however, subtle and often difficult-to-detect dysfunctions might appear in the sphere of learning, memory, and impulse control. This isn't intended, incidentally, as a complete explanation of why some children hate learning and "quit school" as soon as the law will allow. But it should provide a check on a parent's exasperation and impulse toward name-calling. "He's so stupid" may in the future be translated into "He has difficulty with mathematics, sitting still, and spatial visualization because of brain impairment limited to subcortical structures and the corpus callosum linking the two hemispheres. This resulted from brain damage between thirty-three and thirty-four weeks of development."

CHAPTER 23

Individuality

If you close your eyes and hold in your hand a fetal brain that has been suitably preserved you can identify by the tips of your fingers some of that brain's larger indentations. Each has a name, a separate identity. The brain tissue on each side of these indentations (variously called a gyrus or a convolution) also has a name. In short, each brain has a topography, a cerebral geography.

Before the midpoint of pregnancy the brain is smooth and without indentation or furrow. By midpoint in the pregnancy only the larger fissures have appeared: Sylvian, central, calcarine. The names are crisp, laconic. Slightly beyond the midpoint, additional finer divisions can be appreciated by the palpating finger. Between fetal weeks twenty-six and thirty-five there is a flowering, a cascading of fissures and sulci. By the last fetal month all of them are there.

Two thirds of the cortex of the brain ends up hidden within the depths of these fissures. And all the cells that this particular brain will ever possess have been generated before the formation of the brain's convolutions. Indeed, all the cells in our cerebral cortex are generated by and before fetal week twenty—just before the halfway point.

What would be the effect, neuroscientists wondered, if part of the cerebral cortex were for some reason to disappear before birth? Would the brain generate additional nerve cells to replace the missing ones? Such questions were unanswerable for a long time. There simply was no way of altering the fetal brain without at the same time producing the death of the fetus—a researcher's variation on "the experiment was a success but the patient died."

With the development of increasingly sophisticated neurosurgical techniques it became possible in the early 1980s to remove the fetus of a monkey at various points during the pregnancy, alter the fetal brain, return the fetus to the womb, and examine the brain once again several months later at the conclusion of a normal, uncomplicated birth.

Prenatal neurosurgery was first carried out by a husband-and-wife team at Yale University, Patricia S. Goldman-Rakic and Pasko Rakic. They discovered that if the brain of a monkey so operated upon is examined even years later vast alterations can be appreciated in the architecture of that brain. Additional sulci, crevices, and gyri, mounds of brain tissue, appear that weren't found in a brain spared the neurosurgeon's before-birth intrusiveness. The brain has reorganized itself in a most peculiar way. Not only are there alterations in the area of immediate interest but far distant sites within the brain are altered as well. If the cutting occurred toward the front of the brain (the frontal and prefrontal fibers), alterations can be detected toward the side (temporal lobe) or at the back (occipital lobe).

Ponder the implications of this for a moment. A fetal surgeon removes a brain part toward the front. Alterations are produced in the front, side, and back. The brain looks different, feels different; these differences in feeling and looking are not parceled out according to the location of the original surgical interference but spread around. Succinctly put, How can the disruption of a small part of the cortex produce widespread changes that encompass the entire cerebral surface of both hemispheres? Not an easy question to answer. Not easy especially if the ponderer and the questioner insist on a model of the brain in which brain parts form, are shuffled about a bit, settle, and stay settled. The answer to the enigma occurred to the Rakics and other insightful ponderers when they set down on paper, pondered, discussed, argued about, and then further pondered the significance of the following facts.

Fissures within the fetal brain emerge at about the same time that fibers from deeper underlying brain areas (the thalamus especially) invade the cortex and establish their thalamic-cortical connections. The importance of such connections? A foot steps on a thorn and an impulse is relayed into the thalamus; it's further relayed into the cortex and that foot is picked up with a vigor. "Damn!" Impulses travel from foot to thalamus and you have your pain. Impulses travel from thalamus to cortex and that pain is further elaborated and you have your "Damn!"

Removal of brain tissue at a time when connections are being established results in an imbalance. The fibers no longer connect since the cortical tissue they would ordinarily connect with have been purloined. Also, under normal conditions, connections are established from one cortical area to another. These, too, are disrupted and run afoul in the event of the surgical removal of part of the cortex. Nerve fibers are shunted elsewhere, connected with cells they would ordinarily have no intercourse with.

"At least some classes of convolutional abnormality [brains that look and feel different from ordinary] in man can be caused by selective elimination of cortical-cortical connections," the Rakics tell us.

Eliminate or alter part of the fetal brain and you may bring about changes in parts of the brain you never intended to alter. Neurons can control other neurons in other areas of the brain. "Competitive activity," "common synaptic territory"—such are the phrases implored to explain why no brain researcher can be absolutely certain of all of the ramifications of his actions when he sets out in the interest of scientific investigation to alter one fetal brain, even that of a monkey.

Examination of the folds and ridges of the human brain, whether by vision alone or vision aided by palpating fingers, reveals an individuality unguessed at by earlier investigators. No two genetic programs or environments or life experiences are ever precisely alike, or could ever be. Provide small fluctuations in the environment or diet, the opportunity to be picked up as an infant, cuddled, loved, cared for in ways that extend beyond the mere custodial—and that brain takes a different turn, a different physiognomy of bumps and crevices. Alter these determinants and you may alter the brain in ways that can't always be discovered but that can be speculated about without doing violence to the tenets of logic.

"Environmentally determined variations may play a major role in determining the unique features of each individual," write the Rakics. Experience, fate, environment, and chance exert their effects on the fetal brain, mold it, shape it and, indeed, sculpt it toward a pattern that, however many brains may be examined until doomsday, will be found in that brain and that brain alone.

CHAPTER 24

Sensitivity

In 1957 the American Museum of Natural History in New York sponsored a lecture entitled "Evidence of Prenatal Function of the Central Nervous System in Man." The speaker was Davenport Hooker, who over the previous two decades had carried out a series of experiments on the human fetus.

Working with fetuses that had been aborted "when the therapeutic termination of pregnancy was deemed necessary by a committee of consulting obstetricians," Hooker placed his tiny still-living subjects into a fluid bath especially prepared to mimic as closely as was then possible the conditions existing within the womb.

Hooker and his associates kept a fetus alive in this contraption for several weeks. During this period a thirty-five-millimeter World War I surplus camera was pressed into service in order to record the fetus's movements. Hooker's observations were made by periodically prodding the skin of the fetus with a fine hair (an esthesiometer) calibrated to exert pressures ranging from ten milligrams to two grams. By 1939 Hooker had carried out this procedure on a sufficient number of fetuses to provide the material for his major opus, *A Preliminary Atlas of Early Human Fetal Activity*. It was in order to speak of these experiments that Hooker had been invited to come to the museum.

The value of Hooker's experiments depended principally on one thing: Hooker and only Hooker had the tenacity, intellectual curiosity, ethical insensitivity or, most likely combination thereof, to carry out on living fetuses procedures other researchers had only fantasized about. Further—and this is the point—Hooker had something original to report on fetuses smaller in size than the head of a pin.

At seven and a half weeks of age the fetus will turn its head to the side opposite a stimulus applied to one side of its mouth. Touch the mouth region on the right with one of Hooker's tiny hairs and the fetus bends its head to the left. Muscle contraction is limited to those muscles served by the upper part of the spinal cord. Conclusion? Motor expression is dependent upon maturation of the nervous system. In those areas where synaptic connections have been formed, movement-behavior is possible.

At a slightly later point (eight and a half weeks, twenty-five millimeters in length) the same stimulus (a touch to the mouth region) produces a more widespread reflex: the trunk and pelvis also tilt to the opposite side, the fingers spread apart, and the mouth opens. At between nine and nine and a half weeks the pelvis and both upper and lower extremities are more active, the mouth opens more completely —the lips separate at the corners as well as the midline.

With these observations Hooker confirmed what previous investigators had debated about over many years. The fetal brain, Hooker established, is the determinant of behavior. Only those muscles can move that are served by the brain areas that have already established synaptic connections.

If Hooker's research had stopped there, Hooker would most likely be regarded today as a kind of Evel Knievel-turned-neurobiologist. But Hooker, to his credit, took to heart the most important injunction of medical research: observe, observe, observe. And observe he did.

• Hooker observed that in response to the touch of a hair the embryo initially reacts as a whole. At first the behavior is limited but this limitation is based solely on the differences in brain development from region to region. When additional regions have matured sufficiently— when there are a greater number of synaptic connections—additional areas of the fetus react to the same stimulus: the head and trunk, the four extremities including the hands and fingers, and even the jaw—all in response to the touch of a tiny hair to the tiny mouth.

• Hooker observed that as the greater surface of the skin became sensitive, inhibitory reactions developed. At this point focal reflexes, the movement of just an arm, began to take precedence over movements of the whole body or even one side of the body. This localization of response occurred in a definite order—the legs, then the lower trunk and pelvis dropped out first, next both arms stopped responding together and started responding separately.

• Hooker observed that parts of an arm or leg began separate movements at about the same time those parts became responsive to touch.

• Hooker observed that as time went on specific body parts tended to ally themselves movementwise. By twelve and a half weeks stimulation of the palm of the hand produces a turning of the face to the same side accompanied by opening and closing of the mouth and associated tongue movements. This intimate relationship of hand and mouth continues after birth: the baby grasps at the breast with her hand so that she may thereby suck easier.

Lips, palms of the hands, genital areas, areas of the face particularly around the eyes—this is the sequence of responsiveness observed by Hooker. This sequence was quite a surprise, incidentally. It might be expected that surface sensitivity would spread regularly from around the mouth downward over the body and extremities. Not at all. The palms of the hands react to stimulation much earlier and more sensitively than do the shoulder, upper arm, and forearm. Touching the genitals provides a reflex long before stimulation has any effect on the back, chest, or abdominal wall. Likewise the soles of the feet were found to be sensitive earlier than either the thighs or the legs.

If you study Hooker's findings, which at first seem paradoxical and seemingly arbitrary, they begin to make sense. This is the famous homunculus created by neurosurgeon Wilder Penfield as a result of his operating room experiments. During the course of an operation, Penfield would stimulate a part of the brain and determine whether or not the patient detected a stimulation. The homunculus is a scaled drawing which represents the various body parts in relation to the total brain area as determined by Penfield's gentle probing. The hand and soles of the feet, lips, and tongue are overrepresented in relation to their size or compared to the shoulders, thighs, trunk, and so on.

Penfield's homunculus depends on the fact that greater numbers of fibers serve the lips, tongue, palms of the hands, and soles of the feet. This arrangement has practical implications as well. Babies can be quieted by giving them a nipple, stroking their feet or palms, and in some cultures, I am told, stroking their genitals. A moment's thought about the matter will convince you that the same hierarchy of pleasure centers persists within the adult.

When Hooker's findings are looked at in their entirety, certain trends become clear. First, the anterior end (mouth) and posterior end (genitals) of the fetus become sensitive long before the intervening regions. Likewise, the palmar surface of the hands and the plantar of the feet are more sensitive than the backs and considerably more sensitive than the more proximal parts of the arms and legs.

Does the fetus taste and smell, does it lose its balance, can it see? Hooker examined each of these questions, too, with the following findings.

Taste buds are mature enough to function as early as thirteen weeks, a later period than tongue movements and swallowing. The addition of sugar to the amniotic fluid of the fetus near term increases swallowing. A newborn's rejection of quinine and enthusiasm for sugar is most likely a continuation of this taste ability that begins early in the womb.

√Smell? There is no evidence to support the fact that the fetus can
smell. Both nostrils are plugged up well into the sixth fetal month.
Besides, smell requires currents of air passing across the epithelium of
the nose, a requirement that must await delivery from an aquatic to an
aerial environment.

Abundant stimulation of the balance (vestibular) reflex exists within
the near-weightless environment of the womb. Indeed, movement of
the fetus may be nothing less than the fetus's response to vestibular
stimulation.

Overall, Hooker's research led him to a series of speculations. Reflex
activity before twenty weeks is executed, Hooker believed, by means of
the midbrain, lower brain stem, and spinal cord and does not involve
the cerebral cortex or subcortical regions. But after twenty weeks
neural circuits within the subcortical areas become functional to an
increasing degree. For example, a premature infant's failure to maintain adequate body temperature indicates, according to Hooker, in-
complete functional development of the hypothalamus. With the passage of time the circuits within the hypothalamus become activated
and, presto, the slightly older premature baby can now regulate its own
temperature.

Hooker's ideas on the brain's gradual development (like a chrysalis
which opens slowly and only partially at a given moment) convinced a
whole generation of infant researchers that brain development occurs
in steps and, further, that at certain of these steps the infant is nothing
more than a "brain stem preparation," a catchphrase implying that
only the brain stem of the infant is operative.

Brain scientists no longer believe, as Hooker did, that the infant
brain operates in a piecemeal fashion: spinal cord, brain stem, midbrain, subcortex, cortex. Would that matters were so simple! Instead,
brain development continues throughout fetal life and beyond, well
into young adulthood and, if one believes as I do, in synaptic facilitation (those synapses that are used are thereby maintained . . . new
uses lead to new synaptic channels), perhaps brain development continues to our final gasp.

But there are other issues raised by Hooker's work on what has been
euphemistically referred to as "exteriorized fetuses." I am uneasy regarding research that fails to make a distinction between a tadpole and
a human being.

C. P. Snow was wrong. There are not two cultures (science and
humanism) but only one of two alternative cultures: a culture in which
science is carried out according to humanistic principles and a culture
that sustains a science wherein anything goes.

Is brain research sufficiently important to justify the temporary sus-

tenance of the fetus solely for the purpose of prodding, poking, observing, publishing, and lecturing on the results of the researcher's
manipulations? In 1957 the American Museum of Natural History
answered that question in the affirmative. How would you answer it
today?

CHAPTER 25

Accommodations

"The sometimes quick, sometimes slow, mostly uncoordinated, but sometimes coordinated extension and flexion of the arms and legs of the newly born are nothing else than a continuation of the intrauterine movements," wrote an early infant observer in 1890. At the time this was a revolutionary suggestion. It still is. Corroboration of this suggestion comes from studies of premature infants.

First, the movements of premature newborns are strikingly similar to fetal intrauterine patterns. Second, premature infants approaching term do not suddenly alter their repertoire in any way. There are no indicators for a "readiness to be born."

At first glance this thesis of seeming similarity seems counterintuitive. The fetus experiences so many changes in the passage from womb to delivery room. For instance, instead of submergence in amniotic fluid, the newborn is exposed to the full force of gravity. Touch, vision, noise, and temperature are also altered. Instead of a continuous supply of oxygen and the removal of carbon dioxide, active breathing movements must be called into play immediately upon birth. The free ride is over; energy must be expended in order to obtain additional sources of energy. And this nutritive process is no longer a continuous taking and passively receiving. Instead, food must be imbibed through the mouth by means of active sucking at intervals set by hunger, maternal convenience, and happenstance. Frustration is inherent in this makeshift arrangement. Too little food, too little attention, too little love—any one or all of these can tip the balance toward discomfort, more discomfort, raging hunger pains, then outright misery. In the presence of so many negative factors both real and potential, it's a wonder the newborn ever adjusts.

"An enormous adaptive capacity is required," according to developmental neurologist Heinz F. R. Prechtl. "The term infant certainly has this capacity, but it does not simply emerge around 40 weeks of gestation; it does so gradually from a much earlier age, so providing a kind of safety range which also enables the preterm infant to survive."

If a newborn is examined soon after birth, a host of "reflex" responses can be elicited that will disappear over the next several months. Rooting (turning the mouth toward the nipple), sucking, automatically grasping objects placed in the hand, flexion, and stretching the legs—each of these behaviors is exhibited by the fetus in the last several months before birth. They continue for a while after birth and then eventually disappear except in those furry primates where clinging and clutching and grasping are an adaptation to close contact with the mother's body and, hence, necessary for survival. With loss of fur, grasping and clutching become less adaptive.

The persistence in the human fetus and newborn of automatic responses observed in "lower" primates provides support for a theory first put forth by a certain K. E. von Baer in 1828. In *Developmental History of the Animals,* von Baer pointed out that embryos, regardless of species, resembled the embryos of other animals more than they resembled the adults of their own kind. Behavior also conforms to this pattern. Rudimentary and "primitive" reflexes necessary for species survival in other primates make early and brief cameo appearances in the human fetus.

"From the point of view of the nervous system, the newborn and infant in the first month or two tend to maintain many fetal characteristics, which perhaps explains the often stated opinion that the human newborn is a helpless and immature creature," writes Heinz Prechtl.

Could this persistence of fetal characteristics explain the uneasiness and discomfort some mothers feel about their newborns? Certainly during the first six weeks after birth the human newborn operates almost entirely on the basis of reflexes, providing little in the way of nurturing of the parent who expects some confirmation, some indication however slight, that she or he is someone special. But the newborn brain isn't capable of making such distinctions or conferring such kudos. Disappointment is inevitable, therefore, for the parent who isn't aware of the infant's limitations.

Take smiling, for instance. Spontaneous smiling has been observed in fetuses photographed in the uterus, can be elicited soon after birth, occurs irregularly for several weeks and then, finally, at six to eight weeks becomes a *social smile.* It's speculated that the behavioral pattern for smiling is established within the fetus months before birth, expresses itself periodically and without provocation, and only then as a final step becomes an expression of the infant's responses to people and events.

"Preadapted functions" is a term developmental neurologists use to explain why Mary's smile at three weeks shouldn't be taken very seriously as an indication of amusement but should be taken very seriously, indeed, when that smile occurs at three months. Simply put, a behavioral repertoire is established within the neuronal network of the immature brain, is expressed periodically in a kind of testing or "dry run," and only later with all the components operating at their most efficient does Mary smile because at that very moment she is aware that someone is smiling at her and she wants to smile back.

The human brain differs from that of other primates thanks to a process dubbed hominidization—attainment of the erect posture; modification of the pelvis to the mechanical requirements of the upright position; partial loss of body hair; and increase in the relative size of the brain (increased encephalization).

Compared to other primates the absolute size of the newborn human brain is not heavy: brain weight is proportional to body weight. This comparison is somewhat misleading since the human newborn's body weight is much greater in proportion to the mother's weight and certainly when compared to monkey and ape babies and their mothers.

This heavier, bigger human brain creates obstetrical difficulties. In rhesus monkeys the size of the female pelvis and newborn skull matches closely. The breadth of the infant chimpanzee skull is only 72 percent of the birth canal. For these reasons the birth process is quick and comparatively easy in these two species. In humans the newborn skull is 101.8 percent of the width of the pelvic outlet. In addition, the skull along its front to back diameter is even larger, requiring a ninety-degree rotation during passage into the birth canal. If pregnancy were extended another month the infant head size would be sufficiently large to preclude a normal delivery. With the increase in head size of our ancestors the duration of pregnancy was shortened, thereby resulting in the birth of a less mature baby. As a result, the greatest period of brain growth and development occur after birth (a fourfold increase compared to twofold in apes, as mentioned previously). In addition, the newborn's helplessness and immaturity in comparison to other primates is the inevitable consequence of the need to adjust brain and body weight to both maternal pelvic size and the increased energy requirements of a larger, more developed fetus. A bigger baby would also necessarily require a larger placenta, thereby rendering a normal birth even less likely.

Consider the paradox of the human newborn. He or she is larger than the newborns of other primate species but is less equipped to survive. Brain growth, therefore, continues to increase at a frantic rate for one year after birth. As a consequence of this rapid growth any interference with normal diet stunts normal brain development.

In essence, human brain development involves a delicate balance. While it would obviously be advantageous to possess a more mature brain after birth, the possessor of such a brain would imperil its own survival. While less dependency on parents would seem advantageous, the immaturity of the infant brain renders early independence impossible.

Those given to late-night speculations regarding meaning can ponder this: the human brain is the determiner of when we are born, what we can do at the moment of birth, our chances of survival. The poetically or mystically inclined might put it the other way around. All these accommodations and compromises are arrived at or arranged at the behest of the human brain. Nothing should be altered or can be altered very much without compromising the entire enterprise. My brain and your brain may ponder how to arrange the separate components somewhat differently but that pondering isn't likely to affect how the expectant mother across the way is going to be delivered of her infant, nor how that infant's brain is going to develop at a rate that boggles our understanding (in the range of two hundred and fifty thousand multiplications per second). No interference on our part is called for or will be tolerated. Fortunately, the human brain has a way of arranging things in its own good time.

CHAPTER 26

Baby Brain

What is the nature of the baby brain? Is it merely a "primitive," unsophisticated version of the brain of an adult? Descriptions of infant behaviors would lead one to such a conclusion.

The pediatrician supports the infant in his arms and suddenly pretends to be dropping her. The baby startles, sweeps her hands in an arc in the empty air as if clutching for safety at an unseen object. The Moro response. A "primitive" remnant of something from our ancient past, a "reflex" that serves no present purpose and given a few short weeks will disappear into the murky mists of our biological origins. Our pediatrician if pressed on the matter for a specialist examination would say something along the following lines (he would, that is, if he wished to pass his examination).

"The Moro response is present because the cerebral cortex of the baby's brain has yet to exert an inhibitory influence on the lower centers. In a few weeks, the inhibitory forces will hold in check such primitive reflexes that eventually will disappear." Bravo! Our pediatrician has repeated most excellently the standard line and will no doubt pass his oral examination. Even more interesting, it's likely that he will maintain throughout his career this theory that development consists in a gradual increase of cortical influence: voluntary cerebral hemisphere activity suppressing subcortical reflex mechanisms.

Our pediatrician would be surprised to learn that his theory is a hundred years out of date. While physicists and chemists have enlarged the scope of their explanations, plunging deep into the nature of matter to discover a series of "elementary particles" which, once discovered, have only to be replaced by even more fundamental forces, the student of human biology has remained tethered to the mechanistic views of the nineteenth century. During that period physiologists found that the brain of an experimental animal could be altered by surgery to produce a spinal or decerebrate or decorticate preparation,

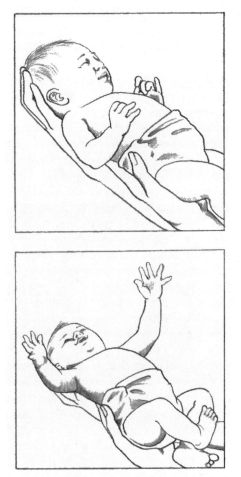

The Moro Response

three buzzwords that correspond to an animal horribly impaired, indeed, mutilated. Although still alive, the animal so "lesioned" has not the capacity for independent existence. It subsists at the experimentalist's whim within the confines of the laboratory and solely on the basis of the functioning of certain areas of the brain below the cerebral cortex. The cat was a favorite subject for such experiments, easy to procure, not terribly hard to subdue, far enough removed, appearancewise, from the experimentalist to preclude any discomforting or invidious comparisons.

Included also in the experimentalist's repertoire was a veritable Noah's ark from which could be selected suitable experimental "subjects" when cats weren't available: pigeons, hens, turkeys, swallows, owls, ducks, or sparrows.

The experiments were based on reasoning along these lines. With destruction of a brain area, whatever "reflex response" could be obtained from the animal must be the result of the operation of the remaining "unlesioned" areas. Indeed, these "reflexes" were, under ordinary conditions, held in check by higher brain areas which, thanks to the experimentalists' scalpel intrusions, had been rendered permanently inoperative. A cat, for instance, could be observed, depending on the site of the "lesion," to right itself when laid on its side. It would also automatically extend its paws and support its weight when contact was made between the paws and the laboratory table.

Another fanciful area for the investigation of "reflexes" was the careful observation of brain-injured adults. A stroke, for instance, might render a patient paralyzed in one arm and hand and yet, mysterious to behold, that same hand might at a later point grasp something placed in the palm. This "grasp reflex" was thought to be the result of the release of subcortical centers from the influence of the now-damaged cerebral hemispheres. While all of this may seem far removed from our understanding of the infant brain, a series of observations in the early part of the twentieth century resulted in the experimentalists gathering together in one unified theory their observations from "lesioned animals," brain-damaged adults, and normal infants.

By the end of the first quarter of the twentieth century several scientists had observed and commented upon the presence of reflexes within the newborn animal similar in their expression to the responses resulting from the placing of "lesions" in various parts of the brains of adults in the same species. Soon, similar observations were reported in human infants and convalescing children. In explanation, the scientists suggested that these reflexes served as the basic units of brain activity which, under ordinary conditions, were inhibited by higher cortical centers. In the human infant the higher cortical centers have yet to develop, hence the appearance and subsequent disappearance of the reflexes. In brain-damaged children and adults the influence of the cerebral cortex was lost, thus permitting an expression of reflexes formerly inhibited by the healthy cortex.

The concept of the human infant as a reflex machine, perfectly compatible with the mercantile mechanism of the industrial revolution, determined not only the interpretation put upon infant behavior but also, and more important, what behavior was deemed worthy of observation.

An infant grasps something in her hand: the grasp reflex. The new-born infant if supported under its arms so that both feet touch the tabletop could walk: the stepping reflex. In their enthusiasm for observing and tabulating reflexes, these early observers failed to notice that very few of an infant's responses are truly reflex in nature. Yawning, stretching, rolling over, smiling when smiled at, fretfulness, laughing—rarely could such behaviors be understood solely on the basis of a reflex response to some external stimulation.

Contemporary developmental neurologists recognize the limitations of attempting to understand the infant brain on the basis of observations of surgically altered animals or sick human adults. Both animals and adults possess biologically different brains. Operated-on animals and neurologically damaged adults possess *damaged brains*. The infant brain is different from that of a surgically altered cat, normal adult, or a neurologically damaged adult. It is nothing less than its own unique self. There is nothing remotely like an infant brain.

"The adult brain is (structurally) different from the brain of an infant, so that it functions differently," according to Dr. Bert C. L. Touwen, a developmental neurologist. "If the adult brain is damaged the remaining parts which are responsible for the remaining functional display are still biologically quite different from the healthy infant's brain. It would be remarkable, therefore, if the functional display of the adult's damaged brain and the healthy infant's brain were similar."

According to Dr. Touwen, the normal infant brain operates on two separate but interrelated channels. The brain generates motor patterns such as sucking, breathing, and stepping while at the same time it responds to people and events in the environment. In the event of damage to the brain, the infant may be capable only of "reflex" reactions. This tells us little or nothing about how the normal undamaged brain operates.

To Dr. Touwen the infant brain functions in a manner similar to Bohr's principle of complementarity: light has both particle and wave characteristics. "The capacity actively to generate rhythmical . . . motor patterns and the capacity of reactive behavior are both required in order to explain the infant's brain."

In addition, I believe there are other reasons for replacing the concept of a hierarchy where the cortex influences the lower centers. Such a view represents the scientific equivalent of a top-downward sociopolitical ideology. A more likely, more "democratic" pattern of control involves the successive development and organization and reorganization of compound centers within the brain which may change in place and number according to the needs of the brain as a whole. One learns to suck and grasp before taking on geometry. Motor development and

control is the most important accomplishment of early life and, therefore, the greater percentage of brain activity is organized for reaching,
grasping, turning, lifting, lugging oneself upward first onto the knees,
and then finally those first lumbering, uncertain steps. The infant brain
is perfectly attuned to the achievement of such milestones. "The
healthy infant's brain is an age-specific and age-adequate organ," Dr.
Touwen tells us with a peremptory erudition.

"Children stand in the place of the chrysalis of the immature animal
that is so far different from its fully grown model as almost to merit the
name of a different creature," wrote pediatrician N. Oppenheim in
1898.

Darwin continued this analogy concerning the human infant. Com-
menting on the birth of a colleague's child, Darwin stated: "You will be
astonished to find how the whole mental disposition of your children
changes with the advancing years. A young child and the same when
nearly grown sometimes differ almost as much as do caterpillar and
butterfly." The stimulus for these infant/caterpillar/butterfly analo-
gies?

In the nineteenth century embryologists noted two lines of development from newborn to adult. The first, the direct form, comprises
animal species in which the newborn closely resembles the adult and
needs only to undergo further growth to attain adult characteristics.
Spiders and guinea pigs, for instance, grow larger but appear essen-
tially the same throughout their life spans. Indirect development requires a dramatic change from the newborn to the adult. The most
familiar example, cited by scientists and laymen alike, is the transformation undergone by the butterfly from embryo to caterpillar to pupa
to adult butterfly. Frogs and salamanders undergo a similar abrupt and
dramatic change as they progress through their life cycles. Which
category is appropriate for humans?

At first glance the infant appears sufficiently similar to the adult that
a direct form of development seems likely. Certainly a human infant
couldn't possibly be mistaken for a member of another species,
whereas the uninitiated would be unlikely to anticipate the transformations undergone by a caterpillar on its path to becoming an adult
butterfly. But there is a problem with such a superficial approach.
Guinea pigs, an oft quoted example of the direct form of development,
are, in terms of brain growth, born almost fully mature. The human
newborn, in contrast, is helpless and fully dependent. Its greatest
period of brain development (the formation of synapses and dendritic
spines) lies in the future. For this reason alone an infant cannot be
considered as an adult merely awaiting further growth. "Children are

not like grownup folks," wrote the psychologist E. L. Thorndike in 1901, "but are in reality different beings. Their bodily makeup is different, as truly though not as much different as is the tadpole's from the frog's."

Considerable light has been shed recently on the relationship of the infant brain and behavior to its adult counterpart. Thanks to the development of ultrasound, the fetus can now be observed directly somewhere between the seventh and twelfth week of life. Its movements and motility patterns can then be compared to those of newborn infants. Such comparisons reveal that fetal movements aren't merely preparations for movements that will occur after birth. Rather they are specific adaptations to life within the womb. Two different movement patterns have been recorded.

In the first movement pattern, the head is flexed backward and turned to one side. This is accompanied by rotation of the trunk and the rest of the body to the same side. In the second movement pattern, leg movements occur, almost as if the fetus were pedaling a stationary bicycle, resulting in a somersault as the legs contact the uterine wall, press against it, and generate an active retropulsive rotary movement. Both of these patterns serve the purpose of stimulating brain development, especially those structures having to do with balance, coordination, and coping with the forces of gravity. The movements also stimulate circulation in the fetal skin and prevent the fetus from adhering to the uterine wall. Both of these movements, incidentally, have served their purposes before birth and disappear thereafter. It's likely that the stepping movements of the newborn are remnants of the propulsive intrauterine movements rather than failed attempts at early walking.

Another group of intrauterine movements are designed for life outside the womb. Fetal breathing, for instance, isn't truly functional in the liquid environment in which the fetus finds itself. Most likely early breathing movements serve as a preparation for that life process upon which all else depends. At birth, if one cannot breathe in, cannot exchange carbon dioxide for the vital oxygen of the environment, life will proceed no further than the delivery room. Tiny tot was born but "didn't make it" are the words of the delivery room nurse. "An anoxic death from cardiopulmonary insufficiency," the pathologist might put it. But the mother and father have no special words for such an event. Their feelings surge upward and make a mockery of any platitudinous phrases that might come to mind in order to attempt to do justice to the painful reality of a newborn's death: to have gone so far, to have come so close, and yet not to have been able to do what seems so elemental—breathe in, breathe out.

Along with breathing come other "respiratory reflexes": sighs, yawns, and stretches. Under ultrasounds such movements have the appearance of all the sighs, yawns, and stretches that are observed in an adult. Despite profound changes in the brain that accompany passage from infancy into adulthood these patterns will remain invariant. Is the fetus at seven months bored? If so, it is not likely to be bored in the same way that a seven year old or seventy year old is bored. You couldn't intuit this, however, from observing this trio for differences in sighing, yawning, or stretching.

Judging from movements, therefore, the human newborn is a hybrid. Some of its earliest movements are unrelated to life outside the uterine liquid world, whereas other movements clearly anticipate, often in startling ways, what can subsequently be observed over that newborn's lifetime. To this extent the human newborn cannot be accommodated within either of the above-mentioned developmental categories. It is unique. While it is true that much of fetal and early infant behavior appears to anticipate adult behaviors, the transitions are often far from easy to discover.

"The state of being a caterpillar always occurs before butterflyhood, but it's difficult to discern the competences that the adult butterfly inherited from the hairy larve," as developmental psychologist Jerome Kagan once put it.

At this point, developmental neurologists are urging an open mind regarding any correlations between fetal, infant, and adult brains. Simply put, the fetal brain reflects the demands of its environment. The same can be said of a newborn, and presumably the adult as well. Much is lost, therefore, when the human brain at an early stage of development is considered solely from the point of view of an inadequate or failed version of what prevails at a later point.

CHAPTER 27

Walking and Reaching

Newborn infants if supported by a proud parent will walk after a fashion. They raise their feet and replace them in regular stepping movements. No weight support is possible, you understand. The legs are too floppy and puttylike. This remarkable behavior soon disappears only to reappear many months later as the culmination of a series of achievements: head raising, crawling, sitting, stumbling and, finally, full-fledged walking. Is the early walking a predecessor of that final walking repertoire that begins in playpens and, in some instances, culminates in the Joffrey Ballet?

In 1952 two French researchers applied themselves to the tricky task of divining the relationship of the earliest walking to its more mature counterpart. They borrowed a group of infants from their mothers and exercised their stepping movements. They discovered that primary walking, if encouraged, endures for a much longer period of time than that in infants where the walking was ignored. More interesting, however, was the finding that the exercised infants learned to walk at an earlier age than expected.

The idea of giving a baby a head start over his or her peers is something inherently appealing, particularly to parents who are competitively inclined. But infant brain development isn't quite that simple. Timetables exist which are immutable.

Take a pair of twins. Subject one member of the pair (the unlucky one) to strict toilet training starting at three months and continuing until just about the child's second birthday. When you are satisfied that the child is almost completely trained, only then start training the twin sibling. This experiment has actually been carried out with the most astounding results. The second twin catches up immediately. Twenty-three months of training produces no higher level of bladder and bowel control than no training at all. (For the moment we'll skip the issue of what other differences might result from twenty-three months of "Sit there until you do it.")

Take another pair of twins, and at forty-six weeks of age introduce one of the pair to some practice in climbing stairs. Six weeks later, introduce the second twin to the practice. Not surprisingly, twin number one outperforms twin number two by about 100 percent. But two weeks later you can't tell one from the other. Climbing ability, it seems, develops without very much practice, nor is it much improved by subsequent practice. That experiment, too, has been replicated but this particular set of twins wasn't nearly as lucky as the toilet-training duo—they were subsequently recruited for a cube-stacking contest.

After six weeks of training the Master Builder was outmaneuvered by the Neophyte with no training. Conclusion: practice doesn't make perfect at least when it comes to stair climbing and cube stacking. Indeed, practice doesn't seem to matter much at all. The brain develops at its own pace (varying from child to child) and not much in the way of environmental enrichment seems to matter a whit.

Some infant behaviors are like stair climbing, cube stacking, toilet training—the skills develop at their own natural rate and not much can be done to influence them one way or the other. Other infant behaviors are more like walking—practice makes perfect or at least serves to improve performance over a period of time. In some instances, the behavior can even be detected before birth. Reaching and grasping, for instance, can be elicited in fetuses between fourteen and sixteen weeks after conception. Immediately after birth the skill is quite impressive. But over the next month the baby stops reaching for objects only to start doing so again when somewhere between four and five months of age.

Accurate reaching demands a combination of skills. Perception of the object must be united with some idea of the position and trajectory of the hand. If you don't believe this, test it for yourself.

Look at an object in front of you about an arm's length away. Close your eyes. Now reach for it. In the absence of neurologic illness, the task is ridiculously easy. One merely consults an inner "feeling" for the hand in space, how much movement is required to travel from here to there, and the thing is done. But it takes precious time early in development to establish such an inner "schema," as the experimentalists refer to it. Later in life it can be lost, too. A stroke can disrupt the sense of hand position so severely that it is necessary to visually track the spoon on the way to the mouth lest the chicken soup wind up on the septogenarian's lap.

In reaching, infants have a difficulty few adults have complained about. Their hand is so *interesting,* so arresting that it captures their attention whenever it enters the visual field. Only the infant truly appreciates the beauty of the human hand—the only hand in created existence that has perfected thumb and index finger opposition. Indeed, a baby is unable to ignore the hand, can't treat it as an object, hasn't the immediate knack of getting along with the business of grasping whatever it is the experimenter wants it to grasp. The baby will start to reach, encounter the hand, and ponder "What's that!" Moments later, attention will shift to the toy once again and reaching will be resumed only to be interrupted yet another time by the Beautiful Hand.

Up until five months of age the hand competes for the infant's attention. Indeed, there are few things in life more intriguing and inherently fascinating than one's own hand. But in the interests of getting along in the world most of us relinquish this fascination in favor of whatever fascination we can extract from the objects we reach out for. But this shift in allegiance takes five months to appear. By seven months the baby can keep track of the hand and the object at the same time—can ignore the Hand and get on with the business of reaching, grasping, and mouthing. By seven months Hand has been demoted to, simply, hand.

In an interesting experiment conducted by infant researcher T. G. R. Bower of the University of Edinburgh, five month olds were shown a toy. The lights were then extinguished. Without hesitation the infants reached out and grasped the toy. Direct visual registration of the hand was not important here. At five months, visual control is helpful but not necessary. Once seen, an object's position can be intuited within the darkness and grasped. Older infants (seven months) can't do this, or are unwilling to try. But by one year of age reaching in the dark reappears, performed as accurately and deftly as at five months.

Appearance. Disappearance. Reappearance. The pattern repeats itself throughout the life of the infant. Input from the ear is fed within the brain to areas concerned with moving the eyes: the baby looks to the source of a sound. A newborn will do that. Nobody has taught that one can expect to see something in the direction from which one has heard something. Sound arouses the curiosity of sight. Expectation within the brain is as real as neurons, as palpably present as neuronal circuits.

Baby reaches out for an object, grasps it, bellows if the object feels different than it looks. This, too, is "hard-wired," not taught (unless one engages in metaphor considering Mother Nature or some other anthropomorphism as Teacher). How else could one explain the behavior of a blind infant? He, too, "looks" toward a sound, "looks" at his hand, and reaches out for objects that were once heard, until one

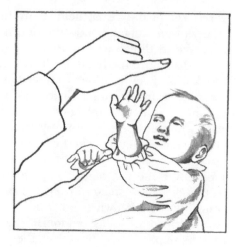

A young infant is often unable to ignore the sight of his or her own hand when it intrudes in the visual field during the act of reaching.

day, suddenly, sadly, all this behavior stops. By four months of age the sighted infant in darkness stops turning to look toward the source of the sound. That, too, he now recognizes as pointless, but for different reasons than the pointlessness of a blind infant's turning.

With time the responses of the infant become more specific. Only those senses that count are brought into play. Baby can't see in the darkness. Ergo Baby stops turning his eyes to the source of a sound in a darkened room. At birth and for some time thereafter, perception operates at the level of global response, "There is something off to the right." Eyes, ears, hands, nose, and everything else that can be mobilized turn toward that thing. In time, by three to four months, reality can be parceled to some extent. "I hear a sound off to the right" doesn't necessarily produce eye movements or reaching movements. Baby simply listens.

CHAPTER 28

Touching

Compare the persuasiveness of touch to that of sight. Bishop Berkeley (the very same who questioned the reality of matter and in the process formulated the theory of idealism which Samuel Johnson refuted by kicking a stone and thus establishing that lofty axiom, "He who kicks a stone ends up with a sore foot") held that "touch teaches vision." Berkeley believed that we see a thing a certain way because of spacial considerations. "Tactile-kinesthetic perception of spatial extension is primary, whereas visual perception of space is secondary," as the psychophysicists put it. But Aristotle fifteen hundred years earlier knew better. Could he have learned it from studying babies? Aristotle discovered the crossed-finger illusion: a single object, say, a pencil, when held between crossed fingers yields a felt perception of two objects. But if the pencil is seen as well as felt, the illusion disappears. One pencil. "Vision teaches touch."

Place a newborn so that its hands and arms are free to move if the infant is so inclined. Outfit the infant with a pair of special glasses that permits the perception of a virtual image (a toy appears but no toy is present, merely the image of a toy projected into the empty air). The baby reaches for the toy, grasps only air, and howls in rage and frustration. Here, too, we have evidence, cruelly obtained, that the senses are unified. Even a newborn expects there will be something to grasp when there is something to see. He wasn't taught this expectation. Seen objects must be tangible, the infant believes, says the experimenter.

A six-month infant displays a craftiness unavailable to her at birth. Although still put off by a toy that could be seen but not grasped, the older infant fails to close her hand after one or two determinations that there's nothing there to grasp her hand on. The infant may shake her head back and forth. "Is the problem in my hand or in my head?" After one or two unsuccessful tries, the infant stops competing with the White Coats. "Doesn't reach out. Doesn't howl. Doesn't care anymore." The infant detects somehow that the toy isn't real. Vision, not touch, is now the dominant sense.

Imagine that I place a coin in your hand. You don't have to see it to remain aware of its presence. Its feel, its contour on your palm attest to its presence. But not so with the baby at six months. If a handkerchief is thrown over the hand grasping a coin, the baby will drop the coin. Even the disappearance of the coin as the baby closes her hand over it may cause her to drop it. Reality is *seen* reality. The unity of the senses is unbalanced. Attention remains riveted on what can be seen. This is the determination of what is real. Later, the unity returns once again. The adult pattern. An adult can hold something in the hand, not see it, still know it's there, still know that concealed in the palm there's a coin to drop into the fare box while stepping onto the bus. Just when the shift from the baby to adult pattern occurs isn't known with any certainty, perhaps it isn't attained at all in a certain percentage of otherwise "normal" adults. "Seeing is believing," such adults assure us. The frequency of that "seeing" varies from one person to another, some requiring almost a continual regard of the object or person in order to continue to believe in its existence. "Out of sight, out of mind" isn't at all confined to babies. Our language betrays which of our senses carries the most weight. "I *see* what you mean," one businessman says to another over lunch and the contract renegotiation. "It *looks* different from your point of view. Now I get the whole *picture.*"

Seeing is touching, the six month old's *grasp* on the world, remains etched in our language, too. "She couldn't take her eyes off him. Suddenly their eyes met. In a rapid glance they sized each other up," writes the scriptwriter for a daytime soap opera. Like language, infant development isn't a gradual accretion, the sophisticated replacing the primitive. Rather, the simple and subtle coexist. Sight and touch are intermingled. Both are derived from the same neuroectoderm: Eye is a sophisticated elaboration of the brain. The first eye developed from a tactile system then developed independently in order to learn about objects at a distance.

Doctor holds a tiny pea-sized brightly colored rubber ball in his hand. He places it on the table. Two-year-old Natasha reaches down, daintily grips the ball between thumb and first finger. She picks it up and laughs. Doctor nods and writes on Natasha's health sheet "pincer grasp intact."

A monkey or an ape couldn't do what Natasha has just done— oppose the thumb to the other fingers to allow picking up a rubber ball or a raisin or a nut. Indeed, Natasha couldn't do it herself until a few weeks ago. And that new ability speaks volumes about Natasha's brain; it justifies a whole cascade of inferences about that brain.

Consider some of the processes that Natasha's brain must carry out in order to pick up that tiny object. Visual depth perception must be perfectly linked with binocular vision and eye movements to retain the ball in sharp focus. There must exist a finely tuned control of body posture—body upright and balanced in the beginning of Natasha's reaching, followed by an anticipatory shift from the center of gravity split seconds before Natasha's arm goes out. Once started on its excursion the arm must be maintained on a track all the way to the target; the arm and finger movements must be smoothly directed under the guidance of direct vision and the "feel" of the arm's position in space. A failure in the execution of even one component of this sequence results in Natasha's missing the ball, swiping it off the table, and falling forward or dropping it. Those who favor comparisons of the brain with a computer might describe Natasha's performance as involving an assemblage of independently developed modules. One module is involved with depth perception, another with body posture, yet another with the maintenance of balance. Indeed, a computer linked to a mechanical arm could be programmed and has been so programmed to pick up that colored ball.

Doesn't it strike you as odd that a mechanical arm, operated by a computer, can accomplish what is denied to the hand of a monkey or an ape? One must recall that a computer is always designed by a human brain, is instructed in the skills of doing some of the things a brain can do, and whenever possible in the same manner. Besides, watching such a computer-driven device, as I have on occasion, reveals the poverty of the mechanical device compared to Natasha's ability. So many centimeters forward, so many centimeters to the side until, finally, the computer arm hovers over its object (you can hear the whir of the motor). Next, so many centimeters downward until the object is encountered, grasped, and lifted. How different, how clumsy all of this is compared to Natasha's beautiful Hand swooping in under the control of Natasha's brain which milliseconds before the movement started had already computed the angle of approach. Throughout that flight of hand through space, information is forwarded back, "programmed," and employed to fashion those small corrections that will be incorporated to keep that hand perfectly on target. It's this combining and superimposing of many different components involving many different parts of the brain which, in the final analysis, separates the performance of Natasha's brain and hand from any computer-driven mechanical device that has as yet or likely ever will be developed.

Processes seemingly remote from grasping, for example, the maintenance of balance when leaning forward, are called into play in order that the colored ball may end up being held and stared at from a distance of six inches from Natasha's face. Shift the position of the ball on the table, shift the position of Natasha in relation to the table, it doesn't matter. Natasha's brain will instantly adjust to these alterations. Her center of gravity shifts or she leans forward an additional few inches, hand now completely straight at the elbow, successfully advancing horizontally through space against those implacable gravitational forces that would pull it downward.

Notice that Natasha's doctor didn't enter in his chart "pincer grasp *reflex* present." If he had he would have done so in defiance of the commonly understood meaning of a "reflex." Strike Natasha's knee with a small hammer and it will jerk outward like the knee of a recruit at his induction physical. *That's* a reflex—present in two-year-old Natasha, present in the anxious and slightly frightened recruit. The knee jerks out slower or faster, or if there's something terribly wrong in brain or spine it may not jerk out at all. Natasha's hand isn't like that. If the observer is observant enough he will notice that Natasha never reaches out for her prize exactly the same way twice. With so many variables it's impossible that everything could be exactly the same from one reaching out to another. The infant brain—one day to be an adult brain—functions, indeed, must function, to handle remarkable degrees of novelty. The "same movement" isn't, in fact, the same at all. The brain must be capable of "programming" tiny differences in distance, timing, angle of approach, weight, gravitational forces, and a repertoire of other factors too numerous and in some cases too complicated to allow for easy explication.

During early development the brain does not mature simultaneously in all regions. Rather, those parts first mature that are necessary for the functions befitting a baby. Sucking, grasping, reaching out, reaching toward—these are the "thought processes" of the infant. The infant is the quintessential existentialist. Future and past—mere conceptualizations born of the ruminations of the present—have no existence to this creature who has yet to learn a language. With language, a new brain organization will emerge; life will no longer be defined in terms of "reach out and pick it up."

If the development of the nervous system progressed in tandem in all parts of the brain, the brain of an infant would be a miniature of the adult brain. This is clearly not the case. There are different interests, different capacities, different specializations. The infant can reach out and grasp at a rattle, take it, and stare at it. An adult won't reach for such an object and grows bored if a rattle is placed in his hand. The infant brain will undergo a long series of changes before boredom occurs. Why then do we speak of the "immaturity of the brain of the newborn"? Mistakenly we consider the adult brain as the culmination, the final product, the end point toward which the infant brain has been evolving. Such hubris! To appreciate the infant brain it is necessary, Dr. Heinz F. R. Prechtl tells us, "to look at the properties in the nervous system and appreciate its qualitatively different organization. At the onset of extrauterine life the neural mechanisms for vital functions such as breathing, rooting, sucking and swallowing, crying, spatial orientation, sleeping and waking are fully developed as very complex control systems."

While many of the structures of the infant brain mature early, the sequence doesn't at all involve a hierarchy: lower leading to higher leading to still higher "levels" of the brain. The infant brain isn't "higher" or "lower." Nor is it any more or less "mature" than its adult counterpart. Instead, the complex control systems mentioned by Prechtl and present from the moment of birth and earlier exist in order that the infant might have the best chance of enduring within the environment in which that infant finds itself.

CHAPTER 29

The Magic of Touch

Imagine some early form of life, perhaps no more than a loose association of cells clinging to one another. Imagine that creature wriggling and squirming and withdrawing whenever it comes into contact with light or solidity or chemicals. Not that much different from our eyes blinking themselves shut in the brightness of the sun for the few seconds it may take for us to reach for our designer sunglasses. Not that much different from the hand withdrawing from the hot stove, the heat informing the skin informing the brain to pull away split seconds before we consciously feel the pain. Energy at certain frequencies translates into lights, sounds, and touchings. Additional energy directed to the same receptors yields pain, discomfort, withdrawal—the limits of the sense organ have been exceeded.

Over millions of years the original primitive unitary sense has split off into photoreceptive organs of sight, mechanosensitive organs of touch and hearing, chemosensitive organs of taste and smell. Within every embryo this process of differentiation can be observed.

At first there is only ectoderm. And then endoderm, but the former undergoes splitting into skin, brain, eye—the instruments that "palpate" the environment. Each of these senses employs similar mechanisms since, in the final analysis, all senses are originally composed of neural tissue. Receptors differ to be sure, because eyes, ears, and skin are specialized for transforming different types of energies into neural activity. But farther along within the brain—the common destination of all energies conveyed by whatever receptor—one sensory pathway becomes indistinguishable from another. A neuron is a neuron. One electrochemical signal is like another.

Hearing and touch share a common ancestry in the lateral line organs of fish. On either side of a fish's body, starting near the eye, runs a longitudinal groove, the lateral line, containing sensory cells that respond to gentle pressure, especially low-frequency vibrations.

In the primeval soup the earliest fish employed this arrangement to inform themselves about movement of objects and fluid in the immediate vicinity. More advanced systems followed thereafter. Sensitivity to mechanical stimulation of sound waves at a distance projected through water and, at a later point, through air. Sensitivity at a distance—the key to liberation from the confines of immediacy and expediency. The organism that can see and hear achieves a quantum leap over that dumb brute, fish, or fowl that can only feel, palpating only immediacy, precluded from contact at a distance.

The senses' common heritage has been explored. Children, "primitive" people, and the brain-damaged enjoy the mixed blessing of synesthesia, the transformation of images from one sense to another.

Clues to the senses' common heritage persist within our language. "His ties are too loud." Or in the more formal language of Swinburne:

> "Summer and noon, and a splendor of silence, felt,
>   Seen, and heard of the spirit within the sense."

Swinburne, again:

> "And now the heaven is dark and bright and loud."

Forgetting Swinburne for the moment (what could he possibly know about the brain's responses, says our scientist), picture in your mind this experiment carried out a quarter of a century ago.

A man sits quietly in a dark room, viewing a rod that glows in the dark. Through earphones a loud tone is conveyed. If the loudness is greater to one ear than the other, the rod's orientation seems to shift to that side. A tiny electric pulse delivered to the muscles on one side of the neck accomplishes the same thing: the rod appears to move when no movement takes place. The shock, visual tilt, and sound interpenetrate one another's domains and tug at our emotions in the process. The clap of thunder: fear. The movement of a breeze through willows: peace. The white knuckles and clenched fist: anger or anxiety. Emotions involve us entirely. A group of volunteers asked to press one finger on a piano key to express an emotion (love, grief, or anger, for instance) exert reliable patterns of pressure corresponding to the particular emotion evoked. Emotion informs touch and touch must be exactly right.

We sit breathlessly in the concert hall as the pianist begins the *Goldberg Variations*. His touch on the keyboard must be exquisitely tender and soft and delicate. If it's too hard, the notes grate on our ears. Touch, the pianist's touch, is translated into mechanical energy, sound energy which must waft with sufficient subtlety into our ears and across our tympanic membrane lest, impatient, we get up from our seats and bolt from the concert hall.

With the infant, too, touch must be exactly right. Not too harsh. Not too soft. The quality of a touch, the location, the rhythm and intensity —these are the determinants of the message received. By six weeks a baby can distinguish Mother from Father from stranger by the quality of touch. Part of the reason for this early prescience is that Mother and Father and stranger touch an infant differently. When Mother touches the baby she does so in order to control, comfort, awaken. Fathers rarely do that, says pediatrician Dr. T. Berry Brazelton. "Their attempt in touching is to jazz the baby up. They are more likely to poke and touch abruptly. Baby, in turn, responds by laughter and excitement. The infant comes to expect these predictable behaviors from each parent."

Dr. Brazelton has studied how hundreds of fathers and mothers touch their infants. Sexual stereotypes aside, Brazelton has found differences between how fathers and mothers go about something as elemental as touching someone. "The mother and father set up a different expectancy for touch, starting at birth, and we find that their behavior is likely to be sex-linked."

How does one prove that differences in touch make any difference? The infant can't be queried. Perhaps the experimenter reads more into the infant's facial expression and responsiveness than that infant intends, suggests the skeptical observer. Within the past decade advances within intensive care nurseries have provided the kind of "proof" favored by scientists.

In 1972 German physicians R. Huch and A. Huch developed a special electrode that measures oxygen tension on the skin. It can be left in place providing a continuous monitoring of an infant's blood oxygen. In 1978 this technology of using the skin as a "window" through which to monitor blood oxygen tension was introduced into American hospitals. This eliminated the need for a technician to visit Emily every two hours, jam a painful needle into one of her arms, and leave Emily in a turmoil of fear and anger. Thanks to transcutaneous oxygen monitoring, none of that is now necessary.

Pediatric neurologists have learned a lot from transcutaneous oxygen monitoring. Contrary to popular belief an infant's normal oxygen tension isn't stable but varies sometimes dramatically from moment to moment. Virtually any maneuver that disturbs the infant or provokes pain will result in a fall of the oxygen tension in the blood. And by "pain" neuroscientists aren't referring to open-heart surgery or a spinal tap. Indeed, something as simple as changing a diaper, weighing the infant, or drawing a blood sample can cause the oxygen tension to plummet. The illustration shows a rapid drop in oxygen tension in response to diapering, the drawing of a blood sample, the infant crying. Although the greatest variation occurs in infants sick enough to require domiciliation in an intensive care unit, lesser fluctuations can regularly be observed in healthy infants (for about forty minutes out of twenty hours a normal newborn may exhibit an abnormally low oxygen tension).

By touching or stroking a sick or a well infant, oxygen tension variations can be avoided. At Boston Children's Hospital the personnel have, on occasion, cut down by as much as two weeks the hospital stay of eight-week-old prematures. They simply stroke Emily in order to soothe her. Only then do they jab with a needle, diaper, turn over, and otherwise intrude. Talking to the infants, caressing, touching, and mouthing soothing words often accomplish the same purpose: the oxygen tension remains steady instead of dipping like a schooner in a squall.

The infant is a labile creature. Disturb him and the heart rate, breathing, and oxygen tension will go out of whack. Disturb him even more and his breathing may go further askew. Of all the physiologic processes carried out and abated by the infant brain, respiration is undoubtedly the most sensitive. This sensitivity begins before birth.

If a pregnant woman smokes one cigarette, her fetus will stop breathing for five minutes. If her blood sugar goes suddenly up or down the fetus's breathing will also stop. The same sensitivity continues for many infants, particularly prematures when they move from the intensive care of the womb to the intensive care of the nursery. Handle them too much or too roughly and they become hypoxic (lacking in oxygen). What is so bad about recurrent episodes of hypoxemia, you may ask?

Imagine forcing all the air out of your lungs and then inhibiting inspiration for twenty seconds. (You may pass out, so I don't recommend trying it.) Even if you don't pass out, you'll likely consider this experience extremely stressful. Yet your oxygen will have dipped only ten or fifteen units, starting at a baseline of ninety units. In an infant, the drop is thirty or more units from a starting point of forty or fifty units, an oxygen level, incidentally, that can render mountain climbers and airline pilots immediately unconscious.

If an infant stops breathing, the pressure in the ventricles of its brain rises along with accompanying boosts in blood pressure and carbon dioxide. Intracranial blood flow is thereby increased. This increased pressure on the infant's fragile blood vessels, can, according to the most recent thinking, result in a cerebral hemorrhage.

Disturb the infant—interrupt the rhythm of the infant's respiration,

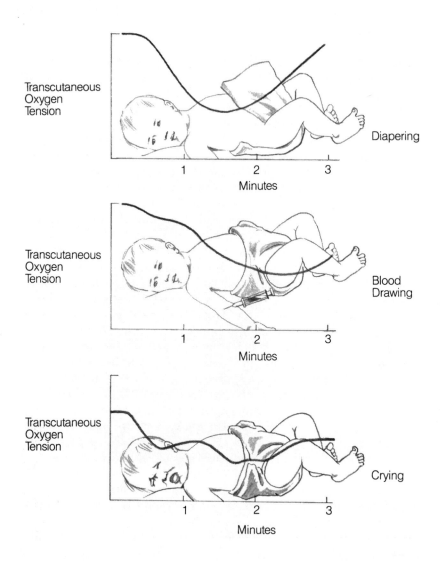

Transcutaneous Oxygen Tension — Diapering — Minutes

Transcutaneous Oxygen Tension — Blood Drawing — Minutes

Transcutaneous Oxygen Tension — Crying — Minutes

Every procedure that disturbs a young infant or causes pain results in a fall in oxygen tension in the blood. In sick or physically unstable infants this falloff in oxygen tension can be quite dramatic.

produce low blood pressure, raise intracranial pressure, rupture the fragile blood vessels in the infant brain—this is the disaster scenario that haunts the sleep of the directors of intensive care nurseries throughout the world.

How much easier and safer it is to intrude less, to let the infant alone. In order to avoid unintended harm, neonatal specialists are encouraging a return within hospital personnel to the wisdom of early nursing practitioners. "If you don't have a good answer to the question 'Why are you disturbing that baby?' then don't do it!"

"As a result of too much intrusiveness on the part of the hospital personnel, an oxygen lack may actually be worsened," says Dr. Brazelton. "Despite our good intentions we may not only be doing harm but causing infants to miss major opportunities for organization of the central and autonomic nervous systems."

Using technology such as the transcutaneous oxygen monitoring, specialists caring for extremely young infants may find themselves in a Catch-22 situation.

"As a neonatologist I feel I am sort of trapped because we're responsible for creating these very abnormal environments," says Dr. Jerold Lucey, professor of pediatrics at Medical Center Hospital of Vermont. "We did it with a goal in mind and we've had some success. We really can't operate without a lot of people or silently and in the dark. We're in a spot. If we do a lot, we can be criticized for doing too much, and if we don't do anything, then we're back to where we were before."

But Dr. Lucey along with many other specialists on the infant brain believes that the overall picture remains a hopeful one. "I think the situation is rapidly changing. In the next decade, I think nobody will die of prematurity. Brain care will be the name of the game."

In the 1970s Harry Harlow and an associate Stephen Suomi directed their attention to the effects of isolation on maternal behavior. They found that isolated monkeys make poor mates and, it turns out, abusive parents. But if the female monkeys are allowed as little as forty-eight hours with their infants they can become adequate mothers.

"The best predictor of whether a female that abused or neglected one infant is going to be a good mother to another is the amount of time the female spent with the first infant," says Suomi, who speculates that contact—simple touch—may make the difference. "This little bit of experience, even later in life, may be sufficient to make such contact acceptable to the female after subsequent births. It may be like a priming mechanism."

The separation of female monkeys from their infants and the subsequent abusive behavior that ensues can be experimentally induced even in females who have been raised normally. "If a female's first two infants are both taken away at birth, there is a fairly high probability that she'll be a poor mother to the third infant," states Suomi.

Touch, according to Suomi, is an absolutely indispensible component for the establishment of normal feelings of affection and care. Monkeys raised in solitary confinement as infants actively avoid most social contacts as adolescents and adults. Whether or not other monkeys can be seen or heard in the vicinity doesn't seem to make a difference. "It was consistently found that rhesus monkeys reared in total isolation from conspecifics for at least the first six months of life actively avoided most social contact as adolescents and adults, and in their infrequent social interactions they tended to be hyperaggressive." If such monkeys become pregnant (often by artificial insemination) about three quarters of them failed to care for their firstborn offspring.

"In a nutshell, tactile contact is obviously a very basic and necessary component of normal rhesus monkey social life: The stimulation provided through tactile contact with conspecifics seems crucial for normal development."

Watch a mother monkey or mother human touching her infant. The infant is soothed by this. In the case of the mother monkey, scientists have carried out a series of perfidious experiments; they have separated mother and child and observed what happened next.

Monkey infants separated from their mothers exhibit a protest-despair or agitation-depression reaction that looks for all the world like the reaction of a human infant.

In a typical experiment monkeys are born and raised in their natural social group (still in captivity, the laboratory rather than the "wild"). At four to six months the monkeys are separated from their mothers. Immediately the infants become agitated and upset. They search for their mothers, they exhibit almost continual cooing (the young macaque's distress call), their heart rates increase, body temperatures soar, serum cortisols rise.

Two or three days later a profoundly different reaction ensues: the infant monkey slouches in its cage, won't play, moves slowly and clumsily. The face is sad even by the standards of macaques. This "depression" is accompanied by decreases in heart rate and body temperature, and increases in heart arrhythmias and disturbances in sleep.

For years scientists have noticed physiologic changes in the wake of separation and loss. Morbidity and mortality is increased, for instance, following bereavement in adults as well as in children. Medical disorders of various kinds also increase under such circumstances. Separation leads to irregularities in physiologic functions: heart rate and rhythm, respiration, appetite, sleep, withdrawal, restlessness. Put another way, close physical contact leads to optional integration of these variables.

"A major function of social attachment may be the promotion and facilitation of psychobiological synchrony between individuals," says Dr. Martin Reite, professor of psychiatry at the University of Colorado Health Sciences Center in Denver and the researcher who carried out the separation experiments on infant monkeys.

Reite suggests that touch is instrumental in the development and maintenance of attachment as well as in the maintenance of optimal physiologic function. When the infant monkey can touch and be touched by the mother, psychophysiological variables are regulated. Separation causes these variables to spin out of control, resulting in some instances in sickness and death.

"The experience of touch in appropriate situations may exert a regulating or signal influence on physiologic systems similar to that afforded by the process of 'being attached,'" says Reite. Put at its simplest, touch contact between infant and mother promotes good health in both parties.

Studies carried out by T. Berry Brazelton, chief of the Child Development Unit of the Children's Hospital Medical Center in Boston, have revealed disturbances in the physiology of both the infant and mother at times of separation.

"When a young baby goes into day care, we can expect the child to have sleep problems, feeding problems and immunological problems for the next few months until the adjustment is made. And I know the same thing will happen to the mother: she, too, will have sleep problems, eating problems, immunologic problems for a while."

Brazelton's observations on day care—certain to arouse controversy among believers in substitute parenting—bring the issue closer to home: Is there any reason to believe that the studies of Harlow, Suomi, and others on separation in monkeys have any bearing on humans? A complex and intriguing question.

Picture in your mind a frightened or distressed infant. He or she reaches out for Mother. Mother adopts an open welcoming approach, her face and body turned directly toward the infant. Body-to-body contact is made.

Another mother under the same circumstances arranges things so that the infant is barred from direct contact, actively turning the approaching infant so that its frontal surface doesn't directly touch Mother's. Or the mother may simply make a sour face, wince, or draw away. These maternal responses to the approaching infant may remain consistent over many years.

A team of researchers studied how mothers responded to their stressed infants. They evaluated how often mothers avoided physical contact with their infants during that infant's first three months. The observations were repeated nine months later at about one year of age. The judges attempted to hold value judgments to a minimum: ambiguous responses were ignored, only active rejections of the infant's bid for skin-to-skin contact were tallied. The correlation with the mother's earlier reaction to physical contact with the infant was very high.

Dr. M. Louise Biggar has extended the observations on infant/mother contact for up to six years of age. These studied children actively avoid face-to-face encounters with their mothers. Conversation takes place with the participants speaking to each other at odd angles.

"Returning to a room in which the six-year-old has been examined, these parents approach the child from behind, speak to the child from behind, touch the child only gingerly . . . at six the children seem to join the parents in avoiding a mutual ventral orientation, even across a distance," writes Dr. Biggar.

Dr. Biggar compares the effects of active rejection by the mother to the effects of rejection among other primate species. If an infant monkey is pushed away by the mother monkey, the infant tries all the harder to approach and cling. Indeed, the immediate effect of rejection is to elicit stronger attachment efforts on the part of the infant monkey. With fear, the infant attempts to move closer. The infant is rejected by the mother's turning away or making a face of resignation. The infant pulls away, is further distressed, makes another bid to seek comfort from the "comforting figure" of the mother who because of her difficulty with touch and bodily contact is anything but comforting. At this point, according to Dr. Biggar, the infant's fear turns to anger.

"We found that the greater the mother's observed aversion of physical contact with the infant during the first three months, the more anger seemed to direct the infant's mood and activities nine months later," writes Dr. Biggar. "In addition, the more the mother had shown an early aversion to physical contact with the infant the more frequently the infant struck or angrily threatened to strike the mother."

At six years of age the children of mothers who had turned away, indeed, had rejected their infant's efforts at physical contact during the first few weeks, behaved peculiarly around the parents. Some of them tended to avoid contact with parents by crossing a room or moving away in order not to encounter the parent face to face. Others displayed open hostility. "Leave me alone."

Touch, it turns out, is as necessary to normal infant development as food and oxygen. Mother opens her arms to the infant, snuggles him, and a host of psychobiological processes are brought into harmony. Disrupt this process because the mother cannot or will not caress, touch or otherwise make skin-to-skin contact with the infant and psychobiological processes go askew along the lines described by Martin Reite. The details may vary as they certainly must when infants are compared with other primates. But the general trend is the same: physiological imbalances, behavioral peculiarities, hostilities, suppressed anger and rage.

The infant turns toward the mother. How will she respond? Will she touch him? Will she turn away? How simple the situation, how seemingly devoid of content and importance. But we are deceived by the simplicity of this exchange which takes place within seconds but endures for decades. The mother turns toward her infant and touches him. Neither party speaks. Who could ever have guessed that simply *touching* another human being could be so important.

CHAPTER 30

The Permanence of Objects

Consider this book you're holding at the moment. Consider what happens if you put the book down for a second to answer a phone. Conversation finished, you turn and pick up the book once again. Same book? It would hardly occur to you to consider the book has changed even though it was out of your sight for a few minutes. "Object permanence" is the name Jean Piaget applied to this phenomenon. Babies, too, display, finally, some degree of object permanence. On the way they also exhibit some peculiarities in their thinking about the world that would be of interest to a Brahmin.

Over a nine-year period Piaget published his observations on object permanence among infants. The three books, *The Origin of Intelligence in Children* (1936), *The Construction of Reality in the Child* (1937), and *Play, Dreams and Imitation in Childhood* (1946) are classics not merely in the *Moby Dick* sense but more like the Bible or the Dhamipada. The profundity and breadth of vision displayed by Piaget in these works are those of a seer, a prophet, a guru. Yet the demonstrations are simple; they can be done with any child. They were, in fact, carried out by Piaget with his own children.

Prop an infant of up to four months of age in a sitting position. (You have to do this since four month olds can't as yet sit without swaying.) A toy is displayed. The infant may reach for it. Now cover the toy with a handkerchief. The reaching stops. This is stage 3 of infant behavior (the stage 1 or stage 2 infant doesn't reach for the toy even when it's set out in front of him without any experimentalist machination). In stage 3 the infant will reach for a partially concealed toy but is stymied when the object is completely covered. Finally, the infant in stage 4 will look for an object if it is hidden by a cloth. After several trials, the infant will fail, however, if the location of the toy is shifted under another cloth in close proximity to the first. The child will repeat and repeat and repeat this error. Overall, the infant's performance suggests he proceeds on the assumption that an object, once hidden, will always be found in that very spot for all eternity. To this extent an object doesn't really have an identity of its own independent of location. Recently neuroscientists have suggested a brain mechanism for this classic experiment in infant inflexibility.

A stage 3 infant will reach out and grasp a partially covered object (A) but is unable to take an object that has been completely covered by a cloth (B).

Over the past one hundred years neuroscientists have learned quite a lot about the frontal lobes of the brain, those areas directly above and behind the nasal bridge, at about the height of the hair line. The frontal areas of the brain when injured result in an impairment of our organizational ability. The temporal sequence of recent events is often askew. For instance, show an individual with frontal lobe impairment a series of pictures. Then ask which of the two pictures, randomly chosen, had been displayed first. He or she can't do it—can't organize a sequence.

"On tasks of this kind, the impairments observed after a frontal lobe lesion appear to stem from the patient's inability to overcome previously established response tendencies, resulting in the generation of fewer hypotheses and, frequently, in a high incidence of errors involving perseveration [repetition]," write two specialists on frontal lobe disease.

For our purposes think of the stage 4 infant returning to the same spot for the toy even though but a moment earlier—before the infant's very eyes—the object had been moved. Does this imply that infants suffer from "frontal lobe damage"? Not exactly. More likely, the infant displays an immaturity in frontal lobe function, an impairment caused not by damage as with the patient who had suffered frontal lobe injury (a stroke or tumor) but by failure of frontal lobe development, an immaturity that given time will correct itself. Proof for such an assertion (it's always nice to have proof, the stuff that separates the scientist from the mere speculator) comes from an experiment with one of our cousins.

The prefrontal monkey differs from the jungle variety monkey by reason of an experimental alteration, "lesion," which has destroyed the monkey's frontal fibers. This kind of monkey will perform identically to the eight- or nine-month-old baby at the stage 4 level. Choose once, choose twice, choose over and over again even when the choosing repeats the same mistakes over and over again. A monkey captured in the jungle won't do that—at least when it comes to choosing, it is smarter than a human baby. When the jungle monkey sees the reward hidden, it reaches toward the reward which is now out of view. Hide the fancied object in an alternative slot and it changes strategy accordingly. But cut those precious frontal lobes and the monkey is instantaneously transformed into a Perseverer. Baby and altered monkey fail in one of life's most important discernments: the recognition that an object continues to exist in time and space even when it's not in view. Psychologists speculate with good reason that such a basic function may provide the foundation for symbolic reasoning.

"Every cat is an animal; this is a cat; ergo this is an animal," writes the logic student during his first efforts at constructing a syllogism. Indeed, it's hard to imagine a philosopher philosophizing without his frontal lobes functioning normally. Anticipation, reasoning, knowing "right from wrong," the ability to inhibit the urge to be "impulsive"— all this is mediated via the frontal lobes.

Give a pen to a patient with frontal lobe damage and he'll start to

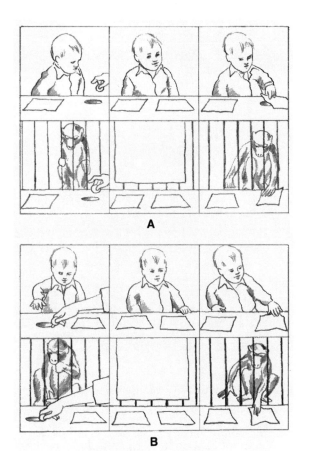

A

B

A normal infant and a monkey with surgically damaged frontal lobes perform alike in a task that involves finding a hidden object after a period of delay. Both the baby and the monkey return to the site where they previously had found the object. In A, this is a correct response. In B, the object is in an altered site. The baby and monkey "perseverate": reach under the left-hand cloth whereas the object is now under the cloth on the right. Failure to inhibit the incorrect response is eventually overcome by the child as his frontal connections are established through brain growth. Later in life, a human with frontal lobe damage will once again "perseverate" the correct response as does the monkey with frontal lobe damage.

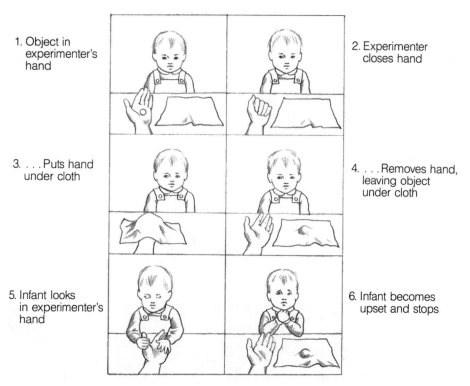

1. Object in experimenter's hand

2. Experimenter closes hand

3. ...Puts hand under cloth

4. ...Removes hand, leaving object under cloth

5. Infant looks in experimenter's hand

6. Infant becomes upset and stops

Infant errors in finding hidden objects.

write something without having been instructed to do so. Often he can't or won't stop the writing even when told that writing isn't called for. Some neuroscientists, though not the majority, hold that compulsive and impulsive behavior stem from frontal lobe damage. They suggest that our prisons and a goodly number of our mental hospitals are filled with individuals afflicted with discernment problems similar to those of the stage 4 infant and the prefrontal monkey. ("Why do you rob banks?" Willy Sutton was once asked. "Because that's where the money is," he answered.)

"Take your pencil and begin tracing through the maze. When you hear the buzzer, stop, since it signals that you've made an error." With frontal damage the person doesn't stop; he can't or won't acknowledge an error, plodding along to the consternation of the bemused experimenter. All this is remarkably similar to the performance of the stage 4 infant.

1. Infant looks at object

2. Object placed under cloth

3. Cloths are switched

4. Infant pauses

5 . . . Reaches under the incorrect cloth

Infant errors in finding hidden objects.

At eighteen months all this ceases. The infant can recover hidden toys and take into account invisible displacements, in fact, feels confident it can do so and thus seems to be a potentially perfect setup for Three-Card Monte or the Three-Shell Game. "Nothing to it, mister. Just watch as I move the shells ever so slowly. Pick the shell that covers the little rubber ball and you'll double your money!"

Such street corner scam artists have rarely read books on an infant's mental development. Intuitively, though, they've grasped the essence of the art of deception: "All objects in the same place are the same . . . an object is the same object as long as it continues to move on the same path of movement . . . all objects on the same path of movement are the same objects." This quotation is from an infant researcher describing the world of the twelve week old. With a mixture of a glib tongue, slippery fingers, and speed, the street corner sleight-of-hand wizard returns us to that magical world. Then takes our money and runs.

"The infant thinks that a single object seen in different places is, in fact, a number of different objects," writes infant researcher, T. G. R. Bower. To prove it, the good professor hooked up an arrangement whereby multiple images of an infant's mother were presented. Infants less than five months of age showed no signs of distress, set off no alarms, engaged in no displays of temper. Mother could be one, could be two, could be three. All three were played with, laughed at, stared at.

Shift the arrangement a bit. Substitute an image of Mother and two strangers. Baby ignores the strangers, spends all its time gazing at Mother. If the Three-Mother Test is carried out with an infant older than five months, that infant doesn't like it a bit. Fussiness and irritability ensues since Baby now knows it has only one mother. Projection of the image of Mother to more than one place doesn't change the fact that Mother is one, her uniqueness imposing an identity more fundamental than any mere position in space. Other "objects" in the infant's world are not so uniquely identifiable, however. Toys look like other toys. "How is the infant to know whether this is the same object that was moved or a new object that has just appeared?" asked Dr. Bower. "The best anyone can do—even an adult—is to make an educated guess."

But the educated guess often goes wrong. "Sorry, man. Wrong card. Better luck next time. Put down your money and try again. Watch the cards *very* carefully."

CHAPTER 31

Memory

Studies on infant memory carried out at the University of Toronto suggest that infants may remember more about events than, only a few years ago, the most optimistic researcher would have thought possible.

Obviously, infants can't tick off a series of letters or words as a proof of memorization. Indeed, until the emergence of language and the ability to form symbols, infants' memories could not, it would seem, be tested at all. Before assenting to this seemingly reasonable proposition, however, consider the rather eerie experiment carried out on adult volunteers.

A string of words and nonsense syllables are presented at the experimenter's whim for the volunteer's inspection. If a string of letters forms a real English word, the volunteer presses a button. If the letters don't form a word, no button pushing is required. Real words and nonsense strings are presented with equal frequency but at different times. The volunteer's response times are then tabulated. With this information as a baseline, the real fun begins.

Half of all the items are re-presented at times varying from a few minutes to several days. The volunteers perform better and faster the second time around. At this point, the experimenters cleverly change the conditions of the experiment. Instead of merely indicating whether or not the letters formed a word or a mere string, the subjects are requested to specify whether or not they have encountered the word before. The performance of all of the volunteers falls markedly.

Question: If the volunteers didn't recall seeing the words the second time around, why did their response time decrease? Clearly, in some way they must have "remembered" previously seeing the words. But if so, why couldn't they consciously recall their previous experience?

To understand the significance of this finding and its relevance to our understanding of infant memory, consider a slight modification of the previous test wherein the experimental subjects include not only normal volunteers but a group of patients with profound amnesia (memory impairment).

A string of forty word pairs (corn-light, mellow-grass) are presented on a screen and looked at for three seconds. Later, the first three letters of one of the words is shown, i.e., cor. Both normal people and amnesiacs performed better if the word fragment is presented along with the word that originally accompanied it, cor-light. But if the subjects are requested to recall the word without any letter clues (——-light) the performance of the normal volunteers improved while the amnesiacs performed no better than random guessing.

On the basis of such experiments, neuroscientist Morris Moscovitch of the Unit for Memory Disorders and Center for Research in Human Development at the University of Toronto suggests that human memory involves an early and late memory system. Further, the early memory system is in place in very young infants. You can test it. Moscovitch has done so. Most intriguing of all, the memory performance of the infant in the first year of life is very similar to that of the adult amnesiac. Or to put the matter somewhat differently, individuals with serious memory impairments later in life revert back to a memory system characteristic of early infancy.

A five month old shown an object hidden behind a screen increases her looking time when the screen is tilted all the way backward—an impossible situation if the solid object is still there. The scientist who carried out this experiment interprets her findings as evidence for a kind of object permanence and, by implication, symbolic representation in a five month old: the infant knows something is amiss, the object can no longer be there, where is it? While this may be attributing quite a lot to a five month old, the experimental facts speak for themselves: somehow five-month-old Martha "remembers" that an object was sitting behind the screen. She doesn't demonstrate her "remembrance" by telling anybody about it. Instead, her physiology gives her away: she looks longer at the experimental setup, her heart rate increases, her galvanic skin response is altered. In essence what happens is very similar to the findings in adults mentioned a moment ago: people can demonstrate quite nicely a remembrance of something (measured by, for instance, a decreased response interval at the second time around) without necessarily being capable or recognizing that they have encountered the stimulus previously. In essence, there is a disparity between one or more bodily processes that indicate recognition and the individual's inability to consciously recall the previous event.

This is what I meant when I mentioned that the experiments were eerie.

On the basis of such findings in normals and amnesiacs, neuroscientists are now postulating that there are at least two separate memory systems. The first, present from birth, enables the infant to achieve memory in the "wide sense." Past experiences exert an effect on current and future behavior. Later, at about eight to nine months, the infant develops what most of us refer to when discussing memory: a memory for a particular event at a particular time and place.

In the experiments I've just mentioned, memory in the "wide sense" was responsible for the improved performance in letter and word recognition. The capacity to recall the words upon request represented memory in the "strict sense." This was greatly impaired in amnesiacs: their performance improved the second time around but they weren't aware, "didn't remember" that they had ever encountered the words previously.

Through the use of laboratory measures of an infant's physical responsiveness, neuroscientists have demonstrated that memory in the "wide sense" is present probably from birth. Indeed, the infant can learn, modify its reactions, and exhibit surprise when something new occurs—none of these responses would be possible if the infant didn't in some way remember previous experiences.

Later, at about eight to nine months, the infant begins to develop memory for specific events, time, place—memory in the "strict sense." What is the relationship of these two memory systems?

Currently, neuroscientists are postulating that memory systems that develop later in evolution also appear relatively late in the development of the individual. Further, the more sophisticated and later developing memory system (memory in the "specific sense") is the first to be affected in the event of an illness that affects memory (encephalitis, Alzheimer's disease). In other words, memory is affected according to the "last in, first out" principle: the last memory system to appear on the scene (the late memory system, coder-of-memory for specific events) disappears first. This intriguing hypothesis has been put to the test using the experimental situation described in the last chapter.

Recall that if an infant between nine and ten months is shown an object and the test object is then hidden in full view of the infant, most infants have no difficulty remembering the location of the object over a brief time delay. After several repetitions of this rather boring procedure, the object is hidden at a different location (B). Most infants continue to search for the object at point A even though the switch from location A to B occurred before the infant's eyes.

A similar performance occurs in severely amnesiac patients. In fact, in one variety of the experiment an object is placed in full view on a desk about halfway between the patients and location A. After a time delay of only two minutes, the patients are given the opportunity to retrieve the object. They direct their search not to the object before their very eyes, but to the original location where, moments before, the object had originally been hidden!

"The parallel performance of the two groups may reflect the operation of a memory system that is degraded in amnesics and is not yet fully developed in eight to ten month old infants," observes Dr. Daniel Schacter of the department of psychology of the University of Toronto.

The time frame in which the two types of memory systems develop (in the "wide" and "strict" sense, respectively) can be correlated with brain development. The amygdala and frontal lobes are known to be important in memory; damage to either structure in adults leads to a greater or lesser degree of memory impairment. They are also known to develop relatively late in infancy. Memory in the "strict" sense must await, therefore, the development of the amygdala and frontal lobes. Before the time when these structures are functioning, only early memory in the "wide" sense is possible. With the passage of time and the maturation of these structures (at about ten months of age) memory in the more common sense of the term appears.

"If we accept the neuropsychological premise that cognitive skills are dependent on the development of neural structures that mediate that skill, then again, one would be forced to conclude that significant transitions in the development of memory coincide with the period during which these structures become functional," says Dr. Moscovitch.

Six-month-old Johnny sits in Grandfather's arms while the old man watches television. Johnny's grandfather has Alzheimer's. He won't remember any more of the program after it's over than Johnny will. He won't remember holding Johnny in his arms while Johnny's mother, his daughter, goes out for a six-pack of beer. Indeed, Johnny and his grandfather experience the world in ways that are strikingly similar. Neither baby nor old man remembers according to the kinds of criteria most of us would require in order to certify the intactness of memory in both of them. What has not yet developed in Johnny has ceased to function in Grandfather. When it comes to memory, each is impaired in the same way: a cruel trick of nature (in Grandfather's case) which, until the experiments I mentioned a moment ago, had resisted the white-coated detectives.

"Once the late memory system is impaired . . . memory performance becomes more and more dependent on the early system and begins more and more, especially in Alzheimer's patients, to resemble the memory processes of infants," says Dr. Moscovitch.

Fitting it is therefore, that Johnny remains cuddled in Grandfather's arms. They're buddies, soul mates, sharers of a memory world that can improve only for Johnny.

CHAPTER 32

Mother Love

Ever since the discovery of genes scientists have tried to distinguish the influence of inheritance from that of environment on human behavior.

Hair and skin color—inherited.

Intelligence—inherited. But, intellectual accomplishment depends too on the environment: how hard Johnny studies, his accessibility to teachers and the right books.

Other influences are strictly environmental—poor nutrition, uncaring parents, accidents.

But the scientists who first formulated this nature-nurture dichotomy hadn't looked carefully enough; they hadn't the sufficient humility to consider all the necessary levels of analysis (molecules, tissues, organs, organ systems, organism) that must be traversed to get from DNA to Johnny failing his first grade reading exam. In their haste to fix blame they forgot or glossed over certain facts. There can be no behavior without Johnny and there can be no Johnny without Johnny's genes. No one has ever encountered a Johnny or a Mary who was partly constituted by genes and partly constituted by the environment. The environment works on genes, the genes only respond to certain aspects of the environment.

A baby is born in a nursery with a tongue-twisting illness, phenylketonuria (PKU). At birth our baby, let's call her Nancy, was perfectly normal. "If my baby could look like this one, maybe I would like to have one too," thinks the nubile nurse while cleaning Nancy moments after the delivery. But this scene of love and harmony is suddenly shattered; the PKU test is positive. Nancy lacks the genetic material to produce an enzyme capable of metabolizing the amino acid, phenylalanine. Half a century ago Nancy would have been doomed. Her infant formula and everything else she would eat after that would contain a nutrient turned poison. Phenylalanine would build up in her brain, eventually leading to severe mental retardation. "Nancy's genes are responsible for her mental retardation," one scientist might have stated after insufficient reflection. But another scientist who thought the matter through a bit more thoroughly and with sufficient reflection would reach different conclusions and thereby save Nancy from an institution.

"If phenylalanine is kept from Nancy's diet then there can be no buildup," and he might add "no mental retardation, no grief-stricken parents, no domiciliation in a home for the mentally retarded." Nancy's genes are enormously important but they can't, in themselves, cause mental deficiency any more than they can cause mental superiority. If Nancy had been unfortunate in other ways she might have been born to parents who didn't smile at her, didn't stimulate her, and didn't really want her. This actually happened several years ago to a child in Los Angeles. The child was confined to a room and denied companionship—even the opportunity to hear human speech. When finally rescued from her mad captors the child didn't speak and was barely recognizably human when it came to social interaction. Did she have the genes for mental superiority? The question is unanswerable.

Nancy is now fourteen years old. She is perfectly normal because from birth she was placed on a diet free of phenylalanine. Applied science has rescued a brain, a mind. To Nancy that is more important than all the space missions that have ever taken place. Nancy and others like her have taught science something too. In some instances the genes are more important; in others some features of the outside world may be critical; in most instances both will be important. Nature-nurture is a falsely facile division. Nancy has one set of genes that must work out their destiny within a specific environment. Her genes set limits, circumscribe what she may be able to do. But no one can ever place blame or heap praise on the genes alone.

Forty years ago psychoanalyst René Spitz set out to discover the ways genes and the environment interact. He was interested, as are all psychoanalysts, in the effects of social interaction on mental development. His interest involved him with women in prison, and the babies of imprisoned women as well as abandoned babies left to languish until someone transferred them to a foundling home. Spitz compared the development of babies raised in the foundling home with the development of their infant counterparts raised in the nursing home attached to a women's prison. Obviously, neither situation is typical of the homes most Johnnys and Nancys encounter, but Spitz wasn't terribly interested in the typical home. Instead, he was curious regarding the effects of various kinds of deprivation. In the prison nursing home, the mothers cared for their own babies, looked forward to the chance to touch somebody, love somebody, or at the very least to get out of their cells or have someone in their cells who loved them and they could love in return.

In a foundling home things were different. There were seven infants for each caretaker—not much in the way of individual attention—no special touching or holding, nobody glad for the opportunity just to be with them.

The two institutions also differed in other respects. In the prison nursing home the cribs were open and the infants could watch the activity around them. Johnny could watch Nancy and vice versa and they both could watch their mothers and the staff go about business. But in the foundling home, the bars of the cribs remained covered by sheets. Nobody saw anybody else and the presence of other babies could only be inferred by baby noises and baby smells. "The babies in the foundling home lived under conditions of relative sensory and social deprivation" is the way one scientist put it.

Spitz observed a few newborns from each of these settings throughout their early years. By four months, the infants in the foundling home seemed to be doing better. As Spitz thought of it, genetic factors didn't favor infants in the nursing home. Not the most favorably endowed mother-to-be wound up in a prison, and so on. But eight months later, at age one year, the nursing home babies had caught up. Indeed, the foundling babies were a pitiable sight: frequently sick with minor infections, withdrawn, lacking curiosity, rarely smiling.

"How could anyone ever let something like this happen? How could the doctors and nurses be so cruel?" you might ask. It's only common sense, you say, that babies ensconced behind bars, covered by sheets, cared for by a succession of strangers—how could they possibly develop normally?

Spitz wrote a paper about his observations, "Hospitalism: an inquiry into the genesis of psychiatric conditions in early childhood." It described two year olds who couldn't walk (twenty-four out of twenty-six were the actual figures). Only two of the children could talk—"baby talk," no sentences, just the most primitive communication. Absent, of course, were any reference to Mama or Dada.

Fifteen years elapsed before much else was done along the lines of Spitz's research. In the 1960s Harry and Margaret Harlow of the University of Wisconsin took things a step further in a study of monkeys. They deliberately placed their subjects into isolation in order to observe what happened. They made movies of their experimentation as Spitz had done, but the drama was less heart-rending (except for members of the SPCA) simply because of a cast change: human babies were replaced by monkeys. But the results were similar to Spitz's.

The baby monkeys ignored the outside world, huddled in a corner of their cages, and rocked back and forth in a manner similar to the behavior of autistic children. When these monkeys were later introduced into a colony they didn't do well at all—didn't mate, wouldn't fight, behaved most unmonkeylike.

Next, the Harlows tested whether or not it made a difference at what point a monkey was placed in isolation. They found that it did. A six-month period of isolation anytime during the first year and a half produced a misfit. Anything after that could be endured. In monkeys and humans there are "sensitive" or "critical" periods for social development. You can stick a man in solitary confinement and he comes out with pretty much the same interests and proclivities. Do it earlier during that person's babyhood and he won't wind up capable later of behavior advanced enough to warrant a hitch in solitary. Although we all need one another throughout our lives, that needing is most acute in the first year. Deprive a baby of light, the opportunity to gaze at a human face, the delight of being picked up, cuddled, cooed at, fussed over, touched—and the infant doesn't abide such deprivations.

Next, the Harlows tried to answer what could be done to prevent the isolation syndrome in the baby monkeys. They put a cloth-covered wooden dummy into the monkey cage and observed how the babies responded. The cloth surrogate drew these monkeys out of themselves in a crude kind of way. They clung and squealed and made a great fuss when the surrogate was removed. Otherwise they stayed isolated. A cloth isn't skin or fur or warmth.

The introduction of another monkey for a few hours each day led to improved socialization. The visitor somehow communicated to the isolate that life wasn't all a dull gray. Some monkeys are better than others at stirring up the interest of their isolated counterparts. These "monkey psychotherapists" (the Harlows' term, not mine) were persistent, gregarious, and drew the isolates into social and aggressive behavior until, finally, the Harlows produced a monkey that acted simply as a monkey.

Thanks to the Harlows and Spitz before them, we, as a society, have learned to treat our underprivileged infants no worse than we treat monkeys. Everyone is now agreed that babies need touching, eye contact, the warmth of a body, the human voice, and a crib from which things heard can be correlated with things seen.

Perhaps Harry Harlow said it best in the title of one of his papers written for professionals but expressed as a mother might describe it. Simply and beautifully put: "The Nature of Love."

CHAPTER 33

An Ode to Prematurity

The brain weight of the mature newborn doesn't differ whether that infant is born in a hospital to well-to-do parents or in a hut to parents whom nature and society may have treated less kindly. Given the chance for a full development within the uterus, the brain will attain the same mass regardless of race or sexual difference. But the brain requires that full nurturing within the womb if it is to develop to its highest potential. Shorten the period, rush things so that the baby brain is forced to deal with the world before that brain is ready and you produce differences nature never intended. For instance, the weight of the brain of premature newborns (a gestational age of less than thirty-eight weeks and body weight of less than twenty-five hundred grams) preterm, and underweight infants varies according to sex and race. The weight is highest for white males, followed by white females, followed by black males, and finally black females.

According to the National Center for Health Statistics, prematurity occurs at approximately a two-to-one ratio when blacks are compared to whites. The percent of white premature babies is 6.4 compared to 13.22 percent for blacks. Among high-risk infants the figures are even more disproportionately distributed between the two groups.

At a regional prenatal health center caring for high-risk cases served by the Case Western Reserve University School of Medicine in Cleveland, Ohio, 75 percent of black males were born prematurely, compared with 80 percent of black females, 48 percent of white males, and 50 percent of white females. Reasons for prematurity? Poor health care of the mother. Smoking and drinking. Malnutrition. Teenage pregnancy. Low income. Little or no education. As a result of these factors, usually more than one, often all of them at once, there emerges a brain that isn't ready, that wants to wait a while but can't. From animal experiments, baby brain specialists know that the spurt in brain growth is determined by the clock. And that clock can't be stopped. The brain must grow in its time lest it not have the chance to accomplish the same thing as well at a later point. Any retardation in brain development, therefore, stands a good chance of never being reversed, with subtle defects remaining in the absence of anything remarkably unusual to the untrained eye.

Learning disabilities, hyperactivity, impulsiveness, attacks of rage— these are some of the disturbances which, later in life, may plague the infant born prematurely. One doesn't need to wait that long to encounter difficulties, however.

In one study 50 percent of the mothers of prematures admitted that "real" affection was delayed for several months. They hadn't felt sufficiently maternal to their early arrivals. In that same study mothers were encountered who feared unnecessarily for their baby's health and safety, perceived the baby as somehow "imperfect," and had difficulty becoming properly attached to it.

A premature brain—a small baby—a "poorly responsive" baby—a "poorly responded to" mother—baby brain affecting Mother followed by Mother affecting baby brain—feeding difficulties at first followed by "temperamental incompatibility"—time spent together by both Baby and Mother not enjoyed or looked forward to by either party. Such can be the tragedy of prematurity.

A low birth weight infant, all things being equal, starts out with the odds against him. Mental retardation, cerebral palsy, seizures, learning disabilities—that baby's brain is at increased risk for all of these. He may have been born too soon (less than thirty-seven weeks rather than the usual forty weeks). Or he may have failed to grow adequately within his mother's womb.

Among a hundred infants who are "undergrown for their gestational age" five or ten of them will have a brain that is defective in some way. If that too-tiny tot is born prematurely, the combination of too small and too soon will produce between thirty and fifty babies with brains less perfect than nature intended.

Mothers who smoke, don't eat as they should, and/or ignore their blood pressure can produce small babies with the potential for imperfect brains. It is interesting that of these three factors only one— elevated blood pressure—is a medical condition, strictly defined. Smoking and eating are behavioral variables that only secondarily produce harmful physical effects. Smoking, nicotine, reduces blood flow from the uterus to the placenta. It cuts down the flow of blood to the baby and injures that baby's brain at the same time it cuts down blood flow to the mother's coronaries and prepares the ground for a heart attack that might not have happened if that mother had only stopped smoking in time.

Malnutrition in the mother is a more complex matter. Not every mother has the last word in what she will eat, how much, how she will pay for it, or whether she can pay for it at all. If a mother doesn't gain enough weight during her pregnancy her infant will be more likely than not to tip the scales at the low end. Malnutrition can be environmentally induced—too little money or too little food or a combination thereof. It can also happen when a mother-to-be, smart enough to know better, attempts to retain what she considers a becoming slimness throughout her pregnancy, starving herself, forgetting that she's now feeding two and not just one.

Caution must be introduced at this point. All the studies on prematures and low birth weight infants rely on statistics. There are plenty of exceptions. Thomas Hardy, for one, was both premature and of a low birth weight. An infant born too small or before his time can, if the circumstances are just right, catch up with his compatriots and conform to the schedules. Only the exceptional infant is that fortunate, however.

"As pre-term infants have been followed into childhood, it has become clear that even children who have had apparently normal developmental progress until school entry are at considerably higher risk for visual motor, attention, language and behavior problems that interfere significantly with adequate school progress," notes Dr. Alfred W. Brann, Jr., a pediatrician and expert on the premature infant at Emory University School of Medicine in Atlanta.

With improvements in the care of premature and low birth weight infants have come corresponding improvements in the "quality" of these infants' brains. The major abnormalities of the past (spastic paralysis, mental retardation, visual and hearing abnormalities, seizures) are rarely encountered today. Instead, the preterm or low birth weight infant suffers from more insidious and subtle difficulties.

"Current investigators report children who developed apparently normal until age eight years, when they first demonstrated significant problems with abstract reasoning," wrote Dr. Brann in 1985.

In one study published in 1981, "Outcomes for infants of very low birth weight," only 76 percent of those born prematurely attended regular schools and exhibited no mental handicaps at eight years of age. In another study premature children on the average scored fifteen IQ points lower than did others who had been born at term.

Obviously a damaged or compromised brain doesn't exist in a vacuum. Each infant—term, premature, or low birth weight—is born into a particular environment which may add to or assuage the adjustment difficulties that brain may encounter. Dr. Gordon Avery of the department of neonatology at Children's Hospital National Medical Center in Washington, D.C. believes that in many cases such things as family stability and maternal intelligence may make the difference between an impaired and a normal brain. "According to the thesis of double jeopardy, biologic brain injury and socioeconomic disadvantage have a greater combined effect than does either alone. Thus, the child with prenatal or perinatal brain insult who is discharged into an unfavorable environment will be at a higher risk for a failure to 'catch up' for school failure and inability to compete."

Put simply, the infant brain, particularly the compromised brain, requires the support of loving parents, good nutrition, stimulation, and love. If ignored or understimulated that brain will never be able to compensate for the subtle functional disturbances that we now know result from low birth weight, prematurity, or combinations thereof.

Care and affection make a difference. Instruction, patience, and stimulation make a difference. Fortunately, the infant brain is incredibly malleable and adaptive; it will make up for what it has been deprived of if given half a chance. There is no room for fatalism or pessimism here. The most important factor of all? Overcoming the disappointment of that mother and that father, consumer-minded, who feel that somehow nature has cheated them by giving them a "defective product." If those parents can be convinced of the nearly infinite restorative powers of the infant brain, that child will have a fighting chance.

CHAPTER 34

States

When one considers that people have been having babies since Adam and Eve, the question arises, "Why only in the past twenty-five years has the neonate been appreciated as a psychological being capable of learning, influencing parents, and being influenced?" Several answers are available that will be satisfactory to varying degrees according to the interests and prejudices of the questioner.

To the technologist, the answer lies with the development of video cameras, intrauterine cinematography, time-lapse photography, and increasingly sophisticated instruments and recording devices. With these instruments the subtleties of infant behavior can be recorded, played back, slow-motioned, analyzed, and reanalyzed in a frame-by-frame analysis.

To the developmental psychologist the technology is less pertinent than theory. Developmental patterns and not cameras are important since someone has to decide what's important enough to be video-recorded and has to interpret what is seen.

But the most important contributor to our understanding of the infant brain and its relationship to infant behavior dates from an elaboration of several everyday observations about infants. Hunger, alertness, whether the baby is lying down or sitting up, time of day, noise in the environment—these and other factors affect whether or not the infant is going to "cooperate" with the researcher. In addition, it must be recalled that newborns spend most of their time—as much as twenty hours a day—asleep.

The infant's alertness, as is the case with an adult, determines to a large degree whether or how he or she will react. While this seems a fairly commonsense kind of notion, it wasn't until comparatively recently that the baby's state was taken into consideration.

Neuroscientists have devised ways of describing the behavioral states of infants. In the full-term newborn we have deep sleep, active

(REM) sleep, and arousal (included here are drowsiness, alert but quiet, alert but fussy). Newborns respond differently in each of these states. Observe an infant without specifying his state at the moment of your observation and you've accomplished little of importance. An alert, wakeful, curious baby can be enticed to look toward a voice or a face. An alert fussy baby won't abide such tinkerings.

For years, before the concept of "behavioral state," investigators of various persuasions attempted to plumb the intricacies of infant behavior. Why Baby Timothy wasn't responsive (retarded? brain-damaged?) when, in fact, Baby Timothy was only tired and bored and wanted to be left alone. Neonatologists are smarter now. Is an inactive fetus and, later, a newborn baby "compromised" or merely sleeping?

Before thirty weeks the fetus exists in a no-man's-land after which it comes to separate and definable states. From thirty-two weeks on, organized and identifiable states occur with variation enough to enable scientists to predict delays or abnormalities in development. In general, if the brain is abnormal, the abnormality is likely to be evident by a variation in the timing or organization of the separate behavioral states. Babies with Down's syndrome, for instance, spend less time in active sleep than do normals of the same age. This correlation between structure and function, between the state of the brain and the state of the baby, continues throughout gestation and for several months after birth. It is yet another example of the continuum that exists between fetus and newborn.

At least seven different ways of classifying newborn states have been proposed. Starting with deep or regular sleep (marked by even breathing and a minimum of grimacing and body movements), classifications have included irregular sleep (uneven breathing, changes in bodily position and facial expression, sometimes tremors and twitches) and light or transitory sleep. Of more interest, obviously, are the various waking states.

In *alert inactivity* the infant is fully awake, eyes open, comfortable, and prepared if the circumstances are right to be "fully cooperative."

In *active wakefulness* the activity consists for the most part of flailing movements of the arms and legs, coupled with twisting of the head and trunk. Much less "cooperative" here. Many a researcher has floundered by conducting tests and basing conclusions on infants who are active and wakeful instead of alert and inactive. In the next stage, active wakefulness merging with agitation, things are simply impossible—the baby is disturbed, bored, perhaps angry, and no doubt uncomfortable.

Adult awareness of infant states made possible observations of what one researcher has characterized as "infant competence." Infants are not "a blooming, buzzing confusion, a blank slate to be written on by his world" (the words of Henry James, a bachelor) or a tabula rasa (the philosopher, John Locke). On the contrary, if an infant is studied with sufficient sensitivity to its mood, wakefulness, inclinations, and brain development, truly marvelous performances can be achieved.

Some years ago a psychologist at Western Reserve University, Robert Fantz, temporarily abandoned a series of experiments he had been carrying out on chimpanzees in favor of more challenging ones on twenty-two human infants. Fantz was interested in visual predilections, specifically in determining whether or not, and if so when, an infant fancied looking at one object rather than another. A simple question but nonetheless a profound one that no doubt would have been of interest to John Locke.

The answer to Fantz's question can be arrived at by considering his experiments of suspending an infant in a type of hammock which is then itself suspended within a box, "the stimulus chamber." In two openings a foot above the infant's head Fantz displayed two "targets" —cardboard squares containing, at various times, a bull's-eye, a strip, a checkerboard pattern, or several geometric shapes. Meanwhile the experimenter, slyly concealed and spying through a peephole in the chamber ceiling, watches a tiny image of the target reflected on the infant's pupil. As the infant switches from one target to another this shift in gaze is matched by a corresponding substitution of the reflected target as seen in the baby's eyes. All very neat, unobtrusive, devilishly clever.

It is worth noting that the newborn's eyes have a fixed focal point of about seven and a half inches (19.2 cm). Targets have to be presented at about this distance, therefore, if the newborn is to see them clearly. Over the first several months the infant's visual performance will become more adaptable because of the ability to converge the eyes on nearby or approaching targets and, second, to accommodation of the lens: changes in lens shape to bring objects at different distances into sharp focus.

Fantz discovered that infants exhibit clear biases as early in development as the researchers can capture their attention. They gaze longer at patterned targets than at plain ones, stripped ones rather than at a bull's-eye. Overall, they seem to prefer patterns of intermediate complexity to either the very simple or the very complex. But in all instances, patterns of any sort are preferred over featureless surfaces. Most arresting of all, however, is the human face. Even a cartoon will do. Newborns spend more time looking at a facelike arrangement of shapes than at the same shapes randomly arranged. It is likely that the baby brain is prewired to prefer the human face over the faces of other species and, most decidedly, over inanimate objects. By one month of age, this preference has narrowed to a specific human face, usually that of the mother.

It is strange but true that looking should merge almost perfectly with the development of the visual system in the infant brain. Infants can't look until the "hardware" and "software" are in place. This occurs between the age of one and three months.

At one month the infant hasn't much in the way of visual interest and doesn't look toward anything. But between one and two months there is no doubt that the infant can see. How do we know? By inference, of course.

An infant is simultaneously presented with a pattern containing stripes and a blank field of matched luminescence. The acuity estimate is taken as the narrowest width of stripe that is preferred to the blank field. A second method employs evoked potential recordings: the smallest check size in a checkerboard pattern that will reliably elicit an evoked response.

✓ Changes toward steady development occur in the infant brain, which explains why three month olds see remarkably well compared to newborns or even one month olds. The optic nerve lacks its myelin covering at birth and undergoes the process of sheathing during the first four months of life. Indeed, the process isn't really totally completed until around age two when the optic nerve is indistinguishable from an adult's optic nerve in everything but size. As with the rest of the brain, the number of cells in the visual cortex is complete at birth. From birth on, "fine tuning" occurs: cell size increases, more synapses form, interconnectivity multiplies a millionfold.

If you implant electrodes in the brain of a cat, specifically in the brain's visual cortex, you can detect firing of specific cells whenever that cat is exposed to vertical lines. Other cells fire in response to horizontal lines. Some cells will fire in response to oblique lines, too, but fewer of them. Such findings in the cat fit with the preferences of infants in the first few weeks for horizontal and vertical lines. They, too, have little interest in the oblique. A philosopher might usefully ponder the implications of such research: in cats and men and women certain brain cells are preferentially attuned to the horizontal or the vertical and are preordained, as a Calvinist might put it, to respond to certain aspects of "reality" over others.

A monkey with its visual cortex destroyed thanks to the perfidy of an experimenter can still, after some training, learn to discriminate lines, high-contrast triangles, circles, and so on. Vision, in short, isn't simply lost entirely. Instead, it's speculated that there exists an alternative visual system within the subcortical areas which enables the "lesioned" monkey (a euphemism) after training to once again carry out the same visual discriminations as previously performed by the visual cortex. What happens to humans when they are deprived of their visual cortices by injury or disease? Studies by Larry Weiskrantz and Elizabeth Warrington in London show that these unfortunate patients often possess a visual sense that these investigators call "blind sight." Our philosopher might also ponder the implications of such a patient who when presented with a visual stimulus denies its occurrence. But when asked to *guess* where the stimulus might be, a patient with "blind sight" often accurately locates the stimulus while all the time protesting that he cannot see it!

To see and not know that one sees, to successfully "guess" at something that eludes one's most volitional efforts—indeed, these are matters to puzzle the philosopher, professional or kibitzer, on a dreary winter evening. *To see* but not know what one sees? How can a person be capable of guessing at the location of a stimulus and yet deny that he sees the stimulus? Strange doings.

At age two months an infant will gaze lovingly at Mother, and Mother, gratified, will gaze back in return. This first sign of "social competence," as the psychologists would put it, depends on the establishment of a more fundamental competence within the developing brain. Not until the infant is sufficiently well along to maintain his or her head in a midline position can an infant gaze into Mother's eyes and prolong that gaze for more than just an instant.

At three weeks and for many infants as late as six weeks, sustained gaze at Mother is impossible; the head lilts or drifts off to one side or the other. But at eight or nine weeks all of this has changed. Baby is more sociable. Baby can hold her head pointed forward and maintain that forward-pointedness. Neuroscientists don't understand how such postural mechanisms can develop in the human infant. At the minimum, a vast network of connecting fibers within the brain must interpenetrate, coordinating vision with balance and muscle power. Nor can Baby sit till her muscles are sufficiently developed to maintain herself upright. Three months is the magic moment. The brain maturation dictates the time of "social competence" which dictates whether or not and how well that infant is going to get along in its first intimate encounter.

The relationship of posture, attitude, and behavior starts in infancy and progresses throughout the life span. The recruit slumps in his chair until the sergeant pulls him up sharply with an "Attention!" The sassy waitress flaps her hand on her hip as she tells the customer, "I only serve the food, I don't cook it too!" That hand on the hip will be remembered even more than the words at tipping time. Infants, too, signal attitudes by postural tricks.

An infant who wants to be left alone, turns its head away for a little privacy. Mother, though, is insistent. She won't abide any interference with *her* wish to gaze eye to eye at that moment. Mother wants to look at Baby. Baby doesn't want to look at Mother. How will they work that out? Will they work that out?

Sensitive mothers or well-intentioned mothers or mothers combining both qualities know that their infant, a true mime, communicates by gesture and posture. Once this is accepted and applied by the mother, a major step has been taken toward that "swans' mating dance" mentioned by Dr. T. Berry Brazelton. Not one person influencing another exactly, but two people perfectly accepting of the individuality of the other. But Baby can't turn its head and thereby take the first step in communication for two long months. Mother must wait that long for the infant brain to mature that far. Only then is she really convinced that her baby notices her, that she makes a difference. This realization must take place, incidentally, when the time is just right.

By four months, most babies show a marked decline in their fancy for prolonged looking toward Mother's face. In those short weeks between two and four months, therefore, Mother and Baby literally have a once-in-a-lifetime opportunity to simply stare and be stared at without compunction. Peak age for looking toward the mother's face? Nine weeks, a time of major change in the infant's visual function.

Up to two months of age you can scramble a human face (nose under mouth, one eye sitting in the middle of the forehead) and that infant will still smile at that monster. By two months the infant brain has matured enough to reject a cyclops: two eyes and not one are necessary and those eyes must be spread apart at that.

In an earlier and simpler time scientists believed that this capacity to distinguish and delight in the human face provides evolutionary advantages. This kind of reasoning lost its persuasiveness after Konrad Zacharias Lorenz's work with goslings.

When exposed to Lorenz instead of the mother goose, the newly hatched gosling followed Lorenz, considered him "just right." This earned Lorenz worldwide recognition as the bearded man walking through the woods with a train of goslings in tow. It also earned him the umbrage traditionally directed at the seer who insists on pointing out that behavior is biologically determined and not simply learned.

Said Lorenz, "The fact that the behavior not only of animals but of human beings as well is, to a large extent, determined by nervous mechanisms involved in the phylogeny of the species, in other words by 'instinct' was certainly no surprise to any biologically-thinking sci-

entist. It was treated as a matter of course. On the other hand, by
emphasizing it and by drawing the sociological and political inferences, I seem to have incurred the fanatical hostility of all those doctri-
naires whose ideology has tabooed the recognition of this fact. The
idealistic and vitalistic philosophers to whom the belief in the absolute
freedom of the human will makes the assumption of human instincts
intolerable as well as the behavioristic physiologists who assert that all
human behavior is learned, all seem to be blaming me."

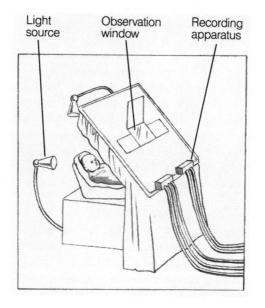

Light   Observation   Recording
source   window   apparatus

An experimental setup for observing behavior without distracting the infant.

Nothing as dramatic as "imprinting" has been demonstrated in humans although folklorists insist from time to time that human infants
have on occasion been raised by wolves. Yet even if these fantastic
stories are true, the "adoption" of the feral children occurred too late
to be explained on the basis of "imprinting" which must take place
very soon after birth.

In recognizing faces, infants under two months ignore information
about internal features and concentrate instead on the outer contour.
The head and face must be shaped just right. "Square heads" won't
do. Starting at one month and certainly by two months the internal
features must also come together in neat anatomic approximation.

This process can be speeded up if oscillating lights are employed to represent eyes and nose and mouth. In this situation the infant switches its attention and takes in both internal and external features. At two months it is no longer necessary to employ lights or tricks of any kind. Not only can a normal face be separated from a scrambled one, but people can be distinguished on the basis of their facial features.

Imagine an experiment in which a mother holds and speaks to a baby. Replace this scene of happy domesticity with a strange woman holding and speaking to the baby. Next, the mother holds the baby but a stranger's voice is substituted by means of a recording. Finally, the stranger holds the baby while the mother's voice is played in the background. This bizarre experiment was actually carried out a decade or so ago and with some surprising, even startling results.

Mother's face combined with Mother's voice: blissful. Stranger's face and Stranger's voice: tolerable but less appealing (Baby looked less at Stranger than at Mother). Mother-Stranger amalgam: simply intolerable (Baby actively turned away from this bizarre combination of sight and sound).

Of course, the only way that Baby could make such distinctions is by learning that Mother's face goes with Mother's voice. Since this association occurs within the first two weeks of life, it suggests that the association tracts between auditory and visual centers in the infant brain are functioning this early.

CHAPTER 35

Imitation

Sensitivity on the part of the newborn toward the behavior of others can be measured by the informal, not so academic, and slightly outrageous exercise of sticking out one's tongue. In many cases an infant as early as a few days after birth will reciprocate this gesture. The mouth opens, the tongue protrudes, the mouth closes. At first this peculiar performance was denied: "the movements are only random, they are part of a feeding response and, therefore, occurred serendipitously."

Perhaps no other performance by a newborn has been so hotly contested by baby pundits as "neonatal imitation." How could little Johnny, so new on the scene, "know" the location of his tongue, correlate this observation with "knowledge" about the tongue of the adult initiating the game and, finally, extrude his tongue in imitation? Does his behavior progress in this fashion? "What is Mother doing? I think she wants me to do the same thing. Let's see now. Where is my tongue so that I can stick it out the way she is sticking out her tongue at me?"

After thinking the matter over (and retesting to assure that the infant can be depended upon to repeat the performance), investigators reached a different and, to me, more sensible explanation of what was going on. Imitation is a dramatic example of the newborn's emerging capacity for empathy.

Yawning when others yawn, feeling anger in response to the anger of others, these are empathic responses familiar to everyone. Neonatal imitation is most likely a similar empathic response, a "resonating" to the behaviors and emotions of others.

Infants tend to cry in the nursery whenever other infants cry. They move their arms and legs in synchrony with the sound of human speech, even when languages are employed that the baby hasn't previously heard. Since this behavior can be elicited in infants only a few days of age, it most likely depends on the contributions from subcorti-

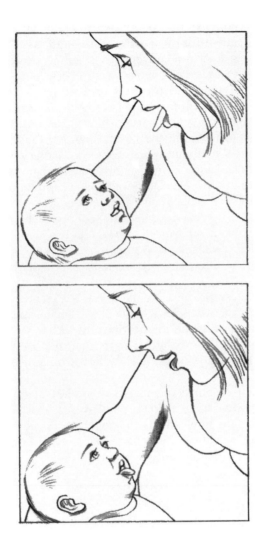

An infant less than a week of age imitates his mother and sticks out his tongue. "Hard wiring" within the brain helps the infant to "know" that a part of her (which he can see) corresponds to part of himself (which he has never seen). He instinctively is able to carry out the same act.

cal rather than cortical structures. Besides, the infant brain is much too immature this early in life to carry out the complex reasoning that I just parodied. Imitation also occurs out of sequence: imitation in slightly older infants begins with those parts of the body visible to the baby. For instance, leg and arm movements occur in preference to nose puckering. This paradox can be resolved, I believe, by assuming that baby imitation (tongue protrusion) is automatic, instinctual, and processed by subcortical centers, while later imitation is processed differently and within the cerebral cortex.

Neurons are born, interact for a while, compete for synaptic connections, then some die off and fewer and more lasting synapses prevail. The infant "walks" and "swims" shortly after birth. These primitive reflexes disappear and, years later, walking and swimming appear once again, only this time embedded within the context of different neuronal networks. Neuronal organization produces behavior. With neuronal reorganization, behavior disappears. Subsequent reorganization leads to the baby walking or swimming or sticking out the tongue again, but for a different purpose and with a different meaning ("That's what I think of you, you creep!").

Baby brain development consists of advance, regression, reorganization, reappearance. Nowhere is the basic dynamism of the brain so clearly evident as with the infant. Starting with a string of reflexes (sucking, grasping), the baby brain reorganizes itself according to circumstance and experiences. Early reflexes disappear or are modified.

Modification in response to experience implies the capacity to learn. Herein lies another mine field of controversy. How does the baby learn? Does learning imply the use of language? (Easier to answer, that one: a dog or a cat can learn to accommodate its master's whim without the employment of language.)

CHAPTER 36

Learning

A baby will suck a pacifier that delivers no milk but is connected to a switch that controls a slide projector. If the infant sucks vigorously enough, the slide that is projected to a screen in the baby's field of vision will change. The baby will soon learn to adopt its sucking to keep the slide in sharp focus. Other arrangements have been tried that link up sucking with brightness in the room. The baby soon learns to control brightness by sucking patterns. If the apparatus is disconnected at any time so that sucking produces no change in the slide, the baby grows fussy, turns away, turns off, and becomes bored. "Habituation" is a more elegant way of phrasing it but "boredom" will do just as well.

An infant, like the rest of us, likes things to change, to feel he or she can have something to say about bringing about that change. Different pictures, different light intensity, different things happening: the baby continues to suck and remain interested—that's learning at its most basic.

Same picture, same illumination, same everything—that is boredom. The most important aspect of all of this? Researchers believe, and with good reason, that the important component is the baby's emerging sense of control over all these things. Contingent reinforcement is what the psychologists call it. "Things that happen in the environment bear a direct, predictable, and immediate reaction to the baby's own actions, thus providing feedback about the baby's own behavior and power to control events," as one pundit explained it.

How early in life can an infant learn? Folklorists claim an infant can learn even before birth and can assimilate aspects of the environment before any direct contact with that environment. Such a proposal can be tested, has been tested, and the folklorists are turning out to be correct.

Place a pair of earphones on a newborn baby and that baby will soon learn to suck in a pattern so as to hear her mother's voice over the earphone (if she sucks at a different rate the voice disappears or is replaced by the voice of another person). Soon the baby learns under such conditions how to maintain her mother's voice via suitable sucking. The newborn will also suck in rhythm in order to hear the sound of the human heart. She had heard the heart for several months in the womb, had gotten used to it, wants to hear it repeated endlessly, and so will learn to suck in a pattern the experimenter fancies in order to hear those sounds once again.

"It looks like auditory preferences after birth are explained by what is heard prenatally," concludes Dr. Anthony DeCasper, a psychologist at the University of North Carolina in Greensboro. It was he who designed the sucking experiments. He based these experiments on a hunch, that newborn babies hear very well, "Why do we come into the world like that? Perhaps we listen in the womb." In order to find out if we do, Dr. DeCasper designed an additional experiment which some scientists knowing nothing about the subject might well have laughed at and, therefore, missed an important point entirely about babies.

DeCasper asked sixteen pregnant women to read aloud a children's book entitled *The Cat in the Hat* twice every day during the last six months of their pregnancy. It seemed silly at the time, a grown woman reading a children's story to an empty room. In fact, the room wasn't empty; there was a listener there, hidden deeply within that slightly incredulous and no doubt skeptical reader. Total reading time prior to birth? About five hours.

When those babies came out, DeCasper hooked them up to the sucking device and earphones. Baby learned immediately to suck in a way so as to produce a tape-recorded rendition of *The Cat in the Hat.* Substituting Mother reading another children's book, *The King, the Mice and the Cheese,* with a different meter failed to elicit the sucking pattern. Baby had learned to suck preferentially so as to hear again what presumably—how else would you explain it?—had been heard during those five hours spaced out over those six months of waiting time. Baby had learned to recognize Mother reading *The Cat in the Hat* and hadn't yet learned to recognize Mother reading a different book or, more likely, simply wanted to hear again what had already been heard many times before. Children of any age will do that. "Tell me the story again, Mommy," and that story will have to be repeated for the nth time. So why not a similar preference at birth for repetition, for that cozy feeling that accompanies hearing the book repeated in a familiar voice? What makes the whole thing incredible, of course, are the assumptions that underscore such an experimental finding: the baby learns in the womb, recognizes its mother's voice, even her intonation and the very book she's reading. At a later point the learning is carried over and can be tested by monitoring one aspect of behavior that the infant has control over from the very first moment—its lips and tongue and the act of sucking at a nipple.

At this point DeCasper and a different associate, Phyllis Prescott, modified their experiment in order to discover what, if any, effect the voice of the infant's father might have on its sucking pattern.

Six men were selected and asked to spend anywhere from four to ten hours simply talking to their newborn sons or daughters. At age two days these babies were outfitted with the nipple and earphones to see if they preferred their fathers' voices to the voice of any other man. They didn't. They could distinguish one man's voice from another but the fathers didn't exert any particular fascination. The dry-as-dust protocols fail to reveal how the fathers took these results. Were they depressed or did they accept without a whimper that when it comes to a baby's learning within the womb the mother has all the odds in her favor? The experimenters didn't say. In any case the fathers' disappointment was no doubt only temporary; within a few weeks the infants were both-parent partial, preferring not only their mothers' voices over a strange woman's but their fathers' voices over another man's as well.

Outside the laboratory, learning takes a different, more urgent form. Baby smiles, Parent smiles back, Parent picks up Baby, Baby feels powerful and important—that's how love is learned. Baby smiles, Mother is too busy and preoccupied with her own problems, Mother looks away, Baby looks away and cries or appears lost in thought (in appearance only)—this is learning of another sort. Smiles don't matter, nothing that Baby Emily does seems to make any difference in the responsiveness of Mother. As a result, she habituates to a dull, dull world in which nothing she can do seems to matter a whit when it comes to how other people behave. In such a situation a baby might understandably wish to be back in the laboratory sucking on a nipple connected to that slide-switching light-dimming apparatus that, if nothing else, confirms that he or she is somewhat autonomous and not a mere plaything of fate.

Reduced to its most basic, love is based on a contingent variation marked by an abundance of reinforcement. Crying elicits picking up which elicits good feelings all around. Romantics may object to such characterization, claiming it's too mechanistic and smacks too much of the mumbo jumbo of the laboratory pedant. But with the advent of instruments capable of monitoring a baby's physiologic response it became possible to measure physiologically things that up until that time could only be guessed at.

Distress of any sort increases the electrical conductance of the newborn's skin by stimulating sweating (heat alone will not do that). Measurement of this electrical conduction, therefore, is a dependable no-frills-attached method of divining how the baby is feeling about the world at the moment. Technology in such instances isn't dehumanizing, indeed, it can be used to increase the humanism of both the infant and those persons in the environment it benefits the infant to get along with.

An infant may quickly learn to respond to the consistencies and inconsistencies of those around it. Consider this scenario. Parent perceives, or thinks so, certain responsiveness (for example, personality) in Baby. As a result, Parent behaves in a kindly way. Soon the relations between Baby and Parent form a kind of dance in which each's response becomes a stimulus to the other's reaction. Baby contingently reinforces Parent and vice versa, as a behavioral psychologist would put it. Advantages of the contingent-reinforcement arrangement: everything. Disadvantages: some dispelling of the mysteries and myths of parent and baby love, the inevitable questions regarding meaning: "Is this all there is? Can love be adequately explained by laboratory legerdemain using instruments and colored lights?"

CHAPTER 37

The Incompetence of Babies

No description of the competence of infants would be complete without some reference to their incompetences. The infant brain isn't merely the adult brain shrunk down. The uniqueness of baby brain sets the conditions for this competence. Most babies are usually passive, malleable, and helpless. Abandon a kitten or a puppy and there's a fighting chance that that tiny, cunning creature might make it. Abandon a newborn human and that tiny, not so cunning creature hasn't a chance. Baby noises—crying, breathing, belching, flatulence—are limited too, much more limited than those of a cat or a dog which at an early age can manage the adult equivalent of a hiss or a growl.

On the other hand, babies may retain fetal behavior that no longer serves a purpose. For instance, a fetus can move itself about in the womb by flexing its head backward and to one side followed by a quick rotation of the trunk to the same side. Newborns will attempt but usually fail at the same maneuver. Monitoring of the electrical activity of the neck muscles of an infant during sleep reveals patterns similar to those seen in the fetus attempting to rotate itself. However, unlike the fetus, the newborn in the absence of the fluid environment provided within the womb can't usually achieve rotation of the trunk following head rotation. The head and body are too heavy for the neck and trunk muscles which for some time after birth haven't the strength to overcome the force of gravity. Indeed, within the first weeks after birth, antigravity mechanisms are strikingly inefficient. The infant cannot lift its head or trunk and, as a consequence, it can't roll over. For this reason, few babies can lift their heads unless born at full-term or close to it.

At its birth, the baby's brain as yet hasn't managed to wrest control over the muscles of the neck and shoulders, but it is working at that enterprise at a mad rate. Whole body movements also can initially be managed. Lay a newborn baby on its face or its back and that's where it stays. Rolling over comes later.

Place the very young or newborn infant on its face at a time when it can't control its head, and that infant might suffocate on a pillow (that's how my grandmother in her generation thought of it). As a result, babies in that generation hadn't any experience with pillows. Sleeping, eating, and eliminating are the three elemental forces that ebb and flow within a baby with such monotony that only a mother or a father can distinguish one baby from another, *their* baby from all the rest.

CHAPTER 38

"When the Baby Is Born It Is Very Little More Intelligent than a Vegetable"

Throughout recorded history the newborn has been regarded as a helpless, insensitive creature not always accorded the status of someone fully "human" yet, at the same time, clearly several notches above anything further down the phylogenetic scale. No doubt this belief in the infant's helplessness and insensitivity served a good purpose—adults experienced less distress when infants died, as they often did. (Infant mortality approached one or two out of every three babies during the medieval period, for instance.) Widespread infant mortality engenders an attitude described by historian Barbara Tuchman: "Owing to the high infant mortality of the times, the investment of love in a young child may have been so unrewarding that by some ruse of nature as when overcrowded rodents in captivity will not breed, it was suppressed. Perhaps also the frequent child-bearing put less value on the product. A child was born and died and another took its place."

Contemporary cultures with high mortality rates often adapt similar attitudes to the newborn, speaking of the infant as a sphinx or postponing the naming process for several months after birth. Such rituals are grief sparing; they foster detachment and acceptance of the inevitable.

In cultures such as ours where, on the whole, most infants survive, reactions to the developing infant have been turned around. Fathers are encouraged to participate in the infant's delivery, mothers cuddle and feed and care for babies from the moment of birth. Even more interesting are the changes in attitude about newborns on the part of doctors and researchers. ♦

In 1963 a textbook, *Cerebral Function in Infancy and Childhood*, suggested to the curious medical student, resident, or practicing pediatrician that infants functioned only on a brain stem level. Testing of the newborn, therefore, was directed to evaluating performances mediated below the cerebral hemispheres. Could the baby breathe harmoniously? Did it withdraw its legs and arms when pricked with a pin or pinched? Did it close its eyes to the flash of a bright light?

Implicit in such questions was the assumption that infants don't experience the same feelings as adults. Indeed, this infant-as-not-quite-human point of view was once sacred dogma to infant specialists. "When the baby is just born it is very little more intelligent than a vegetable," wrote in 1895 a certain Dr. Griffith, a renowned professor of diseases of children at the University of Pennsylvania. "Its soul and its intellect are there, but they are dormant, waiting to be awakened. It has little control over its body and all its movements are automatic or instinctive. Probably there's not a single expression of the face or motion of the arms or legs which is caused by a distinctly willed action . . . a newborn baby probably cannot see except to distinguish light from darkness and will not wink when the finger is brought close to its eyes. It seems unable to hear and, at first, cannot smell. It is, in fact, not directly conscious of anything." This panegyric against infant sensibilities also included this observation regarding the most common behavioral performance of every infant since Cain and Abel: "When it cries it is ignorant of any sensation that makes it cry."

A half century later the status of infants had improved. Dr. Benjamin Spock held that infants could feel pain and discomfort; indeed, in most instances, infant "fussiness" could be traced to hunger, fatigue, or colic. While this represented an advance (the infant could at least experience some of life's more uncomfortable sensations), little encouragement was provided to mothers that their infants might actually be enjoying themselves. "He doesn't know yet that you are a person or that he is a person," Spock promulgated. "He's just a bundle of organs and nerves during his first month."

This "bundle of nerves" orientation persisted throughout the next twenty years and exerted a powerful effect on pediatricians and pediatric neurologists. They approached the baby armed with pins, hammers, flashlights, tongue blades, and tape measures along with a grim determination to employ these instruments in the interest of establishing once and for all the "normality" or "abnormality" of the infant.

Could the baby move, would it cry if pinpricked, would it thrash symmetrically about, would it turn from a bright light, was its head big enough and not too big, when lifted was it limp, did it move on its own or did someone have to initiate the movement? Brain-damaged infants "proved" the wisdom of these procedures, demonstrating distorted or exaggerated reflexes, suppressing stereotyped or obligatory movement patterns—too much, too little, too early, too late, not enough, too much.

The repertoire of infant responses available to the examining doctor was based on a tabulation of results of similar examinations carried out on thousands of babies by similar doctors under similar situations and with similar prejudices. Deviation from this repertoire signaled an alarm: something was wrong or could be expected to go wrong in the future. Would the baby be retarded, clumsy, not intelligent enough in some respects? Would he or she be able to learn, go to Harvard, run a one-hundred-yard dash in respectable time? Parental questions abounded, but answers were few. In most instances, the examining doctors recognized the limitation of pin and hammer to divine who would grow up to be clever.

More astute observers of newborn infants started recognizing in the 1970s that an infant's behavior depended very much on the state of its brain, specifically its state of alertness. Although no one would venture an opinion about a sleepy or drowsy adult's mental or emotional abilities, "baby doctors" have for centuries done just that—routinely carried out their examinations and rituals without reference to the infant's alertness.

Careful observations reveal that infants only moments out of the uterus are alert and wide-eyed (assuming, of course, that their mothers have not been drugged into insensibility by an overly eager anesthetist).

Within minutes the alert newborn can perform a repertoire of behaviors that give the lie to the theories of the once eminent Dr. Griffith. The newborn will turn its head toward the human voice (preferring a female over a male); it will suck in a burst-pause rhythm to the sound of its mother's voice (whereas a pure tone of equivalent pitch elicits a steady, monotonous rhythm, as if the baby recognizes the lack of "information" conveyed by a tone compared to the richness of the human voice); it will stare at a picture or a drawing of the human face; it prefers milk smells and breast smells to mere sugar water; and it can separate human milk from cow's milk formula (via altered sucking patterns).

Simply watch, observe carefully, don't underestimate, don't interrupt, don't overstimulate—these are simple rules but nonetheless ones that many observers of infants over the years have found hard to apply. If you start off assuming that infants know nothing and can do nothing, then by a kind of self-fulfilling prophecy, the infant's competence escapes detection.

CHAPTER 39

Organization

Watch the baby. Do away with all preconceptions. Withhold any judgment. Simply observe. You will see that the head is disproportionately large by adult standards. The facial features are different too: a protruding large forehead; large eyes set below the midpoint of the head; round puffy cheeks. The infant body also differs from that of an adult: thick, short arms and legs; rounded, soft, elastic body surface. Cuddliness, warmth, softness, helplessness. The baby snuggles, conforming to the roundness of the female breast and arms.

Adolescent girls, past puberty, are attracted to babies and want to "mother" them. Adolescent girls not yet pubertal are more like boys in their response: bored, insensitive, oftentimes annoyed if the baby turns fussy. Such findings can stir an infant researcher's imagination: " 'babyness' may correspond to an incentive system in adults for nurturing the young baby," suggests Dr. Robert Emde of the Colorado Medical School.

Mother is awakened on a cold winter night, snow falling softly against the window. She gets up, loosens her nightgown, produces a breast, and half snoozes during the 3 A.M. feeding. Mother feels good about the snuggling, the cuddliness; she isn't merely resigned, she feels, indeed, a kind of joy, although the joy may not be recognized as such at 3 A.M. on a cold winter night.

Baby, if she is to survive, must entice, entrap, and ensnare parental affection. She must create joy and not mere resignation. Baby's thrashing of arms and legs also elicits, in its own way, a tenderness, a moving closer in order to comfort. Helplessness elicits a "tuning in" on the part of parents, a rhythmic to-and-fro adjustment and readjustment of parent to child and child to parent. If this process is interrupted by illness or absence or maternal indifference, the rhythms go awry. Grimacing, turning from the nipple, fussing, crying—these are the disaster signals. Things have "gone sour," the "tuning in" of the parent and infant is no longer operative. Nor is this "swans' mating dance" linked to just Mother and Baby.

Infant researcher Louis W. Sander has a favorite home movie. It depicts a young married couple standing on the lawn outside their house. The woman is holding her eight-day-old baby who, as the film opens, turns fussy and restless. She hands the baby to her husband who casually takes the child and places it in the crook of his arm while continuing an animated conversation with the cameraman. As the film unfolds the father appears to ignore his newborn baby. The baby, too, seems to be unaware of the father. Nevertheless, after just a few seconds the infant stops crying, grows quiet, and finally drops off to sleep.

A slow-motion frame-by-frame analysis of the movie reveals a different story. The father looks down several times at his baby who returns the gaze. The infant and father begin to reach for each other. The baby clasps the little finger of the father's hand and, at that moment, falls asleep.

What delights Sander is the sensibility and sensitivity of the infant, qualities not generally associated with newborns. Such observations, partly made possible by innovative use of videotape, have enabled infant researchers like Louis Sander to depict the subtleties of infant communication which, it turns out, is two-way: the infant to parent, the parent back to the infant. Organizational complexity is present from the moment of birth.

Traditionally, scientists envision organization as proceeding from the simple to the complex. For instance, a number of cells organizes themselves into a tissue which then further specializes into organs with the organs relating to one another in such a way as to produce an organism. But studies of embryonic development reveal that organization in living systems does not develop that way. Rather, life begins with a highly complex organization. The cell itself exhibits a daunting complexity along with a precise organization.

How does one complex organization, a cell, meet and interact with other equally complex organizations (other cells) to then engage in a further heightening of organizational complexity?

"How can we get from something which is endlessly varying to something that is a stable configuration?" asks Louis Sander. "Structures are really functions capable of maintaining stable configurations. I am reminded of Goethe's response in viewing a rainbow in the mist of a great waterfall. He was aware that the drops were constantly churning and falling in the mist: his own preoccupation at that moment was with 'life' and the life process. He said, 'Life is not the light (the sunlight) but the reflected color.' The stability of the rainbow was there in spite of the endless variations and change in the drops of water. What we try to conceptualize is how this endless change can lead to the maintenance of stable configurations."

Dr. Sander suggests that infants cannot be understood if we insist on thinking of them as "simple" creatures gradually progressing to more complex levels of organization. Instead, the infant is awesomely complex from day one.

Observations of infants, hundreds of them, indeed thousands, have convinced Louis Sander of the importance of timing as a regulator of infant behavior. In the movie sequence, the father's hand and the baby's left arm move in synchrony partly conscious but mostly unconscious. The performance of each actor in this minidrama was exquisitely timed yet neither was aware of the exact sequence or synchrony involved. "Fitting together," Sander's term, depends upon a hierarchy of temporal rhythms. Low-frequency rhythms: sleep, feeding, elimination. High-frequency rhythms: sucking bursts, gazing toward, gazing away from—rhythms lasting ten seconds or less.

Low-frequency events provide a background, the stage setting upon which is played out the drama of the infant and mother encounter. If this rhythm is disrupted or, even worse, never set down at all, "fitting together" cannot take place. After a while the infant and mother both "know" that it's time to sleep, to eat, to play, to gaze longingly at each other. But if eating and sleeping rhythms haven't been established, this mutual sharing can't take place. The infant and mother are "misfits."

Under the best conditions a reciprocal effect exists: Infant influencing Mother to hold, feed, not disturb, play with, simply look at—all done in certain ways and at prescribed times.

Mother, in turn, is director, determiner of time and events. It's she who defines precisely the timing of that holding, feeding, not disturbing, playing with, looking at. "We begin with an infant and a mother and then gain, in addition, the highly specific fittedness which allows the regulation of both partners as a system," says Sander.

Infant and Mother: this is a complexity along an order of complexity beginning with cell, progressing to tissue, organ, organs, organisms, social interactors. This hierarchy is not a matter of the simple progressing to the complex but of complexity from the very beginning.

Nothing is more complex than the fertilized ovum, nothing more complex than the neuron. Nothing is more complex than the fetal brain. Infant researchers wrestle with the challenge of how one highly complex organization (the baby) acts with another highly complex organization (the mother) in a highly complex environment (society). Most researchers have sought the answers in simple cause-effect relationships: the mother acts in a certain way and "causes" the infant to develop along certain ways. The mother is impatient and distracted, the baby feels "ignored" and "withdrawn." Years later the psychologist may translate this into "Your mother neglected you. That is the reason for your difficulty." But this interaction of the infant and mother can never be reduced to a level of *this* behavior causing *that* response. Needed for our understanding is a willingness to consider events between the mother and infant as happening in synchrony—one influencing the other and both influencing each other.

"We need new models in the way of thinking about complexities so that we can *begin* with complexity and end with unity. Such is the basic description of every organism from the level of the cell, namely, how unity is achieved in the face of complexity," says Sander.

CHAPTER 40

Boundaries

Anyone who has ever written about, lectured on, or held a seminar on the human baby agrees on one thing: the newborn has no conception of self. Piaget from his Swiss retreat suggested that the baby begins life not even certain where the outside world ends and itself begins. Piaget had a marvelously apt word for this state: adualism. Its aptness derives from the subsequent dualisms the human mind constructs for itself over the subsequent seventy-four years or however long that infant can be expected to endure before returning to the ultimate state of adualism, death. The dualisms of self-other, life-death, brain-mind, subject-object are all, in the last analysis, merely constructions of the infant mind as it gradually emerges over a lifetime from its initial adualism.

Piaget started off as a philosopher, never totally lost his interest in philosophy and, indeed, applied it to observations of his own children and to other children. All that the infant experiences, according to that Swiss savant, are certain sensitivities and experiences without the capacity to tell whether they originate from an external world—the bottle of milk—or from the self—the delight in consuming that bottle of milk.

Piaget was very wise and clever and one hesitates to lock intellectual horns with him. If Piaget says the baby has no sense of self, it's probably safer to go along than to argue. But before giving up entirely on the subject and passing on to other matters, entertain just for the moment a few considerations on the other side of the question.

On first reflection, it seems unlikely that an infant could have an appreciation of the existence of her own head or face. Only with the aid of a mirror might she gradually discover that she is the proud possessor of eyes, ears, a nose, and a mouth to put things in. Movement might also provide confirmation of one's own existence. "Kinesthetic feedback" is the term for such a process. Close your eyes and touch the tip of your forefinger to the tip of your nose. That's kinesthetic feedback. The baby, too, presumably, could learn about herself by means of this feedback of muscle telling the brain about the whereabouts of the arm or hand and then all three components of the kinesthetic system telling the baby who she is.

Despite the appeal of the above formulation, it ignores certain intriguing aspects of our world that are obvious even to little Sarah born but a moment ago while you were reading the above paragraph. The visual field has boundaries which although vague and usually ignored (we've learned to ignore them) are nonetheless boundaries. They consist of our head and our nose. Close one eye and you can see the nose blocking your field of vision closest to the midline. Thus, our nose is a constant feature of our world and is present from the first moment that we, as an infant, open our eyes.

Other parts of the body—the trunk and the limbs—also occlude parts of the visual field, differing from the nose only with respect to their distance from the point of observation. Indeed, the nose, head, and limbs occupy fairly fixed positions. All other objects in the environment will be experienced as a result of the reduction in retinal size as the infant is carried about or as the people and objects move closer or farther away.

Philosophers have often speculated on the reason most people experience themselves as inhabiting and operating from the head. As a possible explanation, try this experiment: turn your head rapidly from side to side. Your eyes and nose sweep across the scene, your eye movements and nose are present everywhere, wherever and whenever you move your head. This omnipresence suggests that the self is in the head rather than the rest of the body.

This ability to sense part of one's self wherever one looks provides the baby with a tool to make some fairly sophisticated discriminations. Whenever the baby moves her head, the position of all objects within the visual field are altered while the projection of head and nose remain constant. But if the mother moves and the baby doesn't, the change is quite different: all other objects except the mother, along with the baby's nose and head, remain steady. Only the moving object —the mother approaching with the bottle—alters its relative position.

If the baby moves only her eyes, the nose takes up a different position within the field of observation than would happen if *both* the head and eyes were moved. These alterations in perception can be tested and confirmed (Test and confirm them); they don't require language or university degrees and just might, therefore, provide the means whereby somebody somewhere sometime may prove Piaget wrong. As with many aspects of babyhood, however, witnesses can't be called, there is no one to depose. Only the baby knows and can't tell us that it's all as obvious as the nose on our face.

Babies discover by accident that they have hands and feet. They encounter these objects floating in empty space and learn to control them and incorporate them into the schema of *me* and *mine*. Hunger, wetness, discomfiture slowly and mysteriously are transformed into "I am hungry, I am wet, I am discomfited." At first there is no *me* or *mine* but only elemental sensations around which are constructed what a Buddhist would define as the illusion of self. Who is the one who is feeling hunger or wetness? Descartes claimed he could locate such a person, inwardly. "I think, therefore I am." But where is this *I* when I sleep? The infant brain hasn't yet developed to the point of acquiring an *I* that feels the need to posit such a question. Experience alone is sufficient. Perhaps the reason why we remember so little of our infancy is that there is no *I* observing at all. Perhaps this explains as well how it is that what we do remember has a crystalline clarity about it that only occurs rarely after the moment when the sense of self and I, me and mine have established themselves. This period was described by that savant, Piaget, as one of egocentrism: the world exists only in terms of the feelings, actions, and experiences mediated by the infant brain. Concepts and abstractions appear later and not to the same degree in each brain.

Over a lifetime it dawns upon the brain of a tiny tot that there's more to the world than what is perceived by himself and that other perceivers might see things differently. Not every person reaches this point. To be able to perceive the world with particularity and yet recognize that that particularity isn't and can't be shared with any other creature —the infant brain isn't ready for such an awesome insight, not yet, and in some cases, never.

Until the moment when self and me and mine mediate and filter raw experience, the infant brain does the best it can without such mediation and filtration. Psychologists speak of this as physiognomic perceiving: the way we see faces or physiognomies. We have no trouble, for instance, recognizing individual faces but have quite a bit of trouble describing in words how one face differs from another. Babies, too, can perceive a face and can do so soon after birth. Infant brain doesn't *learn* this performance, it comes as naturally as breathing in and breathing out. Babies are also sensitive to meanings and we're not talking now of meanings in the semantic sense.

At about one year of age an infant when held in the feeding position will strain toward the approaching bottle. But this recognition is a peculiar matter: that same infant will react the same way to all sorts of substitutes for the nursing bottle. Crumpled-up cleaning tissues, spheres, cylinders, cones—any of these will do as long as they approximate in volume the nursing bottle. Specific recognition hasn't yet occurred, the infant brain is still too inchoate to make the necessary distinction. Instead, a "motor program" for feeding is inappropriately activated in the presence of a stimulus even though that stimulus is the wrong one. Repeat the experiment a few times and the necessary learning takes place. Better yet, combine, as two researchers once did, the color of the bottle with two different formulas. One colored bottle contains a bitter salty solution only a fish could fancy. Another bottle of another color is filled with the standard formula. Soon the infant will select bottle number two in preference to bottle number one by color alone. Integration has taken place in that infant's brain. Color and taste have, for the moment, been associated in the interest of culinary preferences. You only need fashion your experiment so as to make a practical difference in the infant's life and you'll see how much and how early an infant can learn.

An infant can tell its own mother's breast milk from the milk of another woman—it takes only a few days to manage that feat of biochemical divination. The mother's face and her voice are recognized a week or two later. By six months the infant has learned much about voice, face, and touch. With increasing facility in eye/hand coordination (during the second six months of life), the use of the hand for reaching and grasping replaces a mere interest in touching. With this a new dimension has entered the world. But if that infant isn't shown something to grasp after, he or she will not elect to reach forward into a void. Only so much of infant behavior is instinctual. Something must be there, somebody must have put it there. So much more has to be pulled out from a baby, sometimes roughly, most times gently. Nature can't do all of it.

CHAPTER 41

Identity

If a monkey and a chimpanzee are placed before a mirror only one of them, the chimp, recognizes the mirrored image as none other than itself. How do we know this? By inference, of course. If a patch of red dye is painted on a chimp's ear and on a monkey's ear, only the chimp fingers its own ear under guidance from the mirror. From this simple experiment some fairly ponderous conclusions can be drawn.

Chimps, it seems, recognize their mirrored reflection, "know" themselves with a degree of psychological penetration that perhaps matches that of their human counterparts: a teenager scanning her mirrored reflection for zits, the model pulling a mirror from her designer purse to assure herself she looks perfect as always.

The monkey-chimp experiment has been applied to infants as well. Rouge was applied to the infants' faces by their mothers under the guise of wiping the babies' faces clean. The infants were then thrust in front of floor-length mirrors. Not one younger than a year, boy or girl, touched its nose. Between fifteen and eighteen months one fourth of the infants reached up toward the funny red spot. Three quarters of the two year olds reached up and perhaps recognized their mothers' perfidy, although that is clearly reading more into the experiment than the experimenter intended.

Other experimenters have applied the rouge experiments to older autistic toddlers with results that are relevant to our concern about infants not afflicted with such a devastating brain disease. Only a little more than two thirds of autistic toddlers recognize themselves in the mirror and, most distressing to see, they evidence no joy in the process. Typically a child who has self-recognition giggles or appears embarrassed, self-conscious, or shy. Few of the autistic children displayed anything suggesting these feelings. But those who did recognize themselves were considered more "normal" in the responsiveness, less "autistic" than other members of the group which, for want of more precise information about what goes awry in the brains of such children, must still carry the not very informative label, "autistic disorder."

Intrigued with these mirror experiments, other infant researchers devised additional means of exploring who sees what when. Infants between six months and two years displayed a gradual sophistication in mirror performance. Those closest to the six-month cutoff could, if conditions were just right, look at some part of themselves in the mirror. Slightly older infants could locate an object, a hat, suspended over their heads simply on the basis of observing its mirrored reflection above their mirrored reflection. Next mirror experiment: the rouged-face discovery that I just mentioned. Finally, the oldest and most advanced (or perhaps the most eager to please) could respond by mouthing or mumbling something when asked, "What's that?" of their mirrored counterpart.

The mirror experiments are appealing; they don't require a lot of sophisticated equipment. Results are crisp and precise and, most important for the baby and mother, nobody is too discomfited. The experiments are also intriguing. Self-recognition, it seems, is not a eureka experience, a magic moment when self-awareness emerges like a butterfly from a chrysalis. Instead, self-recognition is a stumbling rather bumbling process closely akin, in fact, to walking. That infant barely able to reach up and touch the rouge on her face sits years later in her dressing room applying her own rouge and waiting for the call to step out on the stage and sing the role of diva.

"All very interesting," other researchers responded none too charitably. "But self-recognition involves separating oneself from other people as well. Could the infants recognize differences and similarities between themselves and others?"

An eminently reasonable question, a question certainly worth taking seriously, our mirror experimenters responded sportingly. In order to do so the experimenters confronted infants between seven and nineteen months with other infants as well as with grown-ups. Results indicated that the infants were more distressed by an unfamiliar adult than by an unfamiliar child. Does the infant know that he or she is an infant and not an adult?

If this is true—a reasonable assumption under these circumstances —then wouldn't you agree that this knowledge wasn't gained on the basis of personal experience? Certainly most infants beyond the hospital nursery encounter on the average many more adults than they do other infants. There is a much more sensible explanation, however, one favored by the researchers: the infants were using their own selves as reference points. If true, then it follows that an older child would seem less alien and less frightening than an unfamiliar adult. Somewhere between seven and nineteen months infants acquire the ability to categorize, stereotype, set one person into one group to the exclusion of another. While it's unarguable that much is gained by this capacity, much is also lost. As the infant will soon learn, people tend to slip in and out of categories or stereotypes. Further research, this time using pictures, revealed the sophistication of the infant between seven and nineteen months of age.

Infants tend to look for longer periods of time at pictures of a baby of the same sex as themselves as compared to time spent staring at pictures of babies of the opposite sex. One hesitates to reveal to an androgynous audience the conclusions such experiments suggested to infant development researcher, Dr. P. L. Harris of Oxford University. "Such a result is extremely hard to understand unless we accept first that the infant has some knowledge of his or her own sex, and second, that the infant is capable of recognizing other infants as belonging to the same category."

CHAPTER 42

A Storer of Information

Imagine a blind person to whom full vision is suddenly restored. Place a wooden cube and wooden sphere before him and ask, "Point to the sphere." Could he do it?

This scenario, originally posed to philosopher John Locke, contains a series of hidden assumptions. It seems reasonable to presume the blind person could make the desired distinction by touching the two objects. The key question concerns whether he could do the same thing by sight alone. Does one sense—touch—inform another sense—sight—so as to allow what psychologists refer to as "cross modal transfer"?

If I lose my way in the darkened hallway as I arrive home late at night, I can "feel" my way to the bannister and up the steps. But in my case, of course, I've *seen* my hallway hundreds of times. My "cross modal transfer" is based on direct experience, albeit on different occasions and under different circumstances. But the blind man hasn't seen anything until the moment when his vision is miraculously restored.

Philosophers and, more recently, infant researchers have wrestled with this situation mentioned above, often arriving—to no one's surprise—at opposing conclusions. Despite our assumption that vision and touch are different modes of sensory perception, certain types of information are not exclusively one or the other. For example, information about shapes is available to both vision and touch. Rhythm can be seen, felt, and heard, depending on the circumstances. The "roundness" of the sphere can be assimilated either by touch or vision.

Is it too fanciful, therefore, to assume that the blind person via his past touch experience has assimilated the "shape" of the sphere and thus can identify it via his newly acquired visual capacity? Before assenting too readily to this seemingly reasonable assumption, consider this: on many occasions there isn't a correlation between how something looks and how it sounds or feels. Fake flowers, diminutive people with deep voices (actors usually), large people with high-pitched whiny voices (often hormonal deficients), artificial turf, hairpieces—the way something looks oftentimes provides deceptive clues about how it feels or how it may sound. Despite these exceptions, however, the sights and sounds of human interaction are usually related to one another. The scores for ballet and musical comedies are based on our capacity to detect temporal synchrony between the rhythms of the dance and the rhythms of the music. And there is a measurable, exquisitely timed balance between the movements of a speaker's lips and the sound produced. Recall the irritation of the last time you were in a movie when the sound track and film were out of sync.

An infant researcher tested the capacity of four-month-old babies to detect sight/sound correlations. The four month olds watched two films. In the first film a woman, similar to their mothers, looked out and played a game of peek-a-boo. The other film was a musical and depicted musical instruments with an emphasis on a percussion section. As both films were presented side by side in front of the infants, the sound tracks alternated from film to film. The result: the infants tended to watch the film appropriate to the sound track of the moment.

Another experiment along the same lines: the infants were shown two films of toy animals being lifted and dropped on the ground at different intervals. As each animal hit the ground, a large percussion sound, a thump, or a gong, was produced. Since the animals were lifted and dropped at different rates, the accompanying sound track consisted of percussion sounds occurring in different rhythms. Could four-month-old infants turn their attention to the film and its corresponding sound track? Indeed, they could, and did with additional flourishes the experimenters hadn't anticipated. In general, the infants when presented with a sound track alone immediately honed in on the appropriate movie even when they had no previous exposure to either film. The infants, it seems, could recognize and remember a temporal pattern and subsequently match it to a particular film. With such an experiment, we're edging very closely, indeed, to the "roundness" of the sphere.

In similar experiments carried out by infant researchers worldwide, infants have turned out to be wiser than most of the investigators dared to suggest. "Folklore" or "old wives' tales" seem suddenly not so foolish, so unreliable. Infants can tell who speaks, can separate mothers from fathers, and not simply perceive a mother/father amalgam. This, too, has been proved. In the experiment the mother was slightly nervous and the father impatient because he was forced out of his office and into the company of "baby doctors." Both sat silently before their baby, neither speaking, on the orders of the researcher.

Suddenly the room was filled with the recorded voice of only one of the parents, the mother, emanating from a source between and equidistant from the mother and father. Whom do you think baby of three and a half months looked toward? Suddenly the mother became less anxious, the father less impatient to be back at work. They smiled and congratulated each other on having the good judgment to have produced such a genius!

In other experiments toys are placed in the hands of an eight month old with a screen in front of the baby so that what's felt can't be seen. The object is made to produce a captivating sound. Later the infant is shown two objects. It isn't allowed to touch them, only to see them, neither of which is visually familiar. Almost unfailingly the infant reaches for the toy that it had felt earlier, presumably wanting to hear that captivating sound again. John Locke should have tried such an experiment and could have actually, since nothing in the way of fancy equipment or rejected grant proposals precluded such an experiment. All that was necessary was to reassure a mother in eighteenth-century London that it was proper for a philosopher to maintain such an interest in babies. After all, what does a baby know? And what can the children of the ignorant or the poor teach the Wise or the High and Mighty?

But let me tell you of another experiment Locke would have found even more fascinating, which perhaps would have startled him and no doubt disturbed his sleep and his composure. Babies less than four weeks old are provided with a pacifier either round and smooth or stippled with tiny protuberances on it. After ninety seconds of sucking, the pacifier is taken away in the interest of the "experiment." Can the babies distinguish the smooth from the stippled pacifier from pictures alone? They can. What does it prove? That the neonate is a storer of information, can transform aspects of his world into representations, manipulate these representations, and infer that something felt in the mouth looks a certain way and no other. Piaget would also have trouble with this nipple experiment. The babies didn't perform their feat by perceptually associating the look and feel of the pacifier. It's hard to see something stuck in your mouth, and later nothing was in the mouth when the pictures were flashed on the screen. Whatever associations were formed took place within the baby brain.

Feeling guides seeing, seeing guides reaching, hearing guides looking. The infant observes a toy, reaches for it, expects something to be at the ends of his fingers. The infant hears his mother's voice off to the side and turns expecting his mother and nobody else. All very neat and non-Piagetian except for one troublesome discovery that would have delighted the heart of Piaget because it partially vindicates him.

If the baby reaches for something that appears soft (a nipple) and finds instead that it is hard (a plastic imitation), he expresses no surprise. We reach for an apple on a friend's dining room table only to pick up a plastic imitation more perfect than any apple nature ever intended. Our face registers surprise, embarrassment that we could so easily be duped. Not the baby, however. There are no signs of distress or discomfiture. The baby feels what he feels and nothing else, eschews comparison between what is and what was expected to be. This is very close to Piaget's theory—the baby doesn't realize yet that the sight and feel of an object adhere to a common space and are, in fact, identical aspects of one thing. Our Swiss savant spent his life establishing that such correspondences are only gradually constructed. He missed out or glossed over two important tools the baby employs to establish these correspondences. The baby can guide perception in one sphere (sight, sound, touch) by any one of the others. Second, the infant can identify objects by sight that were once only felt, and vice versa.

Which brings us around to John Locke's dilemma of the blind man forced to choose between the cube and the sphere. If Locke had only consulted the newborn, simply observed what the infant can accomplish between breast and nap, he would have found his answer. Infants can use information from one sense to guide another: sound guides looking and sight guides reaching. The infant may not be surprised at a mismatch (plastic apple) but still can use one receptor (sight) to guide another (reaching for the apple). What happens next differs from infant to adult: the adult is surprised by a mismatch while the baby isn't. That comes later.

"Most indubitably, the blind man would be able to distinguish between these objects," the well-informed ghost of John Locke whispered in my ear but a moment ago.

CHAPTER 43

Emotions

Greek philosophers pacing the shores of the Aegean lectured their followers on the distinction between thoughts and feelings. Many of them became quite emotional on the topic. Other philosophers believed in a distinction between emotions and passionate acts on the one hand, and rational and voluntary acts on the other. Indeed, the word "emotion" can be traced to the Latin *emotus* which roughly translates into "stirred up."

Our judges and wardens, psychiatrists and parole officers, believe in such a distinction today. They employ it to separate those responsible for their actions from those who acted in an *emotional* state and can be set free to get emotional again and perhaps return at a later point for yet another determination of their emotionality. Until recently emotions couldn't be measured in any satisfactory way. A man's pulse might rise when he gets stirred up but the same thing happens if he wins the lottery or his girlfriend finally stops saying, no, no, no and offers yes, yes, yes instead. As a result of such difficulties one psychologist characterized the emotions as a "wastebasket category of behavior" (to all accounts a most "stirred up" man, himself, whenever the conversation drifted onto the topic of emotions).

Darwin was unemotional when it came to emotions; he thought and brooded on the matter, as his biographers described the process. But most of all, Darwin did what he was best at: watched and observed. In 1872 Darwin's broodings and observations took form in *The Expression of the Emotions in Man and Animal,* a book on how to relate facial expressions and bodily postures to emotional states. As always, Darwin was interested in what these things could tell him about evolution. When a dog growls, bares its teeth, arches its back, and raises its hair and tail, it is inviting somebody to kindly withdraw. A moment later when wagging its tail, barking, and jumping about that same dog is putting forth an invitation to approach. Such behavior, Darwin claimed, promotes species survival: the show of hostility frightens off enemies or competitors, approach behavior facilitates social interaction. So far so good. No one, not even a Greek philosopher, would argue that a growling dog is not communicating a message to "stay away" even though that same philosopher would argue to the death about whether the dog possessed a mind capable of deciding for the best possible reasons who should approach and who should stay put. But Darwin and the Greek philosophers might both agree that it was an "instinct" (a circumlocution if there ever was one).

Twenty-three years after the publication of Darwin's book, emotions played an explanatory role in the theories of Sigmund Freud. "Strangulated affect" was how he accounted for the formation of neurotic symptoms in hysteric patients. Later, Freud recanted all this and wound up proposing that on the whole difficulties could be traced to instinct or drive. This shifted the positions of the cart and the horse: emotion was the *result* of increases or decreases in drive rather than the *cause* of symptom formation.

In the meantime, mothers who didn't care a whit about Freud or Darwin continued their own investigations and drew their own conclusions. Some babies are "happy" babies, don't give trouble, and smile a lot. Others have "nasty" tempers and raise general all-around hell when they don't get what they want exactly when they want it. Babies can be sad, too, infecting their mothers with a solicitude to correct whatever situation it was that rendered their little one so pensive. Of course, all of this was put down to the mother's imagination—the "projection" of the mother's own attitude onto her offspring, and so on.

In the nineteen forties, fifties, and sixties, baby researchers were conducting experiments that proved mothers were right about the emotionality of their infants. Social smiling, separation and stranger anxiety, fear of heights, Spitz's research on anaclitic depression—any and all of these research projects, when properly interpreted, confirmed that infants are capable of emotions, can be "stirred up," as our Greek predecessors put it.

But with few exceptions the researchers failed to draw the proper conclusions from their investigations. The baby cried when suspended over a height; this merely proved that the baby could measure depth and perceive distance. But the crucial observation went unobserved: the baby was frightened, mad as hell, irritated into a paroxysm by the perfidy of the experimenter and his meddling. Indeed, it was usually the mother, not the experimenter, who made the proper interpretation —little Mary or Reginald became even more of a handful than usual to deal with upon returning home after the conclusion of the experiment.

The mother's recognition of her baby's emotional responses was nothing more than a down-home, no-frills-attached reading of the facial and vocal expression of emotion, the same thing done by Darwin minus the ponderousness and the musings on evolution. Babies who are angry look angry, sound angry, move their arms and hands in ways that communicate to the sensitive observer, "If I could only get my hands on you!" In short, emotions can be "read," in the manner of Darwin, from the careful observations of bodily states.

In the 1970s researchers started showing pictures of people in different emotional states to members of various literate cultures. Later they did the same thing with members of illiterate cultures. But the initial efforts were directed to those who could read and write and, presumably, see things pretty much along the same lines as could the experimenters themselves. After looking at the pictures, the subjects chose from a list of emotional terms the one that best described the picture. The results indicated that people everywhere agreed on the facial patterns typical of happiness, sadness, surprise, fear, anger, and disgust.

With illiterates the findings were the same, only the research methods differed. These subjects were requested to pose the expression consequent to the death of a child. They also were asked to select the appropriate photograph to go along with happiness, sadness, disgust, and anger. On the basis of this study, the researcher, Paul Ekman, asserted that four emotions could be reliably recognized across cultures irrespective of literacy, the language spoken, or familiarity with researchers and their methods: sadness, happiness, disgust, and anger. Although Ekman never said as much, his work provides some support for those philosophers who speak of a "human nature." Without waxing too philosophically, Ekman's work provides a powerful argument, if such be needed, that events such as the death of a child imply a certain emotional "stirring up" of its parents whether the parents reside in a mud hut or in Buckingham Palace. Overall, a message emerges in this research too obvious for disputation: pain is pain wherever in the world it occurs. When people hurt, their faces show it unless, of course, they make a deliberate effort to conceal how much they're hurting. In essence, some emotions can be reliably recognized from changes in facial patterning. Once this was established the door was open for hordes of Ph.D. students, statisticians, psychologists, ethologists, and other generally unemotional people to codify, set up rules, measure and mark off in logical no-nonsense units the width and breadth of human emotions. "Facial measurement systems" emerged which merely formalized the unsystematized observations of sensitive people everywhere: sadness implies a pulling down of the corners of the mouth, a pushing up of the chin, a raising of the inner corners of the eyebrows to form an inverted *V.* Eyebrows, forehead, eyes, eyelids, nose, cheeks, mouth—each of these regions assumes a distinct facial muscle pattern according to the emotion ascendant at the time. Each of the fundamental emotions can be identified with specific and exclusive movements in these key facial areas. At this point emotions became very scientific, neat, logical—no more guessing or relying on the testimony of Mama or Papa when it came to whether or not little Reginald is having a temper tantrum.

Facial muscle patterns as indicators of emotional states are more reliable in infants than in adults. For one thing one can't always guess how a grown person may emotionally respond to a given situation: the mother of the bride laughs and smiles at her new son-in-law whom she likes, the mother of the groom sobs, fears, and is angered by her new daughter-in-law whom she doesn't think she likes, not yet at any rate.

In addition, cultures exert a powerful effect on how "stirred up" we allow ourselves to become. The Japanese, on the average, are much more facially expressive when tested alone than when tested in the presence of other Japanese. According to the experimenter, the Japanese are given to masking negative emotions, hiding their dislike or their impatience in the interest of social lubricity. Infants don't do any of these things, they are not yet convinced that they're part of a culture, and even if they were convinced, they might still prefer to blurt out their feelings at the moment. "Only fools and children say what they think" goes the old proverb. That proverb maker should have included infants as well, since their "saying" remains restricted to the totally honest, unalloyed expression of their state of "stirred-upness" at the moment. One final difference between adults and infants: infants are less likely to employ complex combinations of emotions. When they're angry they're angry and not angry-disgusted—disgust combines with anger only after a period of exposure to the real world that no baby has yet undergone.

Take a seven month old and bestow on it the largesse of a teething biscuit. Now take away the biscuit while measuring anger-related facial movements. This experiment carried out in 1982 by three infant researchers was aimed at providing something every mother knows but no one had so far yet proven. Before the removal of the biscuit, only 3 percent of the facial movements related to anger when the experimenter approached. After the removal, the anger-related facial movements increased to 29 percent when he approached. As the trials continued the percentage continued to mount. A mother has reason on her side when she says that she doesn't want to "upset" her baby. Before this experiment was terminated, the babies were prepared in advance for their tormenters: the anger component had risen from 3 to 32 percent when the experimenter came into view. "Forewarned is forearmed."

A similar effect of frustration-producing anger was shown in another experiment involving one, four, and seven month olds. In this instance, one of the infants' arms was restrained. One third of the four month olds and the seven month olds, as measured by facial patterns, became angry at the restraint. The key question is, of course, how far down the developmental scale can one proceed. Infants less than two hours old display distinct facial patterns when presented with pleasant-tasting substances (sugar) as compared to salty or bitter substances. An impartial observer can correctly identify the substance given to the neonate on the basis of facial expression alone. But probably no more should be made of such an experiment than "the newborn knows what it likes and what it doesn't."

Liking and disliking, at least on the conscious level, require the participation of the cerebral cortex, particularly the language centers. These are imperfectly developed in the newborn. Instead, likes and dislikes are linked to the subcortical structures, the limbic system which provides the biological underpinnings of our emotions. These are intact and functioning in the newborn. In time the connections between limbic system and cortex will be functioning. In time Reginald will know that he dislikes something, will screw his face and forehead into a frown, and will be able to explode into a giant No that apprises his mother of his feelings on *that* particular subject. But to the careful observer that No is redundant—the baby's facial expression says it all.

CHAPTER 44

Emotions and the Infant Brain

In Laboratory A, an unemployed actress is earning rent money by making faces. The faces, varying from sad to glad at the experimenter's whim, are displayed to an audience of ten month olds who are lined up one at a time, placed on their mamas' laps, and pointed toward a video screen. Half of the audience views the happy faces, half is exposed to the unemployed actress-as-tragedian.

Gently applied to the infants' scalps are electrodes which record brain activity. Exposure to the positive emotions leads to enhanced left-sided frontal activity. Sad-Face elicits right-sided frontal activity.

From this study (and others involving depressed patients and stroke patients) investigators have arrived at a theory that, when it comes to emotions, the two brain hemispheres perform a delicate balancing act. States of positive emotion show, as with the infants in the study mentioned above, left anterior activation. States of negative emotion are linked with right-hemisphere activities. Further, these emotional states can be reliably detected in infants by simply looking at facial expressions.

An infant two to three days of age will make a gesture of disgust when an unpleasant-tasting solution is placed in its mouth. Substitute a sugar solution and the look shifts to one of interest. Now do the taste test with EEG electrodes in place. Nice-tasting substances are associated with left-hemisphere activity; sour materials lead to right-sided activity.

Interest and disgust are only two of a range of possible primary emotions which include joy, sadness, anger, contempt, surprise, fear, distress-pain, guilt. Why would only two of these, interest and disgust, occur in the newborn?

According to the two researchers who carried out the taste experiments, the emotional expression of very young infants is limited by the lack of communication between the two brain hemispheres. Maturation of the axons from one hemisphere to another proceeds at a snail's pace. Indeed, the process isn't completed until adolescence. The earliest emotions (interest and disgust) elicited, therefore, "may be primarily under unilateral hemisphere control and may not depend upon the functional integrity of the cerebral commissures," explain Drs. Nathan Fox and Richard Davidson, the two psychologists who carried out the taste experiments.

At this point, it appears that hemisphere connections, communications, and the repertoire of emotions are enhanced in tandem. For instance, the emergence of fear and sadness toward the end of the first year might relate, say Fox and Davidson, to the enhancement of information transfer between the hemispheres. Before this, the components of fear are present but simply not organized.

In 1978 fear in a one-month-old baby was inferred by a researcher on the basis of the baby's facial expression. Although some might question the value of such a single observation, no one in the field of infant behavior denies that newborns can imitate facial expressions of happiness, surprise, and sadness. They do not produce these expressions spontaneously, however. It's as if the components are present waiting to be organized, a task the infant cannot carry out until a certain maturation is achieved in the fibers linking one hemisphere to the other. But nature is kind in ordaining this delay. The facial components of sadness can be detected in three month olds who have been abused. How much easier it is for us to believe that the infant only *looks* sad and isn't really experiencing sadness as we would experience it. But in writing these words, I feel vaguely dissatisfied . . . detecting a note of sophistry. After all, how can we really be sure?

Baby A is cuddled and loved, just like all other babies who enjoy cuddling and loving. No sadness. Baby B is beaten and jarred about. Looks sad. Yet "isn't really sad," the researchers tell us. Pardon me, Good Professors, if I withhold a final opinion on this distressing matter.

Less controversial than facial expressions are the various "motor behaviors" that accompany the emotions. From birth, infants will turn toward an interesting stimulus and will pull away from something that may hurt. Too much billing and cooing, too much talk, too much physical closeness—some infants won't meet your gaze under such circumstances. The infant will look away when he or she has had enough. Some parents can't abide such dismissals. They take things personally. "My baby doesn't like me," they mutter. Unfortunately, such mutterings often lead to a corollary that isn't spoken and barely sensed except by the baby. "I don't like my baby either."

Babies, like adults, differ in how much closeness they can tolerate.

When that tolerance has been exceeded, the baby gets grumpy, fractious, and wants to crawl away.

Locomotion, eye-hand coordination, fine motor control—these are mechanisms by which interest is expressed.

Locomotion away from, gaze aversion, head turning—by such means does the baby create distance between himself and his persecutors.

Notice that crawling toward and crawling away from serve polar emotions: "Let me come closer" or "I want to get away from *you!*"

Place an infant of six months on the edge of a visual cliff. If he can crawl, the situation will frighten him. But before the age of crawling the infant shows no fear and doesn't seem to understand what it's all about. Crawling ability, it seems, develops in tempo with fear, a curious association explained by one experimenter: "Infants who are prelocomotive are less likely to be out of reach or sight of the care giver and therefore less likely to be in danger."

Psychoanalyst and infant researcher John Bowlby notes three emotional milestones accompanying the ability to crawl: fear of the unknown (principally strangers); the capacity to protest separation from the him or her important at the moment (the "care giver"); and increased curiosity about the world coupled with a desire to crawl around a bit and explore it. Using these three indicators, Bowlby can label the "security of an infant's attachment."

Exploration and security: two contrapuntal melodies that begin in infancy and continue over a lifetime. The infant reaches out, grasps, crawls, then clutches part of the world to himself. At the same time he looks back at his mother, doesn't totally relinquish the sight and "feel" of her presence.

An infant who can crawl has achieved a level of brain organization above and beyond his noncrawling counterpart. To crawl one must use all four limbs, coordinating them with a balance and rhythm. Both sides of the brain, both hemispheres, must be in communication in order to do that. Development of the nerve tracks linking the two hemispheres makes this possible. Is the same linkage responsible for the emergence of fear, the inevitable accompaniment of the ability to crawl? Fox and Davidson believe so. "In the case of fear, evidence indicates that locomotion is a necessary prerequisite for its activation and may thus require a certain level of functional hemispheric integrity for its full blown expression."

Missing from all of this is an important human capacity: language. Does it make any difference in response to fear whether an infant can understand and use language?

Preliminary investigations indicate that it does. Eighteen month olds

who can speak are less likely to get upset when separated from famil-
iars. Indeed, heightened verbal fluency is directly correlated with the
infant's ability to inhibit his distress. From this finding has emerged a
theory that will gladden the hearts and fatten the pocketbooks of
psychiatrists everywhere. Through the use of language it seems possible to inhibit some of life's more unpleasant emotions. It's speculated
that the left hemisphere's language capacity serves as a check on the
tendency of the right hemisphere to overemotionalize. Inhibition of
emotion in adults is postulated to work in a similar way. In those
individuals with well-developed interhemispheric connections, the left
hemisphere is able to inhibit the emotionality of the right hemisphere.
According to this admittedly speculative explanation, emotional disturbances are correlated not with fantasies, but with an absence of
regulation between the hemispheres.

"The capacity to inhibit negative affect is a major milestone which
occurs in the middle of the second year of life," write Fox and Davidson. "We suggest that two major changes in brain function may play an
important role in the development of this form of affective regulation:
(1) increased functional activity of the left hemisphere reflected in the
onset of language; and (2) increased functional integrity of the com-
missural pathways."

Simply put, brain development, movement, and emotion develop
apace. In time, brain maturation is enhanced. As a result, the infant
shows a correspondingly enhanced ability to reach out, interact with,
and explore.

At first are only interest and disgust—the product of one hemisphere or the other.

Next are fear and sadness—both dependent on the two hemispheres
working together. This also makes movement possible.

Finally is the capacity to master fear and other states of upset: the left
hemisphere inhibiting regions in the right hemisphere via crossing
fibers in the corpus callosum.

Is the above formulation true? At this point neuroscientists aren't
sure. Certainly infant development is consistent with such a hypothesis. Nevertheless, the schema remains just that: a hypothesis.

CHAPTER 45

Maternal Instinct

One person sits in an experimental laboratory and reads a series of letters of the alphabet to a companion. Instead of enumerating the letters in a dull, monotonous manner, however, the speaker reads the words in varying tones of voice. At one moment he "projects" pain, determination, fear, or joy. This experiment—actually carried out in 1939—showed that 75 to 91 percent of the emotions attempted by the speaker can be accurately identified by the listener. A repeat experiment twenty years later by other investigators confirmed the earlier results with ten readily recognized emotions: anger, fear, happiness, jealousy, love, nervousness, pride, sadness, satisfaction, and sympathy.

In another experiment along the same lines, actors or actresses read standard passages in different tones of voice. Indifference was accurately identified 87 percent of the time, anger and grief 78 percent, contempt 84 percent.

Students of human deception (Intelligence agents) have known for some time that a liar can be unmasked much more easily via a telephone conversation than he can in a face-to-face encounter. Presumably the capacity to hide our emotions is much better developed when it comes to facial expression as compared to tones of voice. The investigators speak of "leakage" in the social sphere which can be successfully contained by someone determined to "keep a stiff upper lip."

If a person suffers a stroke in the right hemisphere, he or she often loses the ability to comprehend the emotional meaning conveyed by tones of voice. In other instances the afflicted person can comprehend the intonations of other people but can't generate any emotions in his or her own speech—a curious series of findings. The emotions, it seems, are conveyed not only by what one says but even more by the voice—tones, vigor, resonance, and so on.

Infants, too, convey feelings by vocal inflection. Indeed, in the absence of language their oral communication is limited to this means. In a whimsically entitled paper, "The Natural History of Crying and other Vocalizations in Infancy," infant psychiatrist Peter Wolff separated infant cries into three groups: the anger cry (loud and prolonged); the hunger cry (rhythmic and repetitive); and the pain cry (sudden onset, an initial long cry and extended breath holding). Wolff played to mothers tape recordings of the different cries of their infants. The pain cry produced alarm and apprehension. The mother set out immediately to the infant's room. The anger cry was also effective in mobilizing the mother.

Infant cries are as individual as fingerprints. In a study in Glasgow, twenty-seven mothers volunteered to participate in a test of whether or not each could recognize her own baby's cries. The mother had to distinguish among twenty cries (hearing only fifteen seconds of the cry) and she had to recognize her infant's among cries of five babies other than her own. The main result of this Glasgow study was that more than 80 percent of the mothers could recognize their own baby's cries even though the infants were no more than eight days old and, in some cases, the mothers had had little exposure to their infants' crying.

Mother recognizes Baby, Baby recognizes Mother—the sound waves from Baby's vocal cords strike a recognizable tune on Mother's tympanic membrane. Screeching is transformed into a meaningful neural code which wends its way into the maternal brain. What could be the wisdom of such an arrangement? Sociobiologists might answer, "So that the mother can recognize the sounds of distress and rescue her infant and not another, thus perpetuating her own genes."

A fantasy forms. A fire. A horde of mothers charging into the nursery where each one picks up her infant and dashes out through the flames. Too melodramatic you say? Not close enough, you think, to the warmth a new mother feels inside at the sight or sound of her baby?— that is, if she feels that warmth at all in regard to her baby. Is there a "maternal instinct"? Certainly if such an instinct exists it doesn't currently enjoy popularity. Social influences are more important on molding a mother's attitude toward her infant, sociologists tell us. Psychiatrists add confirmation, encountering on a daily basis mothers who don't feel particularly maternal and would give up their infants if they had the chance, sometimes seek out the chance, ignoring or shutting off or perhaps never hearing at all that meaningful neural code.

"Until the murders she was nothing other than a model parent . . . a doting mother," said the prosecuting attorney about a thirty-year-old mother who had murdered her two small children. "It appears that the killings are the result of some form of sickness, be it mental or emotional," stated the prosecutor. Presumably one must attempt some explanation, however weak, for such a "distortion of the maternal instinct." What did this mother feel when she heard her infant cry? Once again we face the mystery of that meaningful neural code which is never meaningful in precisely the same way from one mother to another, could never be, and perhaps shouldn't be.

Infant vocalization conveys more than any researcher could ever divine. Pitch and tone and timbre can convey messages regarding the states of an infant's nutrition, breathing, and likelihood of recovery from illness. But it's certain that much more is conveyed, adumbrated, than can be precisely described. That meaningful neural code can only be *experienced* and in a manner that will forever allude the researcher's best efforts at explication.

CHAPTER 46

Empathy

One-year-old Johnny or Jennifer is placed at the end of a "visual cliff," a piece of Plexiglas suspended over a checkerboard pattern several feet below. At a certain moment, Johnny or Jennifer looks downward, sees the floor four feet below, and stops crawling lest he or she tumble down into the apparent chasm. Sight and touch are thrown into conflict. Sight says, "Halt." Touch detects no danger—the Plexiglas is firm beneath the hands and knees and feet of the crawling baby. Vision wins out . . . seeing is believing . . . Johnny or Jennifer stops crawling, starts crying, freezes up, and reaches for Mother.

Modify the visual cliff a bit. Make the drop-off not quite so threatening. A curious response is produced: Johnny or Jennifer looks up toward Mama. What to do? At this point things get interesting in the recent experiments of Denver, Colorado, infant researchers Bob Emde and Joseph Campos.

If Mama looks scared, Baby stays put. With an encouraging word, Baby sets out across the Plexiglas, the combination of touch plus maternal assurance winning out over the less preemptory warning of a visual system that has been traduced. Mother, Emde, and Campos are in collusion; the good doctors have suggested that Mother skillfully and deliberately *pretend* an emotion of fear, force a facial expression that would have gratified the heart of that grandiloquent theatrical director, Konstantin Stanislavsky. ("Do every physical action precisely, clearly, logically.")

If Mother is a successful actress and projects fear, not one baby out of seventeen tested will cross over the apparent drop-off. But if Mother looks happy and projects a "nothing to fear" mien, fifteen of nineteen babies will cross. After some practice, Mother discovers that she can widen her repertoire, perhaps be judged worthy of an Oscar. She tries additional emotions. Anger: only 11 percent of a group of infants will cross. Interest: 75 percent of the Johnnies and Jennifers wind up decid-

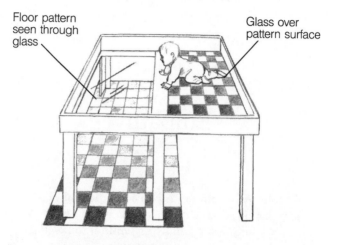

The Visual Cliff

An infant crawls across a heavy sheet of glass toward its mother. Under the glass is a checkerboard pattern. Halfway across the pattern is no longer close to the glass surface but is several feet below.

ing there's nothing to fear. Sadness? Here is a complex emotion indeed. Is Mama sad for herself or for her tiny tot about to plunge over the cliff? Baby can't decide and, therefore, vacillates (only about one third crossed and judging from their facial expression weren't too pleased with the journey). Additional research along the same lines demonstrates that the emotional expressions of other adults, not simply the mother, seem to determine whether the baby will start over the cliff or merely sit at the starting point and fret. "Emotions are social regulators," say the infant researchers. "Indeed, they are," agrees the mother who, along with the rest of us, can look back on a lifetime of deciding what to say or do or not to say or do on the basis of the facial expressions of other people at the moment.

Someone brings a strange toy into a room where a one year old is sitting with Mother. Mother poses a joyful face; Baby approaches, touches the toy and explores the toy. If Mother expresses concern—wrinkles her brow, narrows her eyes into a "watch out it might hurt" expression—Baby won't go near that toy for all the other toys in the wide world. "Emotions are social regulators."

Every good actor or actress expresses as much by the voice as by the face. The mother posing in the laboratory is no different. When asked to speak angrily, fearfully, or joyfully, most mothers can manage a passable performance. An eight month old will stop crawling to a toy if its mother's voice expresses any hint that things might not bode well. Johnny's or Jennifer's hesitancy can be reversed. They'll start crawling to the toy and grasp it if Mother manages a happy voice.

In a "don't talk to strangers" experiment, Drs. Emde and Campos explored the effects of a mother's uttering an unfriendly "Hello" accompanied by a frown at the entrance of a stranger to the room. In this "mother-wary" situation, eight and a half month olds stop smiling, begin to fret, and their heartbeats speed up. But if a mother utters a happy "Hello" accompanied by a smile and gestures that imply "Glad to see you," her baby's heart rate drops, her baby often smiles back.

On the basis of such experiments, infant researchers have turned psychology on its head. Emotions are now considered important again and are thought to determine how people behave, even how they perceive the world.

Talk to people fearful that their houses will be broken into and they'll explain the effects of fright on their interpretation of creaks on the stairs or other unexplained noises in the night. But the testimony of "everyone" isn't enough to satisfy a researcher's requirement for certainty. Only experiments can do that by providing the necessary objectivity: a mother communicating a state-of-the-world to a nine month old by her facial expression and tones of voice.

Three month olds get seriously upset when they encounter their mothers sitting stone-faced and unreactive (once again at the instigation of a researcher). The infant in distress looks to its mother, smiles. If she doesn't smile back, the infant simply gives up, "Something's wrong with Mama."

Researchers have further encouraged the "manipulation" of a mother's emotions; they've told her to pose a depressed face, speak in a lugubrious tone of voice, hardly move at all, or sit like a Great Stone Face—the very personification of depression. Babies haven't enjoyed looking at their mothers as sourpusses. They've looked away, started bellowing, darted from one toy to another without much joy in the process.

No one is certain when a baby starts responding to its mother in all of her individuality. Some infants hardly have a chance or a choice on the matter, having been forced to settle down with a "caretaker" or cast of "caretakers." But if an infant has that chance to enjoy his or her mother in all of her individuality, he or she will recognize the mother's voice, although only in its natural state. If mothers and researchers are in collusion again, with the mother modifying her voice to suit the whims and instructions of the white coats, her baby won't recognize her voice. If she takes on a monotonous, deadly, dull, "Have a good day" kind of voice, after that advice has been uttered for the hundredth time on a day that's been anything but good, her baby won't respond, probably can't respond. It's likely that the mother speaking in her everyday voice is conveying emotion and it is emotion that little Johnny at six weeks can detect, emotion hidden within and behind and interspersed throughout the words that have yet to become meaningful. It's likely that such inferences on the part of the six week old depend on the limbic subcortical connections, which aren't even particularly "human" since even a pet cat or dog responds to the emotions concealed within the words, "Scoot. Out of the room now," said casually, versus the peremptoriness of "Get the ——— out!"

Scientists have come up with a label to describe this process, having borrowed it from poets and psychologists: empathy.

When only a few weeks of age, babies resonate to the emotions surrounding them. Newborns cry when they hear other infants crying, perhaps the earliest response in kind to the distress of another human being, although that is probably reading more into things than the facts justify. Yet what other explanation would you prefer? Not to cry when we perceive others crying, not to share their distress is undoubtedly a learned response (perhaps we would all be better off if we hadn't mastered quite so thoroughly that particular bit of learning).

Responding to the distress of another occurs along a continuum of increasing complexity, says University of Michigan baby researcher Martin Hoffman. A person observing another experiencing an emotion may be reminded of similar emotions, "vicarious emotions," as Hoffman described them.

As far back as 1906 it was suggested by a German psychologist that we humans are capable of experiencing an innate identical response to another person's expression of emotion. Seventy-seven years later other psychologists, Americans, pounced on this theory and incorporated it into their own theory about the infant. An "emotional resonance" exists between people, they assert, which makes it possible to directly experience the emotions of another. Since all of this occurs in early infancy, an exciting possibility presents itself: appreciation of the emotional expression of other people may start to develop during early babyhood. The roots of compassion, love, "doing unto others as you would have them do unto you," "put yourself in my shoes"—while the words used to describe these processes come much later—these underlying feelings start when we're still in diapers, perhaps haven't even made it out of the hospital nursery as yet.

A baby cries in Nursery B—two others join in in a chorus—the nurses check their watches. "Not feeding time yet, surely," but the crying continues and spreads to additional tiny ones. What are these babies *feeling?* We adults aren't certain, separated as we are by such a vast chasm of time—too many words get in our way—only a baby can experience exactly what another baby is feeling.

CHAPTER 47

Infants as Teachers

Since parents are older than their infants it seems reasonable (but isn't) to assume that the parents must be teaching their infants instead of the other way around. Actually infants make great teachers. But as with a lot of teachers the lessons may go unlearned simply because the students aren't listening. This has made for some dogmatic and wrongheaded assumptions about why babies act the way they do, what they "want," how they experience the world around them, and how they eventually "turn out."

Over the past fifty years at least four different theories on infant care have been elevated to the status of Sacred Dogma. At various times during this half century mothers have clutched to their breasts copies of books written by bestseller-seeking savants intent on conveying one of the following four tenets on how to raise little Johnny or Jennifer.

In the 1930s (when Freudianism was at its peak, hard economic times vying with memories of days only a decade earlier when money "flowed like water") mothers were presented with a series of stark alternatives: breast- versus bottle-feeding; demand versus scheduled feeding; gradual versus abrupt weaning; easy versus authoritarian bowel and bladder training. If things went well and the mothers made the correct choices regarding these matters, normal physical and emotional development could be guaranteed for their infants. But woe to the mother whose child became "fixated," immersed, as it were, in a kind of psychological quicksand.

Distinct personality traits were linked with conflicts around feeding (the "oral" personality marked by dependency or verbal aggression) and elimination (the "anal" personality—picture an octogenarian who is stingy, grumpy, compulsive, and as unyielding in his behavior and opinions as he was years earlier with his stool).

If nothing else, this first theory provided a framework for the perpetuation of maternal guilt. Mothers lived in fear that they weren't "doing the right thing" for their infants. Years later their offspring could justify and amplify that guilt, blaming their personal vicissitudes on earlier maternal mistakes involving the breast or potty. This first theory came to an abrupt end in the mid-sixties with the appearance of an authoritative review that showed no apparent relationship between the physical care of an infant and its later personality.

A second and less counterintuitive theory emerged in the 1940s based on the studies of maternal deprivation I have mentioned earlier (principally those of René Spitz). Mother love in infancy is as essential for mental health as vitamins and proteins are for physical health, as one researcher phrased it. But this theory also missed an important point: adopted infants failed to show any harmful effects or developmental lags. Clearly it isn't the mother per se, rather the presence of one or more people willing and able to supply the kinds of attention and care normally associated with mothers. But what aspects of maternal care are the most important so the tiny tot can be guaranteed to grow up "well adjusted"?

"Contact comfort" played a central role in the third theory based on animal research that indicated the positive effects of handling on emotional development and intellectual performance (measured in rats by the "intellectual task" of correctly running a maze). In the 1960s and 1970s when this theory was "the rage" mothers suffered a demotion: "provider of stimulation" replaced the lovely and evocative mother.

If an adult, any adult, holds a baby to its shoulders, the infant becomes more alert and, in the cumbersome language of research papers, "extracts more stimulation from its environment." Even the soothing effects of the mother's heartbeat were reinterpreted; the infant responded, claimed one researcher, not as a result of an association between heartbeat and a nirvana-like state in the uterus but simply on the basis of the heartbeat's continuous repetitive qualities (presumably a metronome would do as well). Mothers, convinced by this third theory, could be found in toy stores buying up mobiles which, they were assured, could be counted on to induce intellectual growth and refine fine motor control. One researcher even went so far as to suggest that infants responded to their mothers simply based on the contingency between the infant's cooing or crying and the mother's caretaking efforts. It was speculated that there was nothing uniquely human about the process. Indeed, one researcher claimed that infants became "emotionally responsive" to their mobiles to the extent that the mothers employed mobiles as "surrogate baby-sitters." Removal of the mobiles led to infant distress, presumably an indication that at least some infants seemed to prefer their mobiles to their mothers.

But subsequent research rescued the mother from the status of a mere biologic mobile. While infants crave stimulation, they also need creature comfort, warmth, cuddling, and a living presence at least once in a while. Indeed, infants, like their adult counterparts, don't fancy interactions that go only one way. How many times can an infant slap at a mobile before something in its makeup yearns for the mobile to slap back somehow? This recognition that all social intercourse involves some degree of reciprocity heralded the fourth and currently most popular theory of infant development.

Work in the wilds led to the development of the science of ethology, the study of the naturalistic behavior of animals with emphasis on inborn determinants. According to the ethologists, social behavior proceeds according to evolutionary principles, mainly the tenet that adaptive behavior increases the fitness of the individual. An infant's response is, therefore, best understood, says the ethologist, when viewed from the perspective of how a helpless, totally dependent creature manages to interest an independent adult in taking care of it.

Since infants are incapable of self-care, it is necessary for them to get into close physical contact with adults who can carry out the functions the infants can't manage for themselves. Further, since infants initially can't walk or crawl, contact depends on the development of a signaling system: crying, smiling, head aversion ("Now I've had enough"), waking, or sleeping (the ultimate turn-off). As with any signaling system, it must operate in two directions. If the infant cries but no one listens, smiles but no one notices, the "evolutionary fitness" of the individual isn't likely to be advanced very much.

Crying infants evoke blood pressure and pulse elevations in their parents. When the infant smiles, blood pressure and pulse rate decrease. The same pattern occurs in the infant's older brother or sister, a neat demonstration that parenthood isn't necessary for the occurrence of these response patterns. Minus the scientific mumbo jumbo, nobody fancies a crying infant, and almost everyone is tickled when a little baby smiles up at him.

Which parent do you think demonstrates the greatest responsiveness (measured by pulse and blood pressure alterations) to its infant's crying or smiling? Mother? Father? For those of an androgynous turn of mind the results must be very gratifying, indeed.

"There were no sex differences in any of the psychophysiologic measures of responsiveness to infant signals," wrote infant researchers Ann Frodi and Michael Lamb. "Our data suggest that there are no biologically determined sex differences in responsiveness to infants but that societal expectations and pressures serve to bring about sex differences."

As a result of infant signaling and adult responsiveness to these signals, infants form attachments, ethologists suggest, to those people who have consistently responded to the "move closer," "feed me," "give me more space" communications. Not that these signals are always easy to read, however. For example, seemingly disparate, even contradictory behavior such as smiling followed by crying and at a later point crawling toward—all are aimed at drawing the parent closer, snuggling up, and decreasing distance. On the other side of the aisle, head turning, sleepiness, and gaze aversion—all tend to "turn off," increase distance, and decrease social interaction.

Smile at an infant of three weeks of age, and he'll more than likely smile back. The infant's mother enjoys special privileges in this regard; he'll smile at her a few hours after birth, although this early smile isn't the kind of smile everyone would be willing to recognize and accept as a true, purebred, "no doubt about it" smile.

Stand over an infant only a few hours old and talk to it. Within a few seconds the infant will start to talk back. Gesture replaces words in the infant's earliest communication repertoire. Films of such dialogue reveal an infant moving in synchrony with an adult's words. Both speaker and listener enjoy a kind of dance. As one moves so the other moves, the moves taking place in synchrony with the speaker's voice. We are talking now of very subtle movements. Indeed, if the movements are obvious they might have been noticed centuries ago instead of only in the past decade. "Interactional synchrony" is the jargon term for this interaction. Only the human voice can initiate it. No other auditory stimulus will do. Nor does it seem to make any difference which language is employed. American babies will move in synchrony with a Chinese speaker as quickly as they will to their native English.

Smiling and "interactional synchrony" are two baby performances only recently investigated along lines satisfactory to the scientifically inclined. Both point in the direction of infants as *social* beings—the presence or absence of other people is important.

The mother and infant take turns as Leader and Follower. The infant imitates, moves its arms in synchrony to a human voice. The mother "reads" the baby's signals: "Get me the bottle." Oftentimes the interactions are less peremptory, more playful.

Smiling in infants has been studied more than any other infant performance. And with good reason. The importance of smiling can hardly be overemphasized. Parents when smiled at suddenly change their minds about the 3 A.M. awakenings, the sense of fatigue and annoyance. Coincident with that first smile, parents start feeling special—smiled at, loved in return.

Week one: a smile appears only when the infant is not fully awake, in a twilight between sleep and waking. Stroke the baby's skin, he'll smile. Hum gently and he'll smile.

Week two: the smile is now more specific, broader, involving the eyes and the crinkling of skin around the eyes.

Week three: now the human voice is the most potent activator of the smile response; it is valued over bells or whistles or rattles.

Weeks four and five: the human voice is still the preeminent elicitor of smiles. But not just any voice. The mother's voice is preferred over other female voices. Any female voice is much preferred over the voice of a male. Indeed, when it comes to eliciting an infant's smile, the father's voice usually plays second fiddle to a woman's, even a stranger's, voice.

Week five: the voice is less important now. Even the mother's voice is less potent a smile getter than is the mother's face, particularly her dancing eyes.

Scientists over the last quarter century have set their sights on discovering and understanding the infant's smile. They have learned that smiles involve an interaction. No baby smiles alone for very long.

One experimenter smiled back each time the baby smiled, talked, then picked the baby up. The baby started to smile more, no doubt fancied being picked up. Every time the baby was put down she smiled; she wanted to be picked up again and had learned how to bring about that positional change. The scientists describe this as an operant conditioning based on a contingency relationship: the baby smiles, the adult picks up the baby, the baby likes it, the baby is put down, the baby smiles again. You'll notice that this behavioral sequence is initiated by the baby and not the adult. The infant is, in fact, eliciting a certain behavior from the adult rather than the other way around.

Imagine an adult who doesn't feel good inside each time the infant smiles, doesn't reach down to pick up the baby, doesn't talk, or doesn't respond in some way. The contingency arrangement is broached. The baby feels cheated, doesn't smile, looks glum. Most distressing of all is the loss, for the baby, of the sense of power—the infant reached out with a smile, the world in the form of another human being didn't reach back.

Power as a determinant of infant behavior? It can be proven and was proven a decade ago. Eight-week-old infants placed in cribs discovered that each time they moved their heads mobiles suspended over their cribs moved in synchrony. Baby movement produced mobile movement. By the second day the babies smiled a lot; they enjoyed the spectacle produced by their own head movement, enjoyed the power that accompanied being able to make something happen. In nearby cribs the mobiles moved independently of the infants' head movements. If the babies moved, the mobiles might or might not stir. No particular smiling response resulted from these infants who perhaps felt powerless.

Encouraged in these results, the experimenter, J. S. Watson, set up the mobile arrangement for an eight month old who never smiled at anyone or anything. After two hours of head-movement-causes-mobile-movement, the infant was smiling and brightening hearts, allowing some measure of hope in experimenters and parents that perhaps everything wasn't irretrievably lost at eight months. The baby could smile and would smile if smiling could be linked to the sense of power.

Combine the mobile results with the contingency arrangement I just mentioned (the mother smiled whenever the baby smiled, talked and picked the baby up). Smiling seems dependent on some type of response to a living, breathing person. Peek-a-boo games elicit the same smiling. The mother's face is hidden and suddenly reappears with a laugh and a smile. The baby laughs and smiles back. In all these exchanges the sensitivity of the mother is paramount. Cold, preoccupied mothers elicit few smiles from their infants.

For example, imagine another infant who signals "approach" by smiling. The parent is preoccupied—things went shabbily at the office earlier in the day, dinner hasn't yet been started. As a result of the parent's lack of responsiveness, the signal isn't reciprocated. Does the infant "try harder" or does it simply withdraw?

Shift the pieces around a bit. The mother coos at her infant at the end of a long day at the office. The baby isn't having any of it: he turns away, closes his eyes, lets out a nasty screech. Does the mother try harder? Should she? Or isn't it easiest to simply turn away and return to the kitchen to prepare dinner?

In both of these situations the infant and mother are drifting apart. The "fit" between what the infant wants and what the mother is willing to give is mirrored by the infant's lack of responsiveness to the mother. Communication, signaling systems, "evolutionary fitness"—all depend on a two-way communication. (If all this seems painfully obvious, contrast it with the mechanical explanations I mentioned about the mother or father doing or not doing certain things at certain times and, therefore, affecting the infant in certain ways. In fact, the infant and parents "do" and "fail to do" certain things to each other. There is no villain, no victim.)

"Among humans, infant-adult proximity depends not only on the ability of infants to emit proximity-promoting signals, but also on the complementary tendency of adults to respond to these signals," says University of Denver infant researcher Joseph J. Campos.

This communication between the infant and mother is the subject of the ongoing research efforts of Daniel Stern, a psychiatrist, psychoanalyst, "baby watcher," and a Burt Reynolds look-alike. Infant smiles during the first two weeks of life, for instance, seem to occur automatically during REM sleep and drowsiness. Rarely do infants at this age smile when awake, Stern has noticed. Indeed, smiling in newborns, "endogenous smiling," as it is called, is an automatic "no mirth intended" reflex unrelated to anything but the brain's intrinsic activity. But a month or so later, starting at about six weeks, smiling starts to become "social." A face, a voice, a tickle—these are the things that make little Hilary smile. The next step is smiling for "manipulating" other people's responses. At this point the infant makes an important discovery: other people *react,* do nice things when they're smiled at (a lesson some babies never forget. Others, however, require periodic refresher courses throughout their lives). Finally, smiles are combined with more complex facial expressions: the haughty smile, the pouting smile, the seductive smile.

If you watch a blind baby four weeks old, it will smile just like its sighted counterparts. By six months, the smile is wan, less expressive, and makes other people feel uncomfortable. This suggests, says Stern, that after a while some visual feedback is required—somebody smiling back or otherwise "acknowledging" the smile. Otherwise the smile fails to increase in complexity. A blind child doesn't as a rule express sauciness by means of a smile.

Smiling is a means of reaching out, "testing the waters," seeing who smiles back and who doesn't. Aunt Mary, who can be made to do anything if she's smiled at, cohabitates with Uncle Fred who blushes and turns away when smiled at—a most "peculiar" man the infant decides, only not in those exact words.

Smiling behavior is a good example ("paradigm," if you prefer to employ the words of researchers) of what happens in the infant's brain as it matures. Intrinsic reflex activity gives way to social responses dependent on the efforts of other people. Still later the smile takes on a purpose, to elicit certain responses from others: "I'll smile and make you happy. Won't you do the same?"

Initially the brain is equipped with the capacity for certain behaviors. These are "rehearsed" during periods of REM sleep. Indeed, a considerable body of research now exists suggesting that REM sleep has no other purpose than to provide an opportunity to rehearse behaviors that will later be carried out in the waking state. Others, by far the minority view, believe that REM sleep is a sign that the three-week infant is dreaming just like his father two doors down the hall. If true, what would little Jason be dreaming *about*? "Can't say," respond the supporters of this view. "Only look at the infant smile, so peaceful, so beatific—smiling perhaps in remembrance of what it was like, you know, *back then.*"

Holders of such an opinion on infant smiling wince when Dr. Stern pronounces at a conference that such REM-related smiles "appear to bear no relationship to anything going on in the external world and are solely the reflection of cycles of neurophysiological excitation and discharges within the brain, unrelated to any other part of the body except the brain's intrinsic activity."

Although the smile is a good example of how the brain "programs" behavior, it is not a typical example. This is because there's nothing "typical" in the brain. Laughter, a kind of hyped-up smile, isn't present at all at birth and doesn't appear until between the fourth and eighth months when perhaps the infant has learned an important lesson useful throughout its lifetime: laugh and the whole world laughs with you, cry and you cry alone.

At first laughter can only be elicited by tickling, later sounds cause laughter. Not until a year of age do most babies laugh at something seen. Blind children laugh, deaf children laugh, as do the retarded and the insane—though it's not always possible to tell in a given instance just what they're laughing about. Even children raised by wolves and later rescued from their jungle lairs have been observed to laugh.

Both smiling and laughter demand reciprocity—by age six weeks smiles elicit smiles in return. When the smiles aren't returned the infant receives a dire message: something is amiss in the world, something so threatening that not even a baby's smile can assuage.

Smiles and laughter draw babies closer to the world, establish comfort and warmth, exile loneliness. Pity, therefore, the baby who smiles but has no one who will smile back, who laughs when there's no one to laugh with him.

CHAPTER 48

Bonding

When ewes are separated from their lambs immediately after delivery they reject the little ones when reunited with them two to three hours later. Nor is this rejection a subtle matter. They butt and shove the lambs aside in a preemptory rejection that doesn't leave room for reconsideration or reconciliation. But if the separation is delayed for perhaps no more than five minutes after birth, the mother lamb will show the typical doting behavior toward her young when reunited two hours later. It's a peculiar situation, noted by farmers for centuries, but not thought to be of much relevance higher up the phylogenetic scale: the birth experience of Mary was thought to bear precious little relevance to that of her little lamb, and vice versa.

Additional observations of other animals suggested hormones may be the critical element in eliciting "maternal behavior." Virgin rats or rats hysterectomized at some experimenter's whim can be rendered "maternal" in their behavior by injecting them with hormones that mimic the final stages of pregnancy.

After giving birth, female rhesus monkeys discover they enjoy looking at infant monkeys more, even infant monkeys not their own. But hormones don't explain everything. If a pregnant rhesus monkey is delivered by cesarean section, it fails to accept its young as readily as a counterpart who does it all by herself without an experimenter's "help."

In the 1970s pediatricians started observing for the first time (or at least putting their observations on paper for the first time) that mothers separated from their newborns for medical reasons (prematurity, a "sickly baby" requiring something in the way of special medical care) often seemed, to the extent that such things can be quantified, less attached to their infants. This caused some pediatricians to ponder a variation of the unthinkable: Did medical interventions aimed at securing the life and well-being of the premature infant do so at the cost of creating "deviant" (their word) maternal attachment?

At this point several pediatricians, principally Marshall Klaus and John Kennell of Case Western Reserve University School of Medicine suggested, on the basis of the aforementioned work done on rats, sheep, and monkeys, that by ensuring physical contact between mothers and newborns in the period immediately after birth "maternal attachment" might prove firmer. To appreciate just how extraordinary this suggestion actually was, it's useful to contrast the Klaus-Kennell hypothesis with the viewpoint on pregnancy and childbirth that has been popular since about the time of the deliverance of Cain and Abel.

Throughout recorded history, childbirth was considered an unpleasant, painful experience, a kind of self-limiting "illness" the mother was advised to reconcile herself to as best she could and get over as quickly and painlessly as possible. Doctors played their part in this rather grim scenario by providing the ultimate in pain-relieving medication. In fact, in the 1950s and 1960s, an obstetrician's reputation often rested upon his skill in drugging the mother to the point that she didn't recall anything from the time of her arrival in the delivery room and her waking up later in the recovery room to hear "Congratulations, you're the mother of a spanking nine-pound baby boy."

On occasion, the obstetrician went a little too far, and the baby was drugged into a stupor or some other iatrogenic (literally physician-induced) fetal distress syndrome. But, on the whole, (the risk being considered a small one) the baby "dried out" after a few hours or days following the chemical onslaught, and the mother was happy to have been spared a universally feared and, to all accounts, painful experience.

Indeed, before the 1970s childbirth was treated as a surgical experience rather than an emotional one. In line with this mind-set, the mother and baby were rarely granted more than a brief glimpse of each other, a glimpse only the mother could take advantage of, albeit through a drug haze, since the infant was routinely frustrated by the implantation in its eyes of silver nitrate (once again a "medical treatment" aimed at preventing the infant from developing a disease it might have contracted during the passage through the birth canal).

All in all, the birth experience was an unpleasant one for mother and infant alike. In those few instances when the anesthesia was "insufficient," some mothers reported they enjoyed seeing their baby moments after birth. On the whole, though, these atypical experiences were discussed more from the point of view of the anesthetist ("perhaps she should have had a bit more gas") than as a clue that, handled

somewhat differently, the birth experience wasn't necessarily the tra-
vail everyone had agreed that it had to be.

Against this background came Klaus and Kennell's suggestion that
the bonding between the mother and infant could be strengthened by
fostering "skin-to-skin contact" within the first few hours after birth.
No less was involved in this suggestion than a totally new way of
thinking—birth as an emotional experience and, with some preparation, an enhancing experience at that.

Since Klaus and Kennell's original work in the early 1970s, other
researchers, egged on by the desire to amplify, confirm, or contradict
the original findings, have, in fact, succeeded to different degrees in
their goals of amplification, confirmation, and contradiction.

One London study looked at the attitude of mothers toward their
infants some time, usually five or six years, after the child's birth. Two
groups were selected for special scrutiny: children born with low birth
weights who had been separated immediately after birth for a minimum period of two weeks; and a control group of normal-weight
infants who had not been separated from their mothers. Both groups
comprised thirty-two mothers and their children.

Among the group that had been separated, six out of thirty-two
showed disturbed relationships: the mothers favored such adjectives
for their children as "destructive," "irritable," "whiny," and "disobe-
dient."

While six out of thirty-two is a fairly impressive figure, seemingly
supporting of the bonding hypothesis, closer scrutiny revealed a sub-
group of mothers who had a monopoly on disturbed parent/child
relationships. Typically the mother was a teenager who had not
planned or wanted the pregnancy, got on poorly with her own parents,
was generally unhappy and, from the first, perceived her child as having a "difficult" or unlikable personality. Not surprisingly, the infants
—all of them of low birth weight—tended toward poor health, temper
tantrums, and a propensity for annoying their mothers, often to the
point of inciting some form of abuse.

"It is concluded that in these cases rejection of a child by its mother
. . . could not be attributed solely to separation from the mother at
birth, since the majority of mother/child couples separated immediately after birth enjoyed good relationships," the researchers concluded.

Disturbed infant/patient interactions stem, it appears, only from
those occasions when *certain mothers* with identifiable problems and
personality features are separated from their infants soon after birth.
Bonding in such instances may play a part in strengthening a relation-

ship which, under conditions of mother/infant separation, deteriorates beyond the point that anything can be done to correct it.

In addition, too much emphasis on bonding contradicts a goodly number of commonsense observations. Adopted children, for instance, get on well with their adoptive parents; their relationships aren't any more or less "disturbed" than those of children born and raised by their natural parents. Besides, even in those instances when infant/mother separation is unavoidable (either the mother or the infant having had a rather bad time of it during the delivery), the majority of mothers and infants don't appear to suffer any consequences. (In the London study, twenty-six out of thirty-two of the mothers separated from their infants enjoyed as happy a relationship with their children as did those mothers provided the opportunity for bonding.)

An unmarried or unhappily married teenage mother-to-be seems less likely to care for herself during pregnancy and, therefore, is more apt to deliver a child of low birth weight who requires medical care and, along with it, separation from the mother. When such a child is returned to the mother, her attitude is often additionally negative since she's been deprived of the opportunity to spend time with her baby. In short, negative maternal attitudes lead to poor health care during pregnancy and increase the likelihood of prematurity or other medical conditions requiring mother/infant separation—a convoluted skein of events in which the lost opportunity for bonding appears to play only a minor role.

"There seems to be an emerging consensus that the effects of early mother/infant contact are weak, short-lived, apply only to some mothers and do not involve biological factors," wrote the authors of one rather skeptical summary on bonding. Inquiry regarding the basis for such a conclusion leads to the usual kinds of experimental hair-splitting that is of little interest to most mothers and to no baby that has ever been encountered. Perhaps, our skeptics point out, mothers desirous of "bonding" with their infants were treated differently by the medical personnel (and perhaps they were), many doctors being partial to mothers who seem attached to their infants and so on. But where does all this leave the mother and her newborn? At this point, no one is seriously suggesting a return to the methods of the past (the mother and infant sharing a drugged stupor and not really getting to know each other for several days after delivery). If nothing else, Klaus and Kennell eliminated a lot of medical protocol and mumbo jumbo, substituting instead encouragement for mothers everywhere to share with their babies warmth and softness and touching.

CHAPTER 49

Sex

In 1978 two researchers at the University of Sussex carried out a "Halloween Experiment." Infant boy babies age six months were dressed like girls, and vice versa. The mothers then handed over their "disguised" babies to women who hadn't been let in on the secret.

Imagine little Johnny dressed in a pink dress with a bow in his hair. Imagine, too, little Jennifer decked out in denim. Finally, imagine a strange woman receiving Johnny or Jennifer from the mother who then promptly leaves the room. What do you think happened?

Videotapes of events at this point reveal that girls dressed up like boys are encouraged to crawl, walk, and engage in other vigorous (for their age) and coordinated physical activity. Boys dressed like girls are treated differently: less encouragement is forthcoming in regard to active kinds of activities. Maternal behavior, we are informed by the two female University of Sussex researchers who carried out the experiment, is heavily dependent on the perceived sex: women tend to treat boys and girls differently according to their ideas of the sex of the infant.

Some feminists point to such masquerade experiments as proof that differences in infant behavior are merely the result of early sexual stereotyping. The mother treats boys and girls differently and, ergo, this is the origin of the behavioral differences between the sexes. But I wonder if these differences are really quite that simply explained. In these experiments replicated and confirmed by other researchers, the stranger spends only a set period of time with the "disguised" babies (ten minutes on the average). How much can you learn about anyone in ten minutes, particularly someone who can't talk back? If the masquerade were continued a bit longer, would Johnny dressed up as Jennifer soon be treated as a boy despite appearances to the contrary? And would Jennifer in her denim outfit eventually be given up on and considered a priss? I don't pretend to have the answer to these questions since no one could or should do extended Halloween Experiments (obviously, yet another participant in the experiment would have to be assigned all diapering and changing activities lest the "game" be given away). But extended experiments have been carried out on less socially loaded adult/infant interactions.

Forget for a moment about such a ponderous imponderable as "sexual identification." Instead, skip down a bit along the phylogenetic scale, down to the level of the rat. Sex is more straightforward here, albeit probably no less complicated.

During copulation Madame Rat adopts a characteristic posture. She stands flat-footed, head thrust forward, back arched, derrière lifted to expose the vagina (no subtleties here). She also flicks her tail to the side to facilitate what happens next. This is the lordosis reflex. Scientists have based doctoral theses on the quantification of this act, graphing and charting Madame Rat's degree of receptivity. In the adult rat, removal of the ovaries abolishes the reflex—sex is no longer of interest. An injection of the female hormone restores that smidgen of romance—the derrière is directed upward once again.

Remove the testicles from Monsieur Rat and he will begin acting like a she. Genetically a male, the castrato adopts lordosis as a sex style. According to experts on the sex habits of rats, the male sex hormone produced by the rat's testes inhibits the female lordosis behavior. Cut off the testes or otherwise block the influence of testosterone and he begins behaving like she in matters sexual.

While the anatomical basis for lordosis remains undiscovered, there are unequivocal differences in the brain of Madame as compared to Monsieur Rat. An area of the hypothalamus, the preoptic area, is eight times larger in the adult male rat than in his female counterpart. But a particular synapse on a preoptic area is 30 percent more frequently encountered in the female than in the male. Castrate the male at birth and these synapses in the adult are increased to the female level. Hormone sculpts brain, brain sculpts behavior. With practice, a scientist can tell fairly rapidly whether he's looking at a male or a female rat brain.

As we make our way up the phylogenetic scale, brain sex differences aren't quite so striking. On the average, male brains are slightly heavier for body weight than those of females. Skull capacity also varies along similar lines. The posterior part of the corpus callosum (the band of fibers connecting the two cerebral hemispheres) is wider in women than in men. And that's about it. No other anatomic brain-sex differences in humans have been demonstrated to everyone's satisfaction. As a result, culture has supplanted biology as the determiner, in many people's minds, of the behavioral differences between the

sexes such as those in the Halloween Experiment. Before closing the
discussion, however, let's consider this experiment on smiling carried
out in Edinburgh.

If infants are cross-dressed (boy dressed as girl and vice versa) other
infants are fooled into mistaking the clothes for the man. Boys look
more at girls in boyish clothes, girls more at boys in girlish clothes (the
opposite of normal adult behavior: as a rule infants prefer to look at
members of the same sex).

If videotapes are substituted for still pictures, however, the deceit is
discovered. Movement patterns of infant boys are different from those
of infant girls. Infants recognize this distinction even though they have
never been taught a word on the subject of kinesis. Since the experiments were carried out on infants who presumably had little opportunity to study how men and boys move and comport themselves
differently from women and girls, how could such a perceptive discrim-
ination be attributable to "social" factors? Before answering that, you
should be aware that the experimenter carried things a bit further
(some might say a bit too far).

The infants had tiny lights attached to each of the twelve major
joints. The house lights were then shut off. The dynamic patterns of
movement, revealed in the darkness by the tiny bulbs attached to the
infants' arms and legs, were sufficient to inform the infant observers
whether they were looking at a boy or a girl. "The origins of the
different movement patterns are at present obscure," comments the
researcher who, perhaps, understandably, doesn't wish to become en-
snared in a bramble bush of controversy. Allow me the foolhardiness
of taking things a bit further and providing a tentative explanation.

The brain is the mediator of movement, the programmer if you
prefer. Neurons connect up with muscle fibers, impulses are generated, movement occurs. In earliest infancy it is difficult, therefore, to
imagine how movement pattern differences could be the result of
cultural forces. For one thing, infants, as I have said, rarely have the
opportunity to study the movements of other infants (on the average,
babies have more experience with adults than they do with other
babies). A more reasonable explanation was suggested by the experimenter.

"The infant's awareness of his or her own movement patterns . . .
can be compared with the perceived movement patterns of another,
giving a match or a mismatch, with the degree of match-determining
interest."

In infancy, like likes like. In adults (heterosexual adults, that is) like
learns to like the unalike. Could homosexuality be a reversion or a

Cross-Dressing Experiment

Two infants cross-dressed for an experiment on gender identification.

fixation to "like likes like"? Do sex hormones modify the developing brains so that under ordinary (some might prefer "normal") conditions little boys become less interested in other little boys than they do in little girls?

CHAPTER 50

Intelligence

A mother stares down at her nine-month-old infant and wonders where will he be two decades from now, how often she will see him, will she like his wife, will he take a wife.

The father stares down at the same infant and sees a future secretary of state or, at the very least, assistant secretary of something important. Each person sees someone who is not there as yet, someone partly imaginative and partly based on what he or she thinks can be inferred from the way Johnny smiles, his responsiveness, the way he moves. Based on subtle distinctions of Johnny's behavior, great plans are nurtured and ambitious goals formulated.

If more "objective observers" are introduced on the scene, they may go about sizing up Johnny slightly differently, without the gleam in the eye, strictly on the basis of the "scientific method," you understand. Johnny will be weighed and his weight compared with his head size. Can he sit up? Can he crawl? Does he smile when somebody smiles at him? Will he take a raisin? Will he place that raisin daintily between his thumb and forefinger with the proper precision? Is he easily frightened? By what?

Based on the answers to such questions the white-coated scientist may seek to modify some of the plans Johnny's parents have for him. Well, not a future secretary of state but perhaps he'll do well enough for medical school. He doesn't smile, you say? He doesn't fancy picking up a raisin? Well, then perhaps Johnny will stop at college. No crawling either? No recognition of Mom or Dad? White coat may tactfully suggest other future plans for Johnny, less academically demanding, for not everyone fancies school, and there can be only one secretary of state at a time, someone drawn from the top of the litter, and so on.

For years scientists believed such prognostications possible: Johnny as tiny tot somehow related directly and predictably to Johnny of two decades later well on his way to the cabinet. Nobody believes that now. Tests measuring the intelligence of infants are of almost no value in determining how smart the future adult can be expected to be. (There is only one exception to this rule: the intelligence of retarded children is reliably predicted by their performance on infant tests of intelligence.)

Currently employed tests of infant intelligence rely on easily measured motor or vocal behaviors. Does the baby move, how often, how far, what sounds are made, to whom? There is little opportunity for the testing of concept formation, symbolization, abstraction—the kinds of things that will predict a secretary of state or the person who shines his shoes.

Nor should this difficulty in distinguishing the gifted from the "shafted" come as a surprise. During the first two years of life everybody is learning pretty much the same stuff: how to move from here to there, how to sit without falling on one's face, how to hold something in the hand. Later these tasks become a little more interesting but not by much: how to move one foot in front of another without tripping over it, how to say, "Mama, Dada, yes," and most importantly, "no no no."

"Individual variation in such skills will show little relationship to the individual variation that is found in the more symbolic verbal and spatial skills that characterize later intelligence," says Dr. Paul L. Harris, infant researcher at Oxford University.

Perhaps this matter of intelligence can be approached slightly differently, some parents have thought. If his mother is professor of romance languages and his father vice president of General Motors, can the infant testers read more into the test results of Johnny at a year and a half? Unfortunately (or perhaps fortunately depending on how you look at it) the correlation between infant intelligence over the first two years and the intelligence of the infant's parents is virtually nonexistent. The same lack of correlation holds if Johnny's father or mother had been tested at two years and their results are now brought forth for comparison. Since Johnny shares on the average half of the genes of each parent, this finding provides little support for the claim that variation in infant intelligence is under genetic control. In short, smart babies don't necessarily turn out to be smart adults and, in general, no one should panic if an infant's "intelligence" doesn't seem to test up to snuff.

If further convincing is required regarding the proposition that

Johnny's IQ during the first two years has nothing to do with how smart he'll be at twenty years, one can look at identical twins. Although there are scientists who believe and have published the opposite conclusion, most studies fail to show that identical twins exhibit similar intelligence scores during infancy. (During adulthood? Yes.)

If you were reading this statement about the twins at all carefully, a question has no doubt arisen that deserves an answer: Why are twin infants unalike in intelligence while years later their intelligence is quite similar?

If you test an adult's intelligence by employing generally available IQ tests, the measurements remain relatively stable, at least over the short term. One wouldn't expect, for instance, a forty-point fluctuation in two IQ tests taken only a month apart for an adult. In infants, however, fluctuations are the rule rather than the exception. Although infants typically pass through developmental sequences (the exact program dependent upon which infant researcher you ask), backsliding from one test occasion to another is very much the rule.

In 1974 three infant researchers tested twenty-four infants between the ages of seven and eighteen months over an eleven-month period. They checked such things as problem solving (the use of a string or rake to snag a toy) and the ability to recognize familiar versus unfamiliar objects. When seven subtests of infant intelligence were compared, only a small fraction intercorrelated with one another.

"It is clear from these data that sensory/motor development is characterized by unevenness and the capabilities exhibited in one area of performance have little relationship to abilities measured in another aspect of performance at a given age," concluded the investigators.

Overall, an infant's mental development is an uneven affair; there are good performances in some areas, mediocre ones in other areas, and no performance at all in still other areas that perhaps don't interest the infant at the time of testing. "We should think of the infant's development as proceeding simultaneously but not synchronously along several relatively independent task sequences," says Oxford University's Paul L. Harris.

Two mothers sit on a bench in the park comparing notes on their babies who, all the while, lie primly in their prams. One will say, "Mama," if sufficiently encouraged whereas the other says nothing however preemptory the encouragement. But little Mark, the one who says nothing, is already trying to sit up while the Orator is "awfully clumsy," says his mother. Which is the smarter? Which one will score higher on his college boards? Who will go to Harvard? Sorry mothers —no one at this point can say. And when you consider the matter, don't you think this simply grand?

When there's no need to worry about who is "smarter," mothers can stop comparing, babies can be simply babies, and Harvard can be left to take care of itself.

CHAPTER 51

Windows on the Infant Brain

The two cerebral hemispheres look very much alike. Only the trained observer—and I'm speaking now of a level of training that requires a decade or more of careful watching—can observe the differences between the left and right hemispheres of the brain. The most striking difference? The speech area is larger on the left side compared to the right. This is no doubt due to the fact that in most people the left hemisphere is more important than the right in the production and processing of speech and language.

The idea that two apparently similar brain areas are not, in fact, similar but different in important and functional ways can be dated back to the mid-nineteenth century. At that period in Paris, Paul Broca, an anatomist and neurologist, was asked to see a patient partially paralyzed on the right side of his body, able to understand what was said to him, but incapable on his own of saying anything other than the simple word "tan." Not surprisingly, the attendants at the hospital where the patient was confined took to amusing themselves by substituting for his real name the nickname "Tan."

Tan's brain, which now rests in a jar in Paris, was discovered shortly after the old man died to contain a cavity filled with fluid located along the lateral aspect of the left hemisphere. When that cavity was drained, the drainers discovered a large left-hemisphere lesion which involved, among other areas, the second and third convolutions of the frontal lobe (there are three convolutions). That same year, 1861, Broca peeled away the scalp bone brain coverings of another patient who prior to death could listen and understand but not speak acceptably. His brain, too, contained a similar "lesion" in the second and third frontal convolutions.

Based on these patients, Broca lectured his colleagues along the lines that a stroke or other damage in a person's left hemisphere, specifically the areas of the second and third convolutions of the frontal lobe, would inevitably lead to a language disturbance. Subsequent investigators confirmed that Broca's area, as it was eventually called, must be working just right in order that one be able to say, "Please pass me the buttered toast and section two of the *Times,*" rather than simply blurting out, "Butter . . . toast . . . paper."

Over the ensuing one hundred years it has become clear that the cerebral hemispheres are functionally asymmetrical: the left hemisphere is dominant for language while the right hemisphere does best with music, the maintenance of attention, spatial orientation, and many aspects of emotions.

Until recently it was believed by professionals and laymen alike that cerebral hemisphere specialization is limited to humans. Within the past two decades, however, canaries have reminded us that we should not be so chauvinistic. In canaries and finches song making disappears in the wake of lesions (deliberately inflicted in the interests of getting the "facts") in the left side of the brain. Similar mucking around in the right hemisphere has no effect on bird song. Researchers have also discovered such similar asymmetries in frogs, rats, giant apes and, as mentioned earlier, men and women as well.

"The demonstration of asymmetry in animals appears to confirm the belief that biologically determined asymmetry has existed throughout vertebrate evolution," said the late neurologist Norman Geschwind, who at the time of his death in 1984 had done more than anyone else to reveal the inherent asymmetries of the brain. "Human asymmetries are not a recent development but only the most recent example of a fundamental feature of anatomy and behavior," observed Geschwind.

Within the fetus the observed asymmetries in brain organization also prevail and resemble the situation found in the adult. Nor does the fetal brain develop at the same rate in all areas. After birth, in the course of the baby's development, the brain tissue develops earlier on the right side, perhaps in response to someone feeling, touching, caressing, and otherwise "handling." In support of this hypothesis are findings in studies of the rat: early handling influences subsequent rat brain growth and development of the right hemisphere. Since the brain and behavior of a rat are in many ways dissimilar to those of a human, this might be as good a place as any to describe the methods and reasoning that neuroscientists apply when they carry out brain research on a "lower" animal and bid us apply these findings to "higher" creatures such as ourselves.

In the 1920s Robert Tryon of the University of California observed that some rats run mazes with greater facility than do others. Separating the two groups, maze-bright and maze-dull rats, neuroanatomist

Marion Diamond observed enhanced development of the cortex of the nimble maze runners. Exposing rats to different environments (enriched, standard colony conditions and impoverished conditions) also affects cortical areas differently. In addition, there are sex differences in cortical thickness: in males, on the whole, the right cortex is thicker than the left. Differences in the architecture of the cortex can also be varied by differing species, sex, age, and environment. What might be the relevance of such an arrangement?

Typically, male rats demonstrate a superiority over females in visual/spatial abilities (running the maze). Is this enhanced performance a reflection of right structural hyperdevelopment in the visual/spatial regions of the cortex of male rats?

"One might offer the following hypothesis for female left dominance [left cortex thicker than the right]," says Dr. Diamond. "The female is not so strong as the male and, therefore, vocalization may be an important means of protection. With language and song predominantly in the left brain of man and birds, respectively, perhaps 'language' (vocalization) is also localized on the left in the female rat."

In female rats that have undergone the removal of their ovaries at birth, a male brain pattern emerges. Does this suggest that brain hormones modify the cerebral asymmetry in the female cortex? Probably so. Removal of the testes of a newborn male rat also leads to a reverse of the male/female asymmetric pattern in several cortical regions.

Comparing rats and humans obviously calls for a degree of caution and restraint. Nevertheless, if one looks carefully enough, subtle brain differences can be found in humans depending on the world in which the human brain finds itself. A German neuropathologist, for instance, has claimed on the basis of his autopsies that the brains of social deviants harbor higher rates of abnormalities than are found in individuals from less socially depressed environments.

The brains of children with severe dyslexia (reading disabilities) contain an abnormal pattern of brain cells in the left hemisphere, particularly in the speech region. If this finding is examined in the light of the differences I just mentioned in the brains of the rats, certain intriguing associations are suggested.

If normal human brain development is interfered with before birth, specifically via a slowing of the rate of migration of neurons to the left cortex, this failure can lead to a localized arrest in brain development. Translation: Johnny can't read.

In recent years neuroscientists have linked early developmental brain disorders with problems in reading, writing, and stuttering. But there are compensations: these disorders are often accompanied by superior performance in other areas. For instance, a young man with a lifetime problem with reading was discovered to be a talented metal-smith. Another dyslexic manifested superior artistic talents. Failure in one sphere such as reading, it appears, can be compensated for by an enhanced performance in right-hemisphere activities (drawing, paint-ing, music). And recently, based on these hemisphere asymmetries, neuroscientists have come to believe they can now explain this puz-zling situation wherein a deficient performance in one sphere often coexists with superiority in other areas.

"If the growth of one part of the hemisphere is delayed, then other regions will be larger than they normally would have been," wrote Norman Geschwind in 1984. "When this increase in size is marked, superior or even remarkable talents may develop."

Superior performance on the basis of brain disease confounds many of our conceptions about the brain. In general, abnormalities in brain development or function result in inferior or deficient performance. Intriguing exceptions exist, however. Ten to 15 percent of autistic children demonstrate remarkable talents (autistic savants). In such situations it is speculated that the brain disorder responsible for au-tism (so far undiscovered) might make it easier for other brain areas to develop more extensively than would ordinarily be the case. Recall the research of the Rakics mentioned earlier in the book on the effect of the removal of brain tissue on one site and the subsequent alternation of the brain in other sometimes far distant sites.

While all of this is interesting and important in its own way, there is precious little of this research that can be applied directly to our understanding of the baby brain. Obviously, experiments cannot be carried out on infants and children involving diet and "enriched" or "unenriched" environments. Besides there is a compelling reason why studying bits of brain tissue under a miscroscope isn't likely to be very rewarding: learning, language, memory, speech—such activities, when they go awry, aren't likely to result in life-threatening situations. Nor does the brain of a stutterer or learning-disabled child often come up for autopsy examination. Few pathologists, therefore, are provided with information that the person stretched out upon the autopsy table was afflicted with dyslexia. No "lesion" is looked for and, not surpris-ingly, no "lesion" is found. What is needed is a dynamic means of measuring function rather than simply structure: what happens from moment to moment within the brain of a living, breathing subject. Three imaging techniques are currently available that can do this: positron emission tomograms (PET scans), radioactive cerebral blood flow studies (RCBF), and brain electrical activity map (BEAM). Each of these methods requires some background knowledge of other techniques such as computed axial tomography (CAT) and magnetic resonance imaging (MRI).

The CAT scan provides a high definition of three-dimensional computer-assisted reconstruction of the brain's absorption of X rays. It is the standard technique for demonstrating normal gross brain anatomy.

The MRI employs a high density magnetic field to provide a three-dimensional reconstruction. As currently employed, the MRI images the concentration of hydrogen ions within the brain. Since the greatest concentration of hydrogen is in water and water is a key component of brain tissue, the MRI can detect changes in brain structure long before such changes occur in a CAT scan. A stroke, for instance, will alter the fluid balance within the affected brain area several days before the resulting dead brain cells can be imaged by the CAT scanner.

While both the CAT and MRI are invaluable tools for imaging brain anatomy, they provide little information about what's happening at the moment. The PET, RCBF, and BEAM techniques are aimed at mapping brain *function* rather than simply structure.

In PET scanning, analogues of glucose are given to a patient after labeling them with positron emitting atoms. These substances enter functionally active brain cells but because they cannot be completely metabolized remain temporarily "stuck" in the cells they have entered. A computer-assisted reconstruction of the radioactivity produced by the isotope-containing substances results in a color-coded map. Those cells that are functionally most active light up as white or red areas. Areas in which the brain cells are comparatively quiescent are coded in "cooler" colors of green or blue. The PET scan, unlike the CAT or MRI, is sensitive to cerebral function. Its main disadvantage is the time required to carry out the test. It takes about twenty minutes for the radioactively tagged glucose to be preferentially taken up by the most active brain cells. Another twenty minutes is required to produce the reconstructed image. A fleeting thought or the impulse of a moment isn't likely, therefore, to be imaged by a PET scanner. Longer periods of testing involving prolonged activities (listening to music) show up nicely in the PET scan image.

RCBF imaging consists of mapping changes in blood flow induced by corresponding changes in the subject's activities. This method is based on the fact that the most active brain areas require additional blood flow in order to provide the active brain cells with sufficient nutrients. Localized changes in blood flow represent localized changes in brain metabolism. The whole process is similar to what occurs in the muscle that burns up more energy in the active stage and therefore requires additional blood flow to provide an excess of nutrients to provide that energy.

Every technological advance is inevitably accompanied by a trade-off: glitches in the technology, risks to the subjects, excessive costs, and so on. PET and RCBF are no exceptions. Both involve exposure to radioactive substances as well as intravenous or even interarterial injections. What is needed, therefore, is a technology sensitive enough to detect moment-to-moment alterations in brain function without at the same time exposing the patient to excessive radiation or making too much of a demand on the pocketbook.

For years neuroscientists recognized that the most promising avenue of approach to a dynamic, safe, less costly imaging procedure would involve a new technique whereby the brain's spontaneous electrical activity could be graphically displayed.

The electroencephalographer who reads a typical EEG pattern representing ten seconds of spontaneous brain activity "eyeballs" the recording in search of deviations from the normal background. The process isn't terribly different from that of a skilled mechanic who starts up a 500 SEL and simply listens to the purr of the motor. Automatically he screens out the normal background sounds of the engine in order to detect deviations. In the same way, the electroencephalographer flips through page after page of an EEG recording often at a breathtaking rate until, suddenly, he stops, his eye attracted to a blip in the recording. While this process is undoubtedly helpful there is a good deal of variation among electroencephalographers regarding what is and what is not normal. In addition, any evaluation of brain wave activity must employ statistical procedures: How much and to what extent does this six-month-old infant's brain wave activity differ from that of a thousand other infants of the same age? No electroencephalographer, however experienced, can incorporate the necessary information or carry out the transformations required in order to decide about all abnormalities, particularly subtle ones. In order to do this, Dr. Frank Duffy, a combination electroencephalographer, neurologist, engineer, and Olympic equestrian, devised in the mid-1970s the technology which is known as brain electrical activity mapping (BEAM). This technique is a quantum jump in mankind's ability to dynamically visualize what is happening in the living brain.

What goes on in his brain when Joseph listens to a story, plays music, tells a joke and makes a fool of himself? With the advent of PET scans and BEAM studies the student of the brain was provided with the opportunity to answer such questions, to study function rather than just form.

All human behavior depends on alterations in ions and neurotransmitters across some defined span of time (we're talking milliseconds here). The mosquito bites. We slap at it, killing it if our slapping is fast enough. We suffer annoyance along with a welt if our responses are wanting in swiftness. Each millisecond of this minidrama is accompanied by alterations in the electrical activity of parts of the brain. Neurophysiologists have known this for over a century but have been able only for about a quarter of a century to take advantage of it, display it, make predictions about it. Computers made this possible.

If you hook up a computer to an electroencephalogram, that computer will average out the "background noise" a brain makes when that brain is doing not much of anything. If you flash a light into the eyes of the person whose brain is idling, the computer will abstract the effect of that light flash from the hurly-burly of ongoing brain waves. After the computer completes this averaging, the effect of that light flash will stand out with all of the clarity befitting a specific event which, because it registers on the brain, has left its own mark however evanescent.

There are specific brain wave patterns corresponding to sounds or light (it matters whether the stimulus consists of discrete flashes or a series of flashing checkerboard patterns—each elicits its own response and provides its own brain "signature").

With the development of these "evoked potential" techniques, neuroscientists added a new dimension: time.

Imagine a series of monotonous tones, each exactly alike. Suddenly introduce a new unexpected note. It's now possible to monitor what happens within milliseconds of such a change, monitoring whether the person is bored, complacently habituated to repetitive stimuli, or surprised by an unanticipated event.

The brain will signal surprise by deflection of the evoked potential recording apparatus. This response can't be suppressed (professionals have tried) and can remain as a kind of lie detector test if the experimenter is so inclined. "Were you surprised in any way by the variation in timbre we introduced a moment ago?"

"Not really," the experimental subject replies, unaware that his evoked potential recording has made him out a liar.

As of 1984 only two research groups in the world had recorded the evoked potentials of infants. "Cortical Responses from Adults and Infants to Complex Visual Stimuli" was the title of one paper by one of these research groups. In this study infants between seven and forty-eight weeks of age were pressed into service to view slides of either cartoon characters or people, defocused slides, flashes of light on the face of one of the experimenters, flashes of light on a doll held by one of the experimenters, or peek-a-boo games. Conclusion? That the

recorded potentials had something to do with ongoing mental processes (concentration, discernment, selection).

"Not so hasty," responded other more skeptical observers. Since the
defocused and focused slides didn't differ in any way in their evoked
potential patterns from those produced by flashes of light on the doll
or the experimenter, the skeptical observer can be forgiven his inherent suspicion that those evoked potential responses were nothing
more than the brain's response to novel stimuli of any type.

The paper, "Event-related brain potentials to human faces in infants," detailed a more subtle and intriguing experiment. Six-month-
old infants were shown photographs of two human faces (the "showing" took less than the blink of an eye—one hundred milliseconds).
One of the faces appeared frequently, the other infrequently. On the
basis of different brain responses to the two faces, the experimenters
concluded that their infants "were able to remember the frequently
presented face from trial-to-trial and to discriminate it from a discrep-
ant face"—something of a mouthful—which translates into "the baby
recognized one face as familiar, the other as unfamiliar, and responded
accordingly." The experimenters even went a bit further, suggesting
that the differences in evoked potential response may be related to the
"clarity, precision, or stability of the memory trace for an event."

In any case, the infant was shown in this experiment to be responsive
to changes in the nature of the photographs that that infant's brain was
exposed to. But whether the infants "recognized" and subtly compared these faces so as to be able to speak about them if that infant
were possessed of the power of language is another matter all together. For one thing, little is known about the physical underpinnings
of event-related potentials. For instance, why does the response differ
between an infant and a five year old, between an adolescent and an
adult?

"We do not know whether the event-related potential changes reflect some kind of maturational change in the brain's structure or a
functional change, such as the transitions in modes of thought postulated by Piaget or an interaction between the two," says Dr. Diane
Kurtzberg of the departments of neuroscience and neurology at the
Albert Einstein College of Medicine in New York.

Dr. Kurtzberg's mention of Piaget reflects the hope among some
neuroscientists that Piaget's stage theory or something like it might
provide a useful theoretical model for understanding how event-related potentials develop from infancy through adolescence. Think how
useful such a correlation would be. As the child advances through the
developmental stages—postulated by Piaget to occur at about two,
seven, and eleven years of age—the evoked potentials vary accord-

ingly. If such a correlation were good enough, it might even be possible, experimenters once hoped, to define a particular child's developmental standing in relation to that child's evoked potential patterns. Alas, that hope has not been borne out. A child's performance on a particular task at one developmental stage fails to provide a basis for predicting how that child will later perform at the next stage. Nor do these changes from one stage to the other occur with the abruptness once postulated by Piaget. Nor do changes in event-related potentials necessarily signal a shift in the child's manner of thinking about the world. Added to this are certain important differences between how the infant brain processes information as compared to, say, the brain of the child or adolescent.

Cognition was once defined as "the activity of knowing; the acquisition, organization, and use of knowledge." By this definition, cognitive activity in adults can occur mentally, strictly on the basis of the internal representation of objects or events. I can mentally picture the inside of my house along with the effects brought about by changes in color or decor. With infants, in contrast, cognitive activities are primarily perceptual.

As mentioned at various points throughout this book, the infant brain's first task is that of gaining information about the world. Who is the person wearing the pretty dress and smiling? Who has the beard and doesn't smile but only stares? Testing of infant brain activity, therefore, must depend on measuring that infant's responses to changes in the environment.

In a typical experiment ten monotonous tones are presented. The baby habituates to the boredom of hearing the same sound ten times. Suddenly there is a new tone. The baby's brain responds to this novelty by putting out a specific evoked response wave. This is the infant brain "thinking" in response to novelty.

In the future—and the not too distant future either—evoked potential recordings will make it easier to decide about the developmental status of the infant brain.

At this point, overt behavior is the only measure by which one infant can be compared to another. Does he follow an object with his eyes? Will she reach out? Does he smile when smiled at? Such behavioral expressions are the tail end of a brain process that begins with perception, includes the transformation of this perception into a meaning, and ends with a response to that meaning: a smile, a reaching out for the familiar, a turning away from the strange. Will these new insights into the infant brain involve the discovery of "new wave forms" or merely a better understanding of how patterns in infancy "mature"?

What is six-month-old Sonia thinking? Is she thinking in ways that bear a meaningful relationship to the thinking of an adult? In other words, does the infant brain proceed as it matures through a series of "stages" that permits comparison between one brain and another? Or is the maturation of an individual brain as individual as the path of a leaf falling from a tree—one leaf's descent appearing very much like another and yet no two leaves progressing along identical pathways? At the moment there are no definite answers to such questions.

In an evoked brain potential, pulses of light are flashed at a subject while the subject's brain electrical activity is recorded from twenty electrodes along the scalp. An arbitrary point in time is selected—192 milliseconds—and the mean voltage values are recorded from the twenty sites. The humps and bumps look pretty much alike in all twenty electrodes. But notice what happens when the head region is plotted on a grid and those regions that fall within the head outline are assigned a value. (Upon this grid can be displayed voltage values fitted to a gray scale.) Even an untrained person can notice in the figure on the opposite page that areas in the frontal and occipital (toward the back) parts of the brain differ significantly from the general "gray" background. In essence, computer transformation can make it possible to display in a colored visual map the brain's electrical activity at any given instant.

By comparing the subject's image with those of a control population variations from normal brain activity can be plotted on a map in units of standard deviation.

"One analogy for this whole system might be that if you took 2,000 separate measurements of points in Vermont and tied them together you could get a topographical map," says Dr. Frank Duffy, the inventor of BEAM. "Then if you had SPM (Statistical Probability Mapping) you could see how Vermont compares with the rest of the country."

Already, children with dyslexia have been discovered to exhibit a unique brain "signature" which simplifies their identification. Generally, the BEAM pattern in control subjects is symmetrical with electrical activity spreading equally on both sides. In dyslexia the pattern is asymmetric with large differences in the medial frontal lobes.

Theories of dyslexia have always postulated that the brain disturbance responsible for this condition resides in the posterior speech region in the left cerebral hemisphere with some extension back into the left parietal lobe. While it's true that disturbances in this area are found by BEAM, additional areas also turned up in the medial frontal lobes, an area not usually considered to be involved in the language process.

Reading, it is turning out, involves a distributed system within the

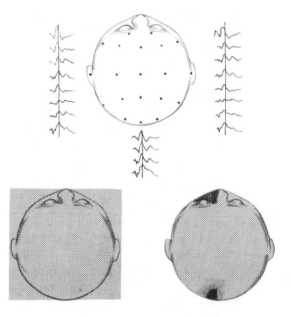

An Evoked Brain Potential Recording

The dark areas toward the front and back on the left side correspond to sites of asymmetric activation.

brain that includes the traditional language area along with areas of the medial frontal lobe which can be shown by BEAM and blood flow studies to be active when a person reads silently to himself, reads aloud, or speaks. Indeed, it was not until the availability of techniques like BEAM that anyone was able to appreciate just how much of the brain is actively involved in reading.

"It may be that dyslexics have a dysfunction in the entire system rather than in just one small area of the brain," says Dr. Duffy. "They may use a different area of the brain than normal subjects to perform a given task and maybe it is not as efficient."

Since dyslexia is a developmental disorder, it is reasonable to assume that given the appropriate technology one could diagnose it at an early point, perhaps even in infancy. Up to 50 percent of prematures, for instance, are known to have learning disabilities including dyslexia compared to only 10 to 15 percent of normal infants.

Could Johnny's difficulty in reading be detected before that first fumbling stumbling attempt to decipher what his brain isn't constitutionally equipped to decipher, at least at a normal rate? "We anticipate that it will be possible to develop a 'signature' of all individual forms of learning disability and that some day it will be possible to quantify descriptors that identify these conditions," claims Duffy.

If Duffy is correct, it seems reasonable to assume that neuroscientists will soon have a "window" on very early infant brain activity. An ongoing project with BEAM seeks to learn whether BEAM patterns will allow predictions to be made as to whether or not newborns will show future mental impairment later in life.

As discussed throughout this book, the infant brain is extremely difficult to assess. Behavioral measurements won't do since even infants with severe forms of brain damage can often perform normally on many commonly employed tests.

BEAM and other visual display systems may make possible the early diagnosis of epileptic disorders, perhaps even before the first seizure occurs. This would be a great advance since it is generally believed that epileptic seizures contribute to further brain deterioration and perhaps even make it easier for additional seizures to occur later. The potential of these imaging techniques is limited only by the age of the patient (so far there is little normative data regarding newborn brain patterns) and the availability of the technology. In the near future it is likely that the infant brain will be functionally analyzed so as to provide a basis for predicting which child is at risk for epilepsy learning disorders and dyslexia. BEAM and other techniques like it just might make possible the measurement of infant brain activity directly without dependence on the behavioral expressions of that activity. The assessment of speech and language, for instance, usually must await the time when the child begins to speak (about a year of age). BEAM could conceivably detect abnormalities within the speech area (left-hemisphere, midfrontal region) before a year of age, perhaps only a few weeks after birth. Think about the implications of such a development.

Within two or three weeks after Ricky has left the hospital with his mother a BEAM test carried out at the request of the obstetrician demonstrates a pattern of brain activity outside the normal range for three week olds. It shows abnormalities in the medial frontal regions. Will Ricky later go on to develop dyslexia? If there are other family members with dyslexia or other forms of learning disability, the odds are increased that the BEAM result is significant. But this leads to an additional problem: What is to be done?

It should not come as a surprise that a condition like dyslexia—which until recently was not even considered a brain disease—has spawned a host of contrasting and often contradictory treatment approaches. It is fair to say in summary that a specific treatment isn't presently available. Some children seem to benefit from intense remedial training in reading and writing. Others fail to show much in the way of improvement under these regimens. "We are going to read it again and again until you get it right" started a long time before pedagogues ever heard the word dyslexia. Until a successful treatment approach to dyslexia is available, therefore, the early diagnosis of the disorder in infancy is likely to continue to be more rewarding for the diagnostician than helpful to the parent of the affected child.

CHAPTER 52

Future Directions

At the end of the long hall on the second floor of the medical school there is a door. Brain Research Institute is the sign tacked onto that door. Within, scientists are at work, scurrying this way and that. Questions need answering which, so far, have resisted the investigator's best efforts. For example: brain malformations are not common in retarded children or in newborns who have died before their time and come under the pathologist's scrutiny. Does this mean, therefore, that brain maldevelopments are uncommon causes of retardation? That maldevelopments causing retardation are too subtle to be detected by current techniques? Or that mental retardation depends on dysfunctions at levels far below the resolving power of the microscope?

In order to address such issues, the scurrying neuroscientists must learn to devise new technologies, to look through "new windows" that are capable of revealing such subtleties as failure of dendritic development, failure to develop normal circuitry, or failure of transmitter or receptor production. In the mid-1980s neuroscientists are only partially able to do these things. Few are skilled enough to detect subtle failures in brain growth, delays in myelination, and abnormalities in the contours and divisions of the brain.

"Even good and careful neuropathologic studies cannot, at this time, account for most of the causes of neurologic dysfunction," says Dr. John M. Freeman of the departments of neurology and pediatrics at the Johns Hopkins Hospital in Baltimore.

At this point research on the infant brain is a curious paradox. While it's possible, thanks to PET scans, to display in color-coded images the ongoing activity of the living brain, neuroscientists remain ignorant of how many cells actually make up this marvelous three-and-a-half-pound mass of specialized protoplasm. While a lot has been learned in the past three decades concerning neurotransmitters and their receptor sites, no one at this point can venture a guess as to how many more neurotransmitters may be discovered. "It is appalling how little we know of the factors controlling, altering, or modifying brain development," concluded a panel convened by NIH in 1985 to comment on knowledge of the infant brain. What can reasonably be expected within the next two decades?

In the near future it will be possible to correlate patterns of metabolic brain activity with infant behavior. A preliminary effort in this regard is already underway by Professor Harry T. Chugani of the departments of neurology and pediatrics at UCLA Medical Center in Los Angeles. In a preliminary study Professor Chugani has demonstrated that in an infant of less than one month of age, metabolic activity, as determined by the PET scanner, is limited to the sensory and motor, cortical and subcortical regions, and midbrain and brain stem, particularly the more ancient areas of the cerebellum. Behaviorally the infant at one month operates principally on reflex responses mediated by these same subcortical brain areas.

By two or three months of age activity shown by the PET scan has blossomed to include additional areas in the brain stem and subcortical regions along with a significant proportion of the cerebral cortex (mainly the frontal area and those cortical areas that link the primary sensory receiving areas: the association cortex). Behaviorally the two- to three-month-old infant is no longer dependent on intrinsic subcortical reflexes. Slowly but surely vision and hearing and touch and movement are integrating so as to produce a unified perception. The electroencephalogram also shows movement toward an adult pattern.

By the time the infant is eight to nine months of age, what is evinced by the PET scan is very nearly mature. This corresponds behaviorally to the infant's enhanced intellectual and emotional development.

"What we're looking for are very early neurobehavioral correlations," comments Dr. Chugani. If his preliminary work is confirmed it may be possible to construct a timetable correlating the unfolding of metabolic activity within the brain with different stages of infant behavior.

Noninvasive imaging tools—technologies that don't involve pain, danger, or radiation exposure—will permit researchers to study the developing brain in its natural environment within the womb. Already the use of ultrasonograms has made possible extraordinarily detailed and informative observations of normal fetal behavior. Additional research on chemical transmitters and biological receptors will help answer questions regarding the role of these chemical messengers in the development of memory, learning, and the relative contributions of genes and environment toward the final "product": the infant brain.

Molecular biology and genetics will play a larger part in the delineation of normal brain development. What aspects of development are dictated solely by the genes? In instances of damage how does the injured brain repair itself? If there is a blueprint, wherein does it reside? What about the genes? The interaction of genetic "instructions" with the specific environment in which the infant brain finds itself? With the techniques already available (PET scans, MRI, fetal surgery, cell cultures) neuroscientists are closing the gap in our knowledge of normal and abnormal brain development, plasticity, repair, and regeneration.

Why is it that the infant brain has an almost unlimited capacity to recover from damage and, eventually, function almost as if nothing has happened? The adult brain, in contrast, recovers incompletely, thus leaving the affected individual grievously impaired. "Plasticity" is the catchword employed to describe this contrast between the infant and the adult brain. But when analyzed further, the term hides an abysmal ignorance of what is actually taking place in regard to brain cell proliferation and brain cell death, how the injured infant brain repairs itself while the adult brain remains largely irreparable.

What factors favor the "plasticity" of the infant brain? Can these be abated? What inhibits them in the adult brain? Is there anything that can be done in an adult brain, injured or otherwise impaired by disease, to restore it to a more "plastic" state? At this point there are no answers to such questions.

Neuroscientists, meanwhile, grapple with the brain's mysteries at the level of individual neurotransmitters and receptors. This emphasis has largely replaced traditional explanations based on anatomy. For instance, if three different brain areas of the primate neocortex are visually displayed in terms of just two neurotransmitters, serotonin and noradrenaline, the frontal and primary sensory cortex fibers are present in all six layers, whereas in the primary visual cortex noradrenaline fibers are largely absent from layer IV and serotonin is barely present in layers V and VI. The primary sensory cortex is thickly and densely innervated whereas fibers in the frontal cortex are sparse and widely separated. These differences in neurotransmitter innervation have practical implications. Damage to the frontal cortex, for instance, produces a loss of noradrenaline fibers not only in the frontal region but in areas farther down in the brain stem where the noradrenaline fibers take their origin (the locus ceruleus, a small compact nucleus in the pons).

In addition, the extent of impairment cannot be approximated unless the investigator takes into account long tangential fibers that cross from one anatomical area to the other, uniting the frontal region with

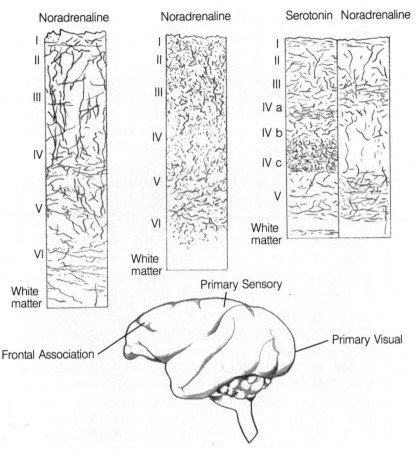

The human brain is not a homogenous structure either anatomically or neurochemically. Here three different brain areas are drawn to illustrate differences in the quantity and distribution of the transmitters noradrenaline and serotonin.

the primary sensory area. Within such a complicated arrangement it's likely that the projection of each neurotransmitter from its own separate and distinct nuclear complex within the brain stem engages a unique set of cortical neurons. Further, each neurotransmitter system influences neuronal activity synchronously throughout the vast expanse of the developing brain.

As an additional complication, the cerebral cortex contains a diverse and varied number of small amino acid messengers (peptides). Information about the distribution of these chemical messengers within the brain remains, at this point, fragmentary. Their action is also poorly understood. What all of this means in practical terms is that in order to understand the infant brain it will be necessary to superimpose biochemical codes on what neuroscientists know about anatomic circuits. It is no longer sufficient or helpful to study the developing brain merely on the basis of cell counts or the development of specific brain areas. Instead, it's necessary to define where different neurotransmitters exert their effects, and how they orchestrate one brain region to act in concert with another.

Imagine trying to plot a map of the traffic patterns in and out of a major metropolitan airport. If you limit yourself to merely observing which planes depart and arrive, noting their origin and destination, a model will emerge similar to the traditional anatomical model of the brain: this area is connected to that area which is connected to . . . and so on.

Now imagine plotting, in addition the origin and destination of all the individual passengers, where they're going, why they're traveling, and the effect their travel will have on various business and personal affairs (contracts signed, visits to relatives, love affairs undertaken, and so on). Within this more inclusive and complicated model, influences are no longer restricted to comparatively simple variables (which plane takes off and lands) but include interactions that couldn't be anticipated or discovered simply on the basis of plotting airplane arrivals and departures. For instance, a passenger in a plane from Tampa may be flying into LaGuardia simply to meet another passenger flying in from Detroit. They may sit in the lounge, discuss and sign a contract, and then return to their respective cities. In the brain, this would correspond to a neurotransmitter influencing the "readiness to respond" of certain neurons in several diverse brain areas simultaneously. In other words, the real action isn't confined to discrete brain regions any more than the purposes of our passengers traveling in and out of an airport can be adequately understood simply by concentrating on traffic in and out of that airport. A neurotransmitter may influence one brain area to respond, its neurons to "fire," at the same time it is inhibiting the responses of neighboring areas. Two or more transmitters may cooperate to heighten the responsiveness of a particular brain region. A peptide may by its presence facilitate or inhibit the action of one or more classical neurotransmitters such as noradrenaline. I should also mention as a final confounding variable that there is some evidence that the activity of a neurotransmitter may alter over time: it may bring about the "firing" of a network of neurons within the infant brain while, at a later point, that same neurotransmitter may inhibit nerve cells in that brain as that infant matures into adolescence and adulthood.

The human brain can be understood only as a dynamic structure that retains throughout life the capacity to alter its workings from one day to another, from one moment to the next.

Indeed, the richness of possible scenarios is limited only by the imagination of the scenarist.

NOTES

PAGE

6 The source regarding the importance of the phrenic nerve for independent life up to three months of age is Michael V. Johnston and Joseph T. Coyle, "Development of Central Neurotransmitter Systems," in *The Fetus and Independent Life* (London: Pitman [Ciba Foundation symposium 86] 1981), p. 267.

7 The Michael Johnston quote is from ibid., p. 263. This chapter was also based on personal communications with Michael V. Johnston, associate professor of pediatrics and neurology, University of Michigan.

9–10 The Michael Johnston quote is from Michael V. Johnston, et al., "Development and Reorganization of Central Neurotransmitter Systems" (Paper given to the author by Michael Johnston).

13 The Philo quote is from David Winston, trans., *Philo of Alexandria: The Contemplative Life, the Giants, and Selections,* The Classics of Christian Spirituality (New York: Paulist Press, 1981), p. 111.

14 The historical references such as B. A. Gudden's drowning are taken principally from Edwin Clarke and C. D. O'Malley, *The Human Brain and Spinal Cord: A Historical Study Illustrated by Writings From Antiquity to the 20th Century,* (Berkeley and Los Angeles: University of California Press, 1968). Also informative and helpful are the historical references in James L. O'Leary and Sidney Goldring, *Science and Epilepsy: Neuroscience Gains in Epilepsy Research* (New York: Raven Press, 1976).

15 Ramón y Cajal quote regarding "Communications More or Less Intimate," from O'Leary and Goldring, *Science,* p. 59.

15 The Marcus Jacobson quotes are from his profoundly influential *Developmental Neurobiology* (New York: Plenum Press, 1978), p. 192.

16 An account of the development of early staining techniques for brain tissue can be found in O'Leary and Goldring, *Science,* pp. 35–60.

18–19 The discussion regarding early brain development in the absence of additional neuronal proliferation after birth is from Pasko Rakic, "Neurogenesis in Primates," *Discussions in Neurosciences* 1, no. 2 (April 1984): 43–48.

22 The zygote at thirty hours with two cells exactly alike in genetic composition is from Keith L. Moore, *The Developing Human: Clinically-oriented Embryology* 3d ed. (Philadelphia: W. B. Saunders Company,

1982), p. 33. The relationship of DNA to protein is taken from a paper, "The Genetics of Human Fetal Growth," by D. F. Roberts, *Postgraduate Medical Journal* 54 (1978): 107–16.

22–23 The comparison of neuron and nephron, nerve cell and kidney cell, and the implications for brain development can be found in Roberts, "Genetics," pp. 111–12.

All of the descriptions of the appearance of the early brain are from Marjorie England, *Color Atlas of Life Before Birth: Normal Fetal Development* (Chicago: Year Book Medical Publishers, Incorporated, 1983.

31 Gastrulation is described in Moore's *Developing Human,* p. 54.

32 The Hans Spemann experiments are described in Eric R. Kandel and James H. Schwartz, *Principles of Neural Science* (New York: Elsevier North-Holland, 1981), pp. 503–19.

33–34 The thymidine data is from Pasko Rakic, "Neuronal Migration and Contact Guidance in the Primate Telencephalon," *Postgraduate Medical Journal* 54 (1978): 25–40.

37 The comment regarding pathologists and psychiatrists in relation to the migrating neuron is in ibid., p. 39.

38 The quote regarding the "normal brain" is from ibid.

38 The cortex generated in sixty days is from ibid.

38 The generation times are from ibid.

38–39 Quotes regarding cell counting as impractical are from ibid., p. 40.

39 One hundred billion neurons generated at two hundred and fifty thousand per minute are from Kandel and Schwartz, *Principles,* p. 506.

40 Marcus Jacobson quotes from *Neurobiology.*

42 Seneca quote from Dale Purves and Jeff W. Lichtman, *Principles of Neural Development* (Sunderland, Mass.: Sinauer Associates, Incorporated, 1985).

42–43 Roux experiments and the Haeckel experiments are from Purves and Lichtman, *Principles,* pp. 4–5.

45 The Wilson experiment is described in Ronald L. Schnaar, "The Membrane Is the Message: Deciphering the Code on the Surface of Cells," *The Sciences,* May/June 1985, pp. 34–40.

46–47 The Roger W. Sperry research is described in ibid., p. 37.

49 "Fate maps" are described in W. Maxwell Cowan, "The Development of the Brain," *Scientific American,* September 1979, pp. 113–33.

53 The Donald Hebb quote is from Purves and Lichtman, *Principles,* p. 294.

53–54 The Hamburger and Harrison experiments are taken from Kandel and Schwartz, *Principles,* p. 524. The Hamburger quote is from Purves and Lichtman, *Principles,* p. 140.

55   The data on Rita Levi-Montalcini is from Purves and Lichtman, *Principles,* p. 158.

55–56   The details of the Hamburger/Levy-Montalcini experiment are from Kandel and Schwartz, *Principles,* p. 526.

56   Ibid., p. 360.

59   The van Leeuwenhoek quote is from Clarke and O'Malley, *Human Brain,* p. 115.

62   The Waldeyer-Hartz and Cajal quotes are from ibid.

63   The Sherrington quote and the reference to Verrall are from Purves and Lichtman, *Principles,* p. 208.

63   The Gary Lynch experiment and citation are from ibid., p. 327.

64   The quote regarding "the pattern of connectivity" is from ibid., p. 301.

64–65   The Purves and Lichtman quote is from ibid., p. 311.

67   The DNA data is from Jean-Pierre Changeux, *Neuronal Man: The Biology of Mind* (New York: Pantheon Books, 1985), p. 185.

71   Data on infant brain and the brain/body weight ratio in selected newborn and adult mammals is from K. W. Cross, *"La Chaleur Animale* and the Infant Brain," *Journal of Physiology* 294 (1979): 1–21; the oxygen consumption data is from ibid., p. 11.

72   Data on Lavoisier is from ibid., p. 8.

78   The data on monkey fingers and brain representation is from Jeffrey L. Fox, "The Brain's Dynamic Way of Keeping in Touch," *Science,* 24 August 1984, pp. 820–21.

78   The quote is from Michael M. Merzenich, "Functional 'Maps' of Skin Sensations," in *The Many Facets of Touch: The Foundation of Experience: Its Importance Through Life, with Initial Emphasis for Infants and Young Children,* ed. Catherine Caldwell Brown (Skillman, N.J.: Johnson and Johnson, 1984), p. 18.

79   The Merzenich quotes regarding the first and second stages of map development are in ibid., p. 18.

79   The cigarette example is from ibid., p. 20.

80   "Darwinian competition," is from Fox, "Brain's Dynamic Way," p. 820.

81   Despite the recent description of structural changes in Einstein's brain, I have great reservations about this work and stand by the statement that "nothing remarkable" has been found structurally in the brain of a genius.

85   The Retzius quotes are from Jacobson, *Neurobiology,* p. 64.

86   The Jacobson quote is from ibid., p. 104. Data on nerve cells per species is also from ibid.

86–87   Cajal quote is from ibid., p. 105.

87   The synaptogenesis reference is from ibid., p. 73.

87   The elephant/shrew brain is described in ibid., p. 108.

87   Figures on size of the brain in relation to the body in ibid., p. 109.

89–90   The twin experiments are described in David S. Tuber et al., "Associative Learning in Premature Hydranencephalic and Normal Twins," *Science,* 28 November 1980, pp. 1035–37.

90   The brain weights of domesticated animals is from Jacobson, *Neurobiology,* p. 203.

91   The Greenough studies are from William T. Greenough, "Brain Storage of Sensory Information in Development and Adulthood," in Brown, *Many Facets,* p. 31.

92   The Darwin quote is from Jacobson, *Neurobiology,* p. 207.

92   The Cajal quote is from ibid.

93   The quote regarding "functional effectiveness" is from ibid., p. 306.

94   The data regarding fetal size and movements are from *Continuity of Neural Functions from Prenatal to Postnatal Life,* ed. Heinz F. R. Prechtl, (Oxford: Oxford Blackwell Scientific Publications, Limited, 1984).

94–95   First movement at seven and a half weeks and its description from ibid., pp. 301 and 304; fifteen weeks with sixteen movements, from ibid., p. 301.

95   The deVries quote is from Johanna I. P. "The Emergence of Fetal Behavior I, Qualitative Aspects," *Early Human Development* 7 (1982): 301–22.

95   "Movements in tandem with developments within specific parts of the nervous system" is taken from deVries, "Emergence," p. 320. The deVries quote is from ibid., p. 304.

95   The Jason Birnholz material is taken from his "Fetal Behavior and Condition," in *Ultrasonography in Obstetrics and Gynecology,* ed. Peter W. Callen (Philadelphia: W. B. Saunders Company, 1983).

96   The citation regarding breathing movements observed nearly a century ago is in ibid. This source is an excellent compendium of early fetal activity including general body movements, eye movements, breathing movements, hearing, and behavioral states. The data on early fetal behavior described in this chapter is taken from ibid.

99   The quote from Burton S. Rosner is in Burton S. Rosner and Neil E. Doherty, "The Response of Neonates to Intrauterine Sounds," *Developmental Medicine and Child Neurology* 21 (1979): 727.

99   The story of fetal heart rate patterns and "the mind" of the fetus is described in Niels H. Laursen and Howard M. Hochberg, "Does the Fetus Think?" *The Journal of American Medical Association* 247, no. 23 (June 1982): 3184–85.

99 & 100   The quotes are from ibid.

100   The Rodier quote from her "Chronology of Neuron Develop-ment: Animal Studies and Their Clinical Implications," *Developmental Medicine and Child Neurology* 22 (1980): 525–45.

101–2   The thalidomide data is taken from D. F. Roberts, "The Genetics of Human Fetal Growth," *Postgraduate Medical Journal* 54 (1978): 107–16.

102   Figure 22 of the major developmental processes in formation of the nervous system is taken from Robert Y. Moore, "Normal Devel-opment of the Nervous System," in *Prenatal and Perinatal Factors Associ-ated With Brain Disorders,* U. S. Department of Health and Human Ser-vices, Public Health Service, National Institutes of Health, NIH Publication Number 85–1149, April, 1985.

103   The study by the neuropathologist at the University of Wash-ington School of Medicine is described in Peter W. Fuller et al., "A Proposed Neuropathological Basis for Learning Disabilities in Chil-dren Born Prematurely," *Developmental Medicine and Child Neurology* 25 (1983): 214–31.

104   The brain developmental sequence of cells and gyri is taken from Patricia S. Goldman-Rakic and Pasko Rakic, "Experimental Mod-ification of Gyral Patterns," in *Cerebral Dominance: The Biological Founda-tions,* ed. Norman Geschwind and Albert M. Galaburda (Cambridge: Harvard University Press, 1984).

105   The "fissures within the fetal brain" information is taken from Geschwind and Galaburda, *Cerebral Dominance,* p. 87.

106   The quote regarding selective elimination of cortical-cortical connections is from ibid., p. 189.

106   "Environmentally determined variations" is taken from ibid., p. 190.

107   The reference to "when the therapeutic termination of preg-nancy was deemed necessary" is from Tryphena Humphrey, "Func-tions of the Nervous System During Prenatal Life," in *Perinatal Physiol-ogy,* ed. U. Stave (New York: Plenum Medical Book Company, 1978).

107   The references to the early fetus and its movement activities are from ibid.; and Davenport Hooker, *The Prenatal Origin of Behavior,* Porter Lecture Series 18 (Lawrence, Kansas: University of Kansas Press, 1972).

112   "The sometimes quick, sometimes slow" information is taken from Heinz F. R. Prechtl, "Continuity and Change in Early Neural Development," in Prechtl, *Continuity,* pp. 1–15.

112–13   The Prechtl quote from ibid., p. 9.

113   The K. E. von Baer quote is cited in Purves and Lichtman, *Principles,* p. 4.

113   The Prechtl quote is from Prechtl, *Continuity,* p. 10.

113 The transition from spontaneous smiling to social smiling is described in ibid., p. 10.

114 The hominidization components are described in ibid., p. 11.

114–15 Data on the brain and head size in different species are from Herman Dienske, "Early Development of Motor Abilities, Daytime Sleep and Social Interactions in the Rhesus Monkey, Chimpanzee and Man," in ibid.

116–19 The quoted material is from Bert C. L. Touwen, "Primitive Reflexes—Conceptional or Semantic Problem?" in Prechtl, *Continuity*.

120–22 The material on the relationship of the infant brain and behavior to its adult counterpart described in this chapter is taken principally from Ronald W. Oppenheim, "Ontogenetic Adaptations in Neural Development: Toward a More 'Ecological' Developmental Psychobiology," in Prechtl, *Continuity*.

123 Secondary walking is described in T. G. R. Bower, *Development in Infancy* (New York: W. H. Freeman & Company, 1982), p. 154.

123 Toilet training experiment is discussed in ibid., pp. 150–51; the stair-climbing and cube-stacking experiments on p. 151.

124 The reaching experiments are described in ibid., p. 180.

127 The virtual image experiment is described in ibid., p. 123.

128 "Vision, not touch, is now the dominant sense." The relevant experiments are described in ibid., p. 126.

132 "Ancestry" of the senses is developed in Lawrence E. Marks, *The Unity of the Senses: Interrelations Among the Modalities* (New York: Academic Press, 1978), pp. 182–83.

133 The luminescent rod experiment is in ibid., p. 184; the piano key/emotion experiment on p. 185.

134 The Brazelton quote and the distinguishing of mother from father at age six weeks is taken from Brown, "Many Facets," p. 17.

134 The transcutaneous oxygen monitoring is described in ibid., p. 75.

135 Boston Children's Hospital experience is in ibid., p. 181.

135 Smoking among pregnant mothers and its effect on their fetuses is from ibid., p. 80.

135 Forced expiration in adults compared to infants is in ibid., p. 79.

137 The Brazelton quote is in ibid., p. 83.

137 The Dr. Jerold Lucey quote is in ibid., p. 83.

137 The Stephen Suomi quote is in ibid., pp. 48–49.

138 The experiments involving monkey infants separated from their mothers are in ibid., p. 61.

139 The quote by Dr. Martin Reite is in ibid., p. 64.

139 The Brazelton quote is in ibid., p. 65.

140 The study of the mothers' responses to their stressed infants is described in ibid., p. 66. This description is based on the work of Mary Ainsworth.

140 The quote by Dr. Biggar is in ibid., pp. 67 and 69.

148 The T. G. R. Bower quote is from Bower, *Development*, p. 217.

149–57 The relevant experiments are described in Morris Moscovitch, "Memory from Infancy to Old Age: Implications for Theories of Normal and Pathological Memory," in *Memory Dysfunctions: An Integration of Animal and Human Research from Preclinical and Clinical Perspectives*, vol. 444 of the *Annals of The New York Academy of Sciences*, 30 May 1985, pp. 78–96. Also see Daniel L. Schacter, "Toward the Multi-Disciplinary Study of Memory: Ontogeny, Phylogeny, and Pathology of Memory Systems," in *Neuropsychology of Memory*, ed. Larry R. Squire and Nelson Butters (New York: Guilford Press, 1984), pp. 13–24.

155 The child in Los Angeles is referenced in Michael Rutter, "The Long-Term Effects of Early Experience," *Developmental Medicine and Child Neurology* 22 (1980): 800–15.

155 The René Spitz data is from Eric R. Kandel, "Environmental Determinants of Brain Architecture and of Behavior: Early Experience and Learning," in Kandel and Schwartz, *Principles*, pp. 620–32.

158 The material on prematurity and sex and race distribution was taken from Khang-cheng Ho et al., "Newborn Brain Weight in Relation to Maturity, Sex and Race," *Annals of Neurology* 10, no. 3 (September 1981): 243–46.

159 The reference to 50 percent of mothers having delays in "real" affection was taken from J. A. Jeffcoate et al., "Disturbance in Parent/Child Relationship Following Preterm Delivery," *Developmental Medicine and Child Neurology* 21 (1979): 344–52.

160 The Alfred W. Brann, Jr., quote is taken from his "Factors During Neonatal Life that Influence Brain Disorders," *Prenatal and Perinatal Factors Associated with Brain Disorders*, NIH publication 85–1149, April 1985, p. 271.

160–61 The Gordon Avery quote is from his "Effects of Social, Cultural and Economic Factors on Brain Development," in NIH, *Factors*, pp. 163–76.

162–63 An excellent description of the behavioral states of the newborn is given in T. Berry Brazelton, "Behavioral Competence of the Newborn Infant," in *Parent-Infant Relationships*, ed. Paul M. Taylor (Orlando, Fla.: Grune & Stratton, 1980), pp. 69–85.

167–68 The Konrad Lorenz quote is taken from Purves and Lichtman, *Principles*, p. 336.

173 The pacifier and slide projection experiments were described by E. R. Siqueland, "Development of Instrumental and Exploratory

Behavior During the First Year of Human Life" (Paper delivered at a meeting for the Society for Research and Child Development, 1969). This work is also nicely described in L. Joseph Stone and Joseph Church, *Childhood and Adolescence: The Psychology of the Growing Person* (New York: Random House, 1984), p. 137.

174 The experiments on learning within the womb are reviewed in Gina Kolata, "Studying Learning in the Womb: Behavioral Scientists Are Using Established Experimental Methods to Show that Fetuses Can and Do Learn," *Science,* 20 July 1984, pp. 302–3. The DeCasper quote is also from this article.

179 The Barbara W. Tuchman quote is from p. 50, *A Distant Mirror: The Calamitous Fourteenth Century* (New York: Alfred A. Knopf, 1978).

179 Historical references and background on early ideas about the infant and fetus are taken from Susan Quinn, "The Competence of Babies," *Atlantic Monthly,* January 1982, pp. 54–62.

181 Observations on infant states and infant activities are from Brazelton, "Behavioral Competence," pp. 69–85.

182 The Robert Emde quote and details regarding "babyness" are from Robert N. Emde, "Emotional Availability: A Reciprocal Reward System for Infants and Parents with Implications for Prevention of Psychosocial Disorders," in Taylor, *Interactions,* pp. 87–115.

183–84 The Louis Sander material and quotes are taken from an interview with the author in Denver, Colorado, July 1984 and from his "Polarity, Paradox and the Organizing Process in Development," in *Frontiers of Infant Psychiatry,* ed. J. Call, E. Galenson, and R. Tyson (New York: Basic Books, 1982). See also my article, "Newborn Knowledge: Infants Arrive Less Wet Behind the Ears Than We Thought," *Science 82,* January/February 1982, pp. 58–65. Other quotes from Sander also are from his "New Knowledge About the Infant from Current Research: Implications for Psychoanalysis," *Journal of the American Psychoanalytic Association* 28, no. 1 (1980): 181–98.

186 "The newborn has no conception of self" is taken from Paul L. Harris, "Infant Cognition," in *Handbook of Child Psychology,* ed. Paul H. Mussen, 4th ed. (New York: John Wiley & Sons, 1983), pp. 689–782, esp. p. 744.

190 The red dye experiments on monkeys, chimps, and infants is described in Harris, "Cognition," p. 746.

191–92 The child/adult recognition experiments and the Harris quote, are from ibid., p. 747.

193 The cross-modal experiments are described in ibid., esp. p. 740.

202 The emotion experiments are described in Joseph J. Campos et al., "Socioemotional Development," in Mussen, *Handbook,* pp. 783–915. Much of this material was also gathered from the author's inter-

views with Joseph Campos and Robert Emde in Denver, Colorado, in July 1984.

203   The material on hemispheres and mood in infants is taken from Nathan A. Fox and Richard J. Davidson, "Hemispheric Substrates of Affect: A Developmental Model," in *The Psychobiology of Affective Development*, ed. Nathan A. Fox and Richard J. Davidson (Hillsdale, N.J.: Erlbaum Press, 1984), pp. 353–81. The Fox and Davidson quote on p. 203 is taken from this source.

204   "Infants who are prelocomotive" is from ibid., p. 370.

205   The quote regarding the capacity to inhibit negative affect is from ibid., p. 375.

206   The experiments on tones of voice and the judgment of emotions is from Campos, "Development," p. 800.

207   The Peter Wolff research is in ibid., p. 803.

207   The Glasgow study on infant cries is from Gisela Morsbach and Caroline Bunting, "Maternal Recognition of Their Neonates' Cries," *Developmental Medicine and Child Neurology* 21 (1979): 178–85.

209   The visual cliff experiment with modifications to test the power of emotional communication is described in Mussen, *Handbook*, p. 108.

212   The description of empathy is developed from material in ibid., p. 808. See also my essay, "Neurophysiological Correlates of Empathy," in *Empathy I*, ed. Joseph Lichtenberg, Melvin Bornstein, and Donald Silver (Hillsdale, N.J.: Analytic Press, 1984).

214   The review of the different theories on infant care is from Mussen, *Handbook*, p. 849.

216   The Ann Frodi and Michael Lamb quotes are from their study, "Sex Differences in Responsiveness to Infants: A Developmental Study of Psychophysiological and Behavioral Responses," *Child Development* 49 (1978): 1182–88.

217–18   The smiling response schedule is from Bower, *Development*, p. 260.

218   The experiment of picking up the baby whenever the baby smiles is in ibid., p. 262.

219   The J. S. Watson experiment is in ibid., p. 264. The material is also from an interview and discussion with Professor T. G. R. Bower on March 29, 1985, in Edinburgh, Scotland.

220   The Daniel Stern material is from his *The First Relationship: Infant and Mother* (Cambridge: Harvard University Press, 1977), pp. 44–47.

222   The bonding experiences are described in Mussen, *Handbook*, p. 875.

224   The London study referred to is Julia Collingwood and Eva

Alberman, "Separation at Birth and the Mother/Child Relationship," *Developmental Medicine and Child Neurology* 21 (1979): 608–18.

225 The quote about "an emerging consensus" is from Mussen, *Handbook,* p. 876.

227 Details on rat sex behavior is taken from Changeux, *Neuronal Man,* p. 194.

228 The cross-dressing experiment is from Bower, *Development,* ch. 8.

231–32 The prediction of later intelligence is from Mussen, *Handbook,* p. 751.

232 The Harris quote is in ibid., p. 752.

236 The canary work is from Fernando Nottebohm, "Learning, Forgetting and Brain Repair," in Geschwind and Galaburda, *Cerebral Dominance,* p. 93.

241 The reference is C. Schulman-Galambos and R. Galambos, "Cortical Responses from Adults and Infants to Complex Visual Stimuli," *Electroncephalography and Clinical Neurophysiology* 45 (1978): 425–35.

242 The reference is E. Courchesne, E. L. Ganz and A. M. Norcia, "Event-related brain potentials to human faces in infants," *Child Development* 52 (1981): 804–11.

242 The Diane Kurtzberg references and quotes are from Diane Kurtzberg et al., "Developmental Aspects of Event-Related Potentials," in *Brain and Information: Event-Related Potentials,* ed. Rathe Karrer, Jerome Cohen, and Patricia Tueting, vol. 425 of *The Annals of the New York Academy of Sciences,* 1984, pp. 300–18.

244–45 The BEAM material particularly as related to dyslexia is from Frank H. Duffy et al., "Brain Electrical Activity Mapping," in Geschwind and Galaburda, *Cerebral Dominance,* p. 53. See, in addition, material from Frank H. Duffy, "Beaming New Light on the Brain," *Discover,* December 1981, pp. 30–33. Several of the Duffy quotes are taken from this article.

248 The John Freeman quote is taken from Brann, *Factors,* p. 19.

249 The Harry Chugani material is from an interview with the author in Los Angeles, September 1985. See also Harry T. Chugani and Michael E. Phelps, "Maturational Changes in Cerebral Function in Infants Determined by FDG Positron Emission Tomography," *Science,* 21 February 1986, pp. 840–43.

INDEX

Page numbers in italics refer to illustrations